Congratulations on your wedding day! Best Wishes Always

Love, The Kirklands

July 12, 2001

A PINCH OF

C · O · O · K · **OF** · B · O · O · K

SALT LAKE

Junior League of Salt Lake City, Inc.

DEDICATION

This book is dedicated to the people of Salt Lake City, a community rich with the spirit of giving, proud of its heritage and progressive in caring for others.

The Associaton of Junior Leagues International Inc. is an organization of women commited to promoting voluntarism, developing the potential of women and improving communities through the effective action and leadership of trained volunteers. Its purpose is exclusively educatonal and charitable.

The Junior League of Salt Lake City, Inc. reaches out to women of all races, religions, and national origins who demonstrate an interest in and commitment to voluntarism.

PROJECTS PRESENT AND PAST

Proceed from A PINCH OF SALT LAKE will be returned to the community through projects sponsored by The Junior League of Salt Lake City, Inc.

AIDS Education
Alliance House
Arts of the Challenged
C.A.R.E. Fair
Child Care Connection
Community Mental Health
Community Training Center
Consumer Health
    Information Center
Court Resource
Domestic Violence
    Victim Assistance
Family Support Center
Here to Help
Heritage Foundaton
Hospice
Junior Science Academy
Juvenile Court
KIDSPACE
KUED
KUER
Lollapalooza

Law Related Education
Museum of Natural History
Neighborhood House
Omnibus
Pine Canyon Boys Ranch
Rape Crisis Center
Ready or Not
Repertory Dance Theatre
Ronald McDonald House
S.O.S. (Seniors on Stage)
Salt Lake Art Center
Shelter the Homeless
S.L. Children's Justice Center
Share Your Heart & Home
Sharing Place
S.M.I.L.E.S.
S.T.A.R.
Utah Children
Utah Youth Village
You're in Charge
Wheeler Farm
Woman to Woman
55+ (Senior Resource
    Directory)

The Junior League of Salt Lake City, Inc.
438 East 200 South, Suite 200
Salt Lake City, Utah 84111
All rights reserved.
Copyright © 1986

Fourth Printing

Library of Congress Catalog Card Number: 86-81537

ISBN 0-961 6972-0-2

For information on ordering additional copies of A PINCH OF SALT LAKE, use the form on the back endsheet or contact Pinch Publications at 801-328-4516.

Cover photograph: Cajun Shrimp, page 147.

A PINCH OF SALT LAKE CHAIRMEN

1995-96	Teresa Suttle Kemp
1994-95	Toni Russell Carter
1993-94	Holly McDavid Virden
1992-93	Teresa Siebert Skaggs
1991-92	Carolyn Godfrey Roll
1990-91	Cari Hansen Tagge
1989-90	Sallee Morgan Middlekauff
1988-89	Krista Szasz Stoker, Kari Waring Schaerrer
1987-88	Laura Benson Headden, Linda Gill Adkins
1986-87	Bette Coleman Ross, Sidney Bullen Dibble

COMMITTEE

Chairman	Kristine Eskelson Widner
Recipe Chairman	Elaine Clinger Clyde
Marketing Chairman	Christie Timmons Mullen
Marketing Assistant	Lisa Brodbeck Fall
Sustainer Advisors	Mary June Vincent Woods, 1985-86
	Marian Watkins Ingham, 1984-85
Editors	Kristine Eskelson Widner, Shonnie Stillman Hays

CHAPTER EDITORS

Beverages & Hors d'oeuvres	Barbara Aspden Gibbons
Brunches & Breads	Bonnie Lindjord Gilley, Shonnie Stillman Hays
Soups & Stews	Lynne Morton
Salads	Janene Cooley Brown
Vegetables & Side Dishes	Janene Cooley Brown, Shonnie Stillman Hays
Seafood	Marilyn Miller Askins
Poultry	Margie Sesler Patton
Meats	Marguerite Marceau Henderson
Desserts & Pies	Karen Cooley Milne, Denise Guiney Black
Cookies & Cakes	Bonnie Lindjord Gilley, Lynne Morton

COMPUTER EDITORS

Kathie Merrill Miller, Patricia Snyder Petersen

■

Graphic Designer	Catherine Green
Photography	Brent Herridge & Associates
Food Stylist	Janet Schaap
Art Direction	Catherine Green
Art Production	Barbara Betthauser
Typesetting	Alphabet Soup
Printer	Quality Press

Salt Lakers are people who relish their diverse surroundings, bask in the four distinct seasons and cook to accommodate their active living. Their cooking is a smorgasbord of styles, complexities and resources dictated primarily by available time, desire and, occasionally, destination.

Each chapter in A PINCH OF SALT LAKE begins by celebrating an activity enjoyed by Salt Lakers and those who visit our attractions, and offers suggestions for foods to complete the occasion.

This collection of recipes is presented by the members of the Junior League of Salt Lake City, Inc., their families, friends and members of the community et al. More than 2000 recipes were submitted and tested by enthusiastic cooks who scrutinized and selected over 400 prize recipes highlighting foods for contemporary lifestyles.

Quick and Easy recipes, those taking an hour or less from start to finish, are identified by a chapter symbol (as on opposite page). This method of recipe description makes the book comfortable and simple to use for cooks new to the kitchen, those who prepare moveable feasts for outdoor entertaining, gourmet chefs and people with pinched time to prepare meals.

It is our sincere hope that A PINCH OF SALT LAKE will bring you a glimpse of our colorful Salt Lake lifestyle, success in cooking and entertaining and a knowledge of your contribution to our community by purchasing this book.

Junior League of Salt Lake City, Inc.

4

CONTENTS

BEVERAGES & HORS D'OEUVRES

Salt Lakers are summoned to Lake Powell where towering spires of nature-carved red sandstone rise abruptly from the depth of turquoise green water. The explorers are intrigued by the hundreds of water canyons offering an opportunity to view ancient Indian dwellings and pictographs. The sports-minded may prefer to cut the glassy water with a pair of water skis, or troll from the stern of a houseboat while anticipating a creel packed with bass.

As the last pinch of sunglow is gradually swallowed by the imposing sandstone horizon, Curried Pecans, Brie Saute', Italian Shrimp Dip and a favorite icy beverage precede a skillet full of the catch-of-the-day.

FRUIT FIESTA

Yield: 20 servings
Assemble: 20 minutes
Freeze: 24 hours

LEMON ICE:
4 cups sugar
4 cups water
4 cups cold water
¾ cup lemon juice

FRUITS:
2 10-ounce packages frozen raspberries
1 16-ounce can pineapple tidbits, drained
6 bananas, sliced
2 10-ounce packages frozen blueberries
2-3 quarts ginger ale or lemon-lime soda

Other fruits in season may be added if desired
** (watermelon, cantaloupe, strawberries, etc.)**

In a large saucepan combine sugar and 4 cups of water. Boil for 5 minutes. Add 4 cups of cold water and lemon juice; freeze. (This recipe makes 2 quarts. The lemon ice may be kept frozen for several weeks. It should be made at least 24 hours in advance of use.)

Remove lemon ice 20 minutes before serving to slightly thaw. When ready to serve, break lemon ice into small chunks in a large punch bowl. Add fruits and combine with lemon ice. Just before serving add ginger ale or lemon-lime soda.

This may also be served in individual punch cups. Lemon ice and fruits are placed in cups and then ginger ale is added. This drink can be used as a heavy slush with very little ginger ale or can be made diluted according to individual preference.

SANGRIA

Yield: 16 servings
Assemble: 2½ hours

1 gallon hearty red burgundy
1 cup sugar
1 cup dry vermouth
5 cinnamon sticks
Lemon, orange and apple slices with a clove in each
Crushed ice

Combine burgundy, sugar and vermouth; mix well. Place in punch bowl or other serving container. Drop in cinnamon sticks and fruit. Allow flavors to blend for at least 2 hours.

When ready to serve dilute with 5 to 6 cups of crushed ice.

LIME TEA REFRESHER

Yield: ½ gallon
Assemble: 1 hour
15 minutes
Chill: 1 hour

2 cups boiling water
2 tablespoons loose tea
½ cup sugar
2½ cups carbonated water or ginger ale
2½ cups lemon-lime soda
2 lime skins
½ cup lime juice (3 large limes)
½ cup corn syrup

Pour boiling water over tea and let steep for 5 minutes; strain. Add sugar and lime skins and let stand 1 hour. Remove skins from tea and add lime juice, carbonated water, lemon-lime soda and syrup. Serve chilled.

BANANA SLUSH

Yield: 20 servings
Assemble: 20 minutes
Freeze: 2 hours

4 cups sugar
6 cups water
2½ cups orange juice
½ cup lemon juice
4 cups pineapple juice
5 medium bananas, mashed
Lemon-lime soda or ginger ale

In a large saucepan dissolve sugar in water and bring to a boil; cool. Blend remaining ingredients in a large bowl. Combine with sugar water. Freeze in large plastic container. Stir occasionally while it freezes. Spoon into punch cups and pour lemon-lime soda or ginger ale over slush.

EASY CHAMPAGNE PUNCH

Yield: 7 quarts
Assemble: 5 minutes
Chill: 2 hours

2 quarts apple juice (not cider)
2 fifths light rum
2 quarts champagne
Club soda
Ice block

In a large bowl mix apple juice and rum together. Chill several hours. Just before serving, pour rum mixture into a large punch bowl over ice block. Add champagne. This is a strong brew, so add club soda to reduce the "punch."

HOT SPICED CIDER

QUICK & EASY

Yield: 10 servings
Assemble: 15 minutes

½ cup sugar
½ cup brown sugar
Juice of 3 lemons
2 quarts apple cider
1 tablespoon whole cloves
1 tablespoon whole allspice
3 sticks cinnamon
2 cups pineapple juice or orange juice

In a large saucepan combine all ingredients and boil for 5 minutes. Strain and serve hot.

CHRISTMAS TOM AND JERRYS

QUICK & EASY

Yield: 1 pint
Assemble: 5 minutes

BATTER:
1 pound super-fine sugar
3 eggs, separated
½ teaspoon vanilla extract
Nutmeg

LIQUOR MIX:
¼ bottle (fifth) white rum
¼ bottle (fifth) dark rum
½ bottle (fifth) brandy

In a large bowl beat egg whites on high speed until stiff. Add ¾ pound of the sugar. Beat 30 seconds longer; set aside. Beat egg yolks until thick and beat in remaining ¼ pound sugar. Fold egg white mixture into yolk mixture. Add vanilla and let stand at least 15 minutes. Mix rums and brandy together.

To serve, pour 1½ ounces liquor mix in a mug, add 2 tablespoons batter mixture and fill mug with boiling water. Mix with a spoon. Sprinkle nutmeg on top and serve immediately.

IRISH CREAM LIQUEUR

QUICK & EASY

Yield: 12 servings
Assemble: 20 minutes

1 cup Irish whiskey
4 eggs
1 teaspoon vanilla extract
1 tablespoon chocolate syrup
1 14-ounce can sweetened condensed milk
¼ teaspoon coconut extract

Mix all ingredients in a blender. Store in refrigerator.

SUMMER VODKA SLUSH

Yield: 20 servings
Assemble: 20 minutes
Freeze: 2 hours

9 cups water
2 cups sugar
1 12-ounce can frozen lemonade concentrate
1 12-ounce can frozen orange juice concentrate
1 pint vodka
Lemon-lime soda

In a large saucepan boil water and sugar for 15 minutes; cool. Add frozen lemonade, frozen orange juice and the pint of vodka. Place in a large plastic container and freeze. Serve with lemon-lime soda—½ glass slush to ½ glass soda.

SPICED ARTICHOKES

Yield: 4 servings
Assemble: 15 minutes
Cook: 40 minutes
Chill: 2 hours

4 artichokes
Water
¼ teaspoon salt
¼ cup lemon juice
3 slices lemon
6 peppercorns
1 bay leaf
1 clove garlic, sliced in half

Place artichokes in a large covered pot. Add water to cover artichokes. Add all other ingredients, bring to a boil then simmer until artichokes are tender in stem-end when pierced with a fork (about 40 minutes). Drain and chill. Serve cold as an appetizer with Herb Watercress Dip or hot as a vegetable.

HERB WATERCRESS DIP

QUICK
& EASY

Yield: 1 cup
Assemble: 15 minutes
Chill: 45 minutes

½ cup mayonnaise
¼ cup chopped watercress leaves
2 chopped green onions, green tops included
1 tablespoon chopped fresh parsley
1 teaspoon lemon juice
Pinch of salt
⅛ teaspoon white pepper
¼ cup sour cream

Combine all ingredients (except sour cream) in a blender or food processor fitted with a metal blade. Whirl on medium speed until blended and smooth. Fold in the sour cream and chill to blend flavors. Serve with spiced artichokes. This also makes a nice change-of-pace salad dressing.

BACON-STUFFED MUSHROOMS

Yield: 10-12 servings
Assemble: 20 minutes
Bake: 15 minutes

2 pounds fresh mushrooms, cleaned and stems reserved
8 slices bacon
½ yellow onion, minced
Stems from mushrooms, chopped
12 ounces cream cheese, softened
1 cup grated Cheddar cheese

In a medium-size skillet saute' bacon until brown; drain and crumble. Drain grease but do not rinse pan. Add minced onion and chopped mushroom stems to pan. Cook all together until tender. Add cream cheese to mixture and cook until melted. Preheat oven to 350°.

Stuff mushroom caps with mixture and cover with grated cheese. Bake on a lightly greased cookie sheet for 15 minutes.

CHEF DREW ELLSWORTH'S STUFFED MUSHROOMS

Yield: 8-10 servings
Assemble: 20 minutes
Bake: 10 minutes

Note: Chef Ellsworth is noted for his creative classes in continental cuisine.

1 pound fresh mushrooms, cleaned and stems reserved
½ cup butter or margarine, softened
3 cloves garlic, finely chopped
½ cup chopped fresh parsley
½ cup grated Parmesan cheese
6 slices Swiss cheese, slivered
Stems from mushrooms, chopped
3 eggs
2 tablespoons capers

In a medium-size bowl combine butter, garlic, parsley, cheeses and mushroom stems. Incorporate eggs into mixture. (It will be sticky.) Fold in capers. Preheat oven to 400°.

Stuff mushroom caps and bake on a lightly greased cookie sheet for 10 minutes or until brown.

SWEET PUNGENT CHICKEN WINGS

Yield: 8-10 servings
Assemble: 20 minutes
Bake: 1 hour

24 chicken wings with end-joint removed
10 tablespoons soy sauce
¼ cup sugar
½ cup water
1 clove garlic, minced or ⅛ teaspoon garlic powder
1 tablespoon ground ginger

Place chicken wings in a 9 x 13-inch pan. Preheat oven to 350°. Combine remaining ingredients in a small bowl. Mix and pour over chicken. Bake for one hour; baste occasionally. May be prepared ahead and reheated to serve.

BUFFALO CHICKEN WINGS

Yield: 6 servings
Assemble: 30 minutes
Bake: 35-40 minutes

2½ pounds chicken wings with end-joint removed
1 egg, whipped
½ cup oil
1 cup cider vinegar
2-3 tablespoons Tabasco (2 tablespoons give moderate heat)
¼ teaspoon pepper
1 clove garlic, minced
¼ teaspoon onion salt
¼ teaspoon celery salt
Pinch of ground cloves
⅛ teaspoon coriander
⅛ teaspoon nutmeg

Celery sticks
Blue Cheese Dip (recipe below)

Preheat oven to 500°. Cut chicken wings in half at joint. Lay wings in a large shallow pan (9 x 13-inch or larger). Mix next 11 ingredients together in a small bowl. Pour mixture over chicken wings and bake for 35-40 minutes or until crispy. Remove wings and drain on paper towels. Serve wings hot with crisp celery sticks dunked in Blue Cheese Dip to help douse the fire!

BLUE CHEESE DIP

Yield: 1½ cups
Assemble: 15 minutes
Chill: 24 hours

½ cup sour cream
¼ teaspoon dry mustard
¼ teaspoon pepper
¼ teaspoon salt, scant
1 clove garlic, minced
½ teaspoon Worcestershire sauce
¾ cup mayonnaise
2 ounces imported Danish blue cheese

Place first 6 ingredients in a mixing bowl and blend 2 minutes at low speed with an electric mixer. Add mayonnaise and blend at low speed for 1 minute. Crumble blue cheese into small pieces and add to dip mixture. Blend at low speed for 4 minutes longer. Dip should be refrigerated 24 hours before serving. Also delicious over salad greens.

BUFFET HAM BALLS WITH HORSERADISH SAUCE

Yield: 20 servings
Assemble: 30 minutes
Bake: 1 hour

1 pound ground ham
1½ pounds ground pork
2 cups bread crumbs
2 eggs, well beaten
1 cup milk

GLAZE:
1 cup brown sugar
½ cup red wine vinegar
½ cup water
1 teaspoon dry mustard

HORSERADISH SAUCE:
½ cup heavy cream, whipped
1 tablespoon horseradish
1 tablespoon prepared mustard

In a large bowl combine ham, pork, bread crumbs, eggs and milk. Roll into walnut-size balls and place in a 9 x 13-inch baking pan.

In a small bowl mix glaze ingredients and pour over ham balls. Bake uncovered in a 325° oven for 1 hour, basting often. (Ham balls should be sticky when ready to serve.)

Fold horseradish sauce ingredients together in a small serving bowl and place beside ham balls. Use cocktail picks to serve.

HOT CHEESE PUFFS

Yield: 8 dozen
Assemble: 45 minutes
Freeze: 2 hours
Bake: 20 minutes

1 loaf unsliced white sandwich bread
½ cup butter
8 ounces sharp Cheddar cheese or Monterey Jack with Jalapeño peppers
8 ounces cream cheese
2 egg whites, beaten

Remove crusts from bread and cut into 1-inch cubes. In top of double boiler melt the butter and cheeses, stirring well. Cool to room temperature. Fold in beaten egg whites. Dip bread cubes into cheese mixture; cover cubes completely. Place on cookie sheets and freeze. After cubes are frozen they can be stored in plastic bags.

To prepare, preheat oven to 400°. Place frozen cubes on cookie sheets. Bake until slightly browned and puffy (about 20 minutes). Serve hot.

BACON-WRAPPED SCALLOPS

Yield: 4-6 servings
Assemble: 30 minutes
Bake: 20-25 minutes

½ cup flour
½ teaspoon salt
1½ teaspoons paprika
½ teaspoon white pepper
½ teaspoon garlic powder
1 egg
1 cup milk
21 sea scallops
1-2 cups fresh breadcrumbs
7 bacon strips, cut into thirds

Remoulade Sauce (recipe below) or cocktail sauce

Combine flour, salt, paprika, pepper and garlic powder in a shallow dish. Beat egg and milk together in a small bowl. Roll scallops in seasoned flour, shaking off excess. Dip scallops into egg mixture, then coat with breadcrumbs, covering completely. Preheat oven to 400°.

Wrap each scallop in bacon and secure with toothpick. Place scallops on a lightly greased cookie sheet. Bake until bacon is crisp and scallops are cooked through (about 20-25 minutes). Serve hot with Remoulade Sauce or cocktail sauce.

REMOULADE SAUCE

Yield: 2½ cups
Assemble: 10 minutes
Chill: 45 minutes

4 tablespoons lemon juice
4 tablespoons red wine vinegar
4 tablespoons prepared mustard
4 tablespoons prepared horseradish
1 teaspoon salt
½ teaspoon pepper
2 teaspoons paprika
Dash cayenne pepper
½ cup mayonnaise
½ cup finely chopped celery
½ cup minced green onions
½ cup cocktail sauce

Mix all ingredients together in a quart jar and chill. Delicious with Bacon-Wrapped Scallops or as a dip for chilled shrimp or crab legs.

EMPAÑADAS (SOUTH AMERICAN MEAT PIES)

Yield: 16 servings
Assemble: 1 hour
Bake: 15-20 minutes

BEEF FILLING:
1 pound lean ground beef
1 cup chopped onion
1 cup chopped tomato
½ cup chopped green pepper
1 clove garlic, minced
¾ cup chopped pimiento stuffed green olives
¾ teaspoon Tabasco sauce
1 tablespoon flour
1 teaspoon salt
½ teaspoon chili powder

CRUST:
1⅓ cups flour
¼ teaspoon salt
5 tablespoons cold butter
3 tablespoons shortening
6 tablespoons ice-cold water

1 egg yolk
1 tablespoon water

Salsa (page 17)
Worcestershire sauce

In a large skillet saute' beef until almost brown. Drain off any grease. Add onion, tomato, pepper and garlic. Cook until vegetables are tender. Add olives and Tabasco. Blend in flour, salt and chili powder. Cook until thick, stirring constantly; cool.

Combine first four crust ingredients in bowl of food processor fitted with a metal blade (or medium-size bowl). Process or cut with pastry blender into small pieces. Add water, a tablespoonful at a time, until mixture forms a ball. Use immediately or wrap and chill until ready to make Empañadas.

Roll on floured surface until thickness of pie crust dough (approximately ⅛-¼-inch thick). Cut into 6-inch circles. Preheat oven to 425°

In a small bowl mix egg yolk and water; set aside. Place one tablespoon filling in center of each circle, paint edges with egg mixture, fold over and crimp edges with a fork. Prick top with fork to allow steam to escape. Place on an ungreased cookie sheet and bake for 15-20 minutes until crust is lightly browned.

Serve hot with salsa on the side or pass Worcestershire sauce to sprinkle on top.

SALSA

Yield: 3 cups
Assemble: 15 minutes
Cook: 30 minutes

1 tablespoon butter or margarine
½ large onion, coarsely chopped
½ large green pepper, coarsely chopped
1 28-ounce can tomatoes, chopped
1 4-ounce can diced green chilies
6 shakes of Tabasco
Dash cayenne pepper
2 tablespoons catsup

Melt butter in a large skillet. Saute' onion and green pepper in butter for about 10 minutes, but do not brown. Add remaining ingredients and simmer for 20 minutes. Tabasco and cayenne may be adjusted according to desired level of "hot."

May be served hot or cold with hors d'oeuvres, chips or any Mexican food. Keeps refrigerated up to one week.

TACO TARTLETS

Yield: 48 tartlets
Assemble: 45 minutes
Bake: 8 minutes

BEEF SHELLS:
1⅓ pounds lean ground beef
2 tablespoons taco seasoning mix
2 tablespoons ice-cold water

FILLING:
1 pint sour cream
2 tablespoons taco sauce
2 ounces ripe olives, chopped
1 cup crushed tortilla chips

6 ounces Cheddar cheese, grated

Using hands to mix, combine beef, taco seasoning and ice water in a medium-size bowl. Press mixture into the bottom and sides of 1½-inch miniature muffin pan to form shells. Preheat oven to 425°.

Mix all filling ingredients together. Place a spoonful of filling into each shell. Sprinkle cheese over top and bake 8 minutes. With the tip of a knife remove tart and place on paper towels to drain. Serve warm.

TASTY TORTILLA ROLLS

Yield: 60 pieces
Assemble: 20-30
   minutes
Chill: 3 hours

12 ounces cream cheese, softened
2 tablespoons chopped green chilies (fresh or canned)
3 tablespoons finely chopped pecans
3 tablespoons chopped ripe olives
5 tablespoons minced green onions
1 clove garlic, minced
6 8-inch flour tortillas

Salsa (page 17)

In a medium-size bowl combine cream cheese, chilies, nuts, olives, onions and garlic. Spread one side of each tortilla with the cream cheese mixture, covering completely. Roll each tortilla up tightly, jelly-roll style, and wrap individually in plastic wrap. Refrigerate several hours or overnight.

To serve, cut each long roll into ½-inch rounds and place cut-side down on serving tray (A dark tray gives a nice contrast to the light-colored rolls.) Use toothpicks to spear rolls for dipping into salsa.

GREEN CHILI BITES

**QUICK
& EASY**

Yield: 20 squares
Assemble: 15 minutes
Bake: 30-40 minutes

2 4-ounce cans whole green chilies
2 cups grated Monterey Jack cheese
2 cups grated Cheddar cheese
6 eggs, beaten
Pinch of salt
Pinch of pepper

Preheat oven to 325°. Butter an 8 or 9-inch square baking dish. Slice and open chilies and arrange on bottom of baking dish. Mix grated cheeses together and sprinkle over chilies. Add salt and pepper to beaten eggs and pour over cheeses and chilies. Bake 30-40 minutes or until firm when dish is shaken. Cut into squares and serve hot.

PRONTO CHILI CON QUESO

**QUICK
& EASY**

Yield: 8-10 servings
Assemble: 10 minutes
Cook: 20 minutes

3 slices bacon
1 large onion, chopped
1 28-ounce can stewed tomatoes, drained
1 15-ounce can chili without beans
1 pound Cheddar cheese, grated

In a large skillet fry bacon; drain and crumble into small pieces. Remove grease from pan but do not wash the pan. Add onions and drained stewed tomatoes to the pan; simmer until liquid has evaporated. Add chili and cheese and cook over low heat until the cheese melts. Serve warm with tortilla chips.

NORTH-OF-THE-BORDER GUACAMOLE DIP

Yield: 2 cups
Assemble: 30 minutes

8 ounces cream cheese, softened
2 medium avocados
1 medium tomato, chopped
1 medium onion, finely chopped
1 tablespoon lemon juice
1 4-ounce can diced green chilies
¾ cup diced Cheddar cheese
¼ teaspoon garlic powder
3-4 drops Tabasco sauce

Whip cream cheese until smooth and creamy; add a little milk if necessary. Chop avocado and add to cream cheese mixture; beat again. Fold in tomato, onion and lemon juice. Add chilies, cheese, garlic powder and Tabasco. Serve with corn chips.

CHEESY BEAN DIP

Yield: 8-10 servings
Assemble: 15 minutes
Bake: 20-30 minutes

1 9-ounce can bean dip
3 ounces cream cheese, softened
1 cup sour cream
1 7-ounce can chopped green chilies
½ cup chopped onions
1½ teaspoons taco seasoning mix
½ pound Monterey Jack cheese, grated
½ pound Cheddar cheese, grated

Tortilla chips, crackers or vegetable crudite's

In a medium bowl combine bean dip, cream cheese and sour cream; mix well. Add green chilies, onion, seasoning mix; blend well. Spread half of mixture in a 9 x 13-inch oven-proof baking dish. Layer cheeses on top. Spread with the remaining bean mixture. Bake at 350° for 20-30 minutes or until bubbly. Serve with tortilla chips, crackers or fresh vegetable crudite's.

SHRIMP AND CHEDDAR SPREAD

Yield: 6-8 servings
Assemble: 15 minutes
Chill: 2 hours

8 ounces extra-sharp Cheddar cheese, grated
9 ounces canned shrimp, rinsed and drained
1½ tablespoons grated onion
1½ cups mayonnaise
1½ teaspoons Worcestershire sauce
Garlic salt to taste

Warm rye bread rounds

In a small-size mixing bowl mash shrimp and combine with cheese. Mix in the remaining ingredients. Chill, covered for at least 2 hours, but not more than 12 hours.

HERBED CHICKEN BITES

QUICK
& EASY

Yield: 6 dozen
Assemble: 40 minutes
Bake: 20 minutes

4 whole chicken breasts, boned, split and skin removed
1 cup finely crushed Ritz-type crackers (about 24)
½ cup grated Parmesan cheese
¼ cup finely chopped walnuts
1 teaspoon dried thyme leaves, crushed
1 teaspoon dried basil leaves, crushed
½ teaspoon seasoned salt
¼ teaspoon pepper
½ cup melted butter

Sweet Hot Mustard (recipe below)

Cover 2 baking sheets with foil. Cut chicken into 1-inch pieces. Mix cracker crumbs, cheese, walnuts, seasoned salt, thyme, basil and pepper in a large bowl. Preheat oven to 400°. Dip chicken pieces into melted butter, then into crumb mixture. Place chicken pieces about ½-inch apart on prepared baking sheet. Bake uncovered until golden brown (about 20 minutes). Serve hot with Sweet Hot Mustard.

SWEET HOT MUSTARD

Yield: 1 cup
Assemble: 12 hours

Note: This recipe doubles easily and makes a great gift.

2 ounces dry mustard
½ cup malt cider vinegar
½ cup sugar
3 eggs

In a medium-size stainless steel bowl soak dry mustard in vinegar overnight. Pour the mixture into the top of double boiler. Add sugar; beat the eggs in one at a time. Whisk over low heat for 10-15 minutes until mixture has thickened. Place in an 8-ounce jar, cover and refrigerate.

CHA SIU (CHINESE-STYLE PORK)

Yield: 12 servings
Assemble: 10 minutes
Marinate: 12 hours
Roast: 1 hour

Note: Delicious as an hors d'oeuvre or to accompany a Chinese salad.

1 cup soy sauce
1½ cups brown sugar
1½ cups sugar
1 teaspoon red food coloring (optional)
1 teaspoon Chinese 5 spices
1 teaspoon Accent
2 tablespoons oyster sauce
¼ cup white wine
2-4 pound boneless pork tenderloin roast
Toasted sesame seeds
Green onion slices

Sweet Hot Mustard

Mix the first 8 ingredients in a large container suitable for marinating. Marinate roast overnight in the refrigerator. Turn meat occasionally.

Preheat oven to 350°. Remove meat from marinade. Place water in broiler pan and tenderloin on rack of broiler pan above water. Roast 30 minutes on each side. Roll in sesame seeds, slice and sprinkle with green onions. Serve hot or cold accompanied with Sweet Hot Mustard.

BEEF YAKITORI

Yield: 6 servings
Assemble: 15 minutes
Marinate: 3 hours
Grill: 4 minutes

Note: Nice addition to an outdoor buffet table.

3 pounds round steak, ¼-inch thick (as for Rouladen)
25-30 bamboo skewers, 8-inches long
½ cup soy sauce
½ cup vegetable oil
½ cup thinly sliced green onions
2 large cloves garlic, minced
4 teaspoons sesame seeds, lightly toasted
1 teaspoon brown sugar
1 teaspoon grated fresh ginger

Cut steak into 1-inch strips. Thread on skewers, placing 2 strips on each skewer. In a large bowl combine the soy sauce, oil, onions, garlic, sesame seeds, brown sugar and ginger. Stir well. Place the skewered beef in a glass or ceramic 9 x 13-inch pan. Pour marinade over beef and cover with plastic wrap. Refrigerate 3-6 hours. Grill skewered meat over medium coals or under broiler, grilling 2 minutes per side.

CURRIED PECANS

QUICK
& EASY

Yield: 3 cups
Assemble: 25 minutes
Bake: 20 minutes

1 pound pecan halves
½ cup butter
¼ cup peanut oil
2 tablespoons brown sugar
2 tablespoons curry powder
2 tablespoons ground ginger
⅛ teaspoon salt
1 tablespoon chutney

Preheat oven to 350°. Place pecans on baking sheet in a single layer and toast in oven for 10 minutes. Do not allow pecans to brown.

Melt butter and oil in a large skillet. Add sugar, curry powder, ginger and salt; blend well. Add pecans to skillet and stir until well coated. Add chutney and mix well. Place pecans on paper towels; allow to drain, then return to baking sheet. Place in oven but turn oven off. Leave pecans in oven for 10 minutes. Remove and salt lightly. Cool thoroughly. Store in airtight container.

PINEAPPLE CHEESE BALL

Yield: 6-8 servings
Assemble: 15 minutes
Chill: 2 hours

16 ounces cream cheese, softened
1 8½-ounce can crushed pineapple, well drained
¼ cup chopped green pepper
2 tablespoons chopped onion
½ teaspoon salt
1 dash Tabasco sauce
1 cup pecans, chopped
Maraschino cherry slivers

Table water-style crackers

Combine softened cream cheese, pineapple, green pepper, onion, salt and Tabasco. Shape into a ball and refrigerate to set. After 1 hour roll in nuts and garnish with cherries. Serve with crackers.

ZIPPY BLUE CHEESE SPREAD

Yield: 6-8 servings
Assemble: 15 minutes
Chill: 2 hours

16 ounces cream cheese, softened
2 tablespoons crumbled blue cheese
2 tablespoons prepared horseradish

Fresh apple and pear slices
Crackers

In a small bowl mix cheeses and horseradish. Cover and refrigerate at least 2 hours to blend flavors. Serve at room temperature with fresh fruit slices and crackers.

BRIE SAUTÉ

QUICK
& EASY

Yield: 6 servings
Assemble: 10 minutes
Cook: 7 minutes

1 6-inch round Brie cheese, medium soft
1 egg, beaten
1 cup seasoned bread crumbs
4 tablespoons butter, divided
½ cup chopped green onion tops

Table water-style crackers

Dip the unskinned Brie into the egg and coat both sides with bread crumbs. Heat 2 tablespoons butter until it starts to brown over medium high heat. Brown cheese round on both sides. Remove to serving plate to keep warm.

Add remaining butter to skillet. When foamy, sauté the onions for 2 minutes. Pour over cheese and serve immediately with crackers.

CAMEMBERT EN CROÛTE

Yield: 4-6 servings
Assemble: 20 minutes
Chill: 1½ hours
Bake: 30 minutes

¾ cup flour
Pinch of salt
4 ounces cream cheese, softened
¼ cup sweet unsalted butter or margarine
1 4-inch round Camembert wheel
Caraway or poppy seeds

Apple wedges

In a food processor combine flour, salt, cream cheese and butter until mixture forms a ball. If mixing by hand, combine butter and cream cheese, cut in flour and salt. Form a ball. Chill 15-20 minutes.

Roll on floured board into an 11-inch circle. Sprinkle seeds generously on circle within 2 inches of border. Place whole Camembert in center of dough and wrap by bringing ends to top of the cheese and twist like a flower. Refrigerate at least 1 hour.

Preheat oven to 400°. Place cheese en croûte on pie plate or cookie sheet and bake for 10 minutes. Reduce oven temperature to 350° and bake 20 minutes longer. Cool on cookie sheet for 45 minutes before placing on a serving plate. Slice to serve. Apple wedges make a nice accompaniment.

SHRIMP AND ARTICHOKE SPREAD

QUICK
& EASY

Yield: 10-12 servings
Assemble: 20 minutes
Chill: 40 minutes

1 pint sour cream
1 cup mayonnaise
1 teaspoon Worcestershire sauce
1 dash Tabasco sauce
3 tablespoons chili sauce
1 pound small cooked bay shrimp
1 14-ounce can unmarinated artichoke hearts
1 small Bermuda onion, cut into lengthwise strips

1 loaf party rye rounds or pumpernickle bread

Combine sour cream and mayonnaise. Add Worcestershire sauce, Tabasco and chili sauce. Break shrimp and add to mixture. Drain artichoke hearts and cut each into 4 pieces; add to mixture. Add onion strips and combine well; chill. Before serving, butter bread slices and warm slightly in oven. Serve with spread.

SALMON MOUSSE

Yield: 6-8 servings
Assemble: 15 minutes
Chill: 6 hours

3 tablespoons lemon juice
2 tablespoons cold water
2 envelopes unflavored gelatin
⅔ cup boiling water
1 pound salmon steaks, poached (or use canned)
2 stalks celery, chopped
1 small onion, chopped
¼ cucumber, peeled and chopped
½ carrot, peeled and chopped
2 sprigs fresh parsley, chopped
½ cup mayonnaise
1 cup heavy cream
½ teaspoon white pepper
1 teaspoon salt
3 sprigs fresh dill weed or 1 teaspoon dried dill weed

Lemon slices
Crackers

Place lemon juice and cold water into bowl of food processor fitted with metal blade. Sprinkle gelatin on top and let stand 1 minute. Add boiling water and blend for 10 seconds. Remove skin and bones from salmon; cut into bite-size chunks. Add salmon and next 10 ingredients to gelatin and process until smooth. Pour into a lightly greased 5-cup mold and chill for several hours until firm. Unmold on a bed of greens; garnish with lemon slices and serve with crackers.

CHUTNEY CHEESE SPREAD

QUICK
& EASY

Yield: 6-8 servings
Assemble: 15 minutes
Chill: 45 minutes

6 ounces cream cheese, softened
1 cup grated sharp Cheddar cheese
2 tablespoons dry sherry
½ teaspoon curry powder
Pinch of salt
¼ cup finely chopped chutney
1 tablespoon finely chopped chives or green onion tops

Crackers or sliced cocktail bread
Vegetable crudité's (Jicama slices, pea pods, asparagus, sweet
**   potato slices)**

In a small mixing bowl combine cheeses, sherry, curry and salt. Stir in the chutney. Blend mixture well, spoon into a serving dish and chill. Sprinkle with chives and serve with crackers and crudité's. (Flavor intensifies when spread on cocktail bread slices and broiled until bubbly.)

PECAN SPECIAL

Yield: 8-10 servings
Assemble: 20 minutes
Cook: 20 minutes

5 ounces chipped beef, shredded
8 ounces cream cheese, softened
2 tablespoons milk
¼ cup chopped green pepper
2 tablespoons grated onion
½ teaspoon garlic salt
½ cup sour cream
1 4-ounce can diced green chilies, drained (optional)
½ cup chopped pecans

Crackers or corn chips

Pour boiling water over shredded beef; let stand 1 minute then drain. Combine cream cheese and milk in a small bowl. Add shredded beef. Mix pepper, onion and garlic salt into mixture. Fold in sour cream and green chilies if desired. Spoon into a 9-inch pie plate. Sprinkle pecans on top and bake at 350° for 20 minutes. Serve with crackers or corn chips.

LAYERED SEAFOOD SPREAD

Yield: 10-12 servings
Assemble: 10 minutes
Chill: 2 hours

8 ounces cream cheese, softened
3 tablespoons mayonnaise
3 tablespoons sour cream
¼ teaspoon garlic salt
½ teaspoon Worcestershire sauce
8 ounces chili sauce
½ cup chopped green onions
1 cup crab meat or tiny bay shrimp, cooked

Crackers

Combine cream cheese, mayonnaise, sour cream, garlic salt and Worcestershire sauce. Mixture should be creamy, if not, add more sour cream. Pour into a glass pie dish, spreading evenly over the bottom and up the sides. Pour chili sauce on top, carefully spreading over the center without mixing it into the cream cheese mixture. Top with green onions and shrimp. Refrigerate for several hours until cheese mixture is solid. Serve with crackers.

PARTY TURNOVERS

Yield: 50 turnovers
Assemble: 1 hour
Chill: 1 hour
Bake: 12 minutes

CRUST:
8 ounces cream cheese, softened
1½ cups flour
½ cup butter, softened

1 egg, beaten
Filling of choice (below)

Mix cream cheese, flour and butter until smooth. Shape into a ball, wrap and refrigerate 1 hour. Divide dough in half. Roll out half of dough on a floured surface to ⅛-inch thickness. Cut with 3-inch round cookie cutter. Roll and cut until all the dough is used.

To prepare turnovers, preheat oven to 450°. Place approximately 1 teaspoon of desired filling on half of each circle. Brush edges of circle with egg. Fold circle in half, crimp edges with a fork and prick tops. Bake at 450° on ungreased cookie sheet about 12 minutes or until golden.

HERB MUSHROOM FILLING:
½ pound fresh mushrooms, minced
1 large onion, minced
3 tablespoons butter
1 teaspoon salt
¼ teaspoon thyme leaves
2 tablespoons flour
¼ cup sour cream

In medium-size skillet saute' mushrooms and onion in butter for 5 minutes over medium heat. Stir in salt, thyme and flour until blended. Stir in sour cream. Fill pastry rounds as indicated above.

HAM FILLING:
4 ounces boiled ham, finely chopped
6 ounces cream cheese with chives, softened
3 ounces pimiento-stuffed olives, drained and chopped

Combine all ingredients. Fill pastry rounds as indicated above.

CRAB FILLING:
4-6 ounces fresh or frozen crab meat
½ cup mayonnaise
½ cup grated sharp Cheddar cheese
1 tablespoon minced green onion
1 tablespoon capers, drained (optional)

Combine all ingredients. Fill pastry rounds as indicated above.

BAKED CLAM DIP IN FRENCH BREAD

Yield: 10-12 servings
Assemble: 20 minutes
Bake: 2½-3 hours

2 large loaves round French bread
16 ounces cream cheese, softened
2 6½-ounce cans chopped clams, drained with ¼ cup liquid reserved
2 tablespoons milk
2 tablespoons grated onion
2 tablespoons Worcestershire sauce
2 teaspoons lemon juice
1 teaspoon Tabasco sauce
½ teaspoon salt
Fresh parsley for garnish

With a sharp knife cut a large circle into top of one loaf of bread to form a lid. (Do not cut through bottom of loaf.) Remove top and set aside. Hollow the loaf, leaving ½-inch shell inside. Cut remaining bread (removed from inside) into bite-sized cubes; set aside.

In large bowl beat cream cheese until soft. Stir in the reserved clam liquid, milk, onion, Worcestershire sauce, lemon juice, Tabasco sauce and salt until well blended. Fold in clams.

On a baking sheet, make a cross with 2 large sheets of aluminum foil, each long enough to cover loaf. Center bread shell on foil and pour clam mixture into shell. Cover with lid. Wrap loaf with foil. Bake at 250° for 2½-3 hours.

Cut second loaf into bite-sized cubes. Toast all cubes on a cookie sheet by baking at 350° for 10 minutes until lightly browned. Remove top from dip and sprinkle with parsley before serving. Serve with long wooden skewers to dip toasted bread cubes in clam mixture.

CURRY LOVERS' VEGETABLE DIP

Yield: 6-8 servings
Assemble: 15 minutes
Chill: 2 hours

1 tablespoon butter
1 tablespoon vegetable oil
2 teaspoons curry powder
½ teaspoon paprika
Juice of ½ lemon
1 cup mayonnaise
½ cup sour cream
½ teaspoon salt

1 red cabbage
Vegetable crudite's

Heat butter and oil in small saucepan or skillet. Add curry and paprika and stir over medium heat 1-2 minutes. Remove from heat, cool slightly and stir in lemon juice, mayonnaise, sour cream and salt. Cover and chill for at least 2 hours. Serve in a hollowed-out red cabbage with an assortment of vegetables crudite's.

CAVIAR SUPREME

Yield: 12-16 servings
Assemble: 45 minutes
Chill: 12 hours

GELATIN MIXTURE:
2 envelopes unflavored gelatin
⅓ cup water

MAYONNAISE:
1 egg
1 teaspoon fresh lemon juice
1 teaspoon red wine vinegar
1 teaspoon Dijon mustard
1½ cups vegetable oil
Freshly ground pepper

EGG LAYER:
4 hard-boiled eggs, chopped
½ cup homemade mayonnaise
¼ cup minced fresh parsley
¾ teaspoon salt
Dash of hot pepper sauce
Freshly ground white pepper

AVOCADO LAYER:
1 medium avocado, pureed just before using
1 medium avocado, diced just before using
1 large shallot, minced
2 tablespoons fresh lemon juice
2 tablespoons homemade mayonnaise
½ teaspoon salt
Dash hot pepper sauce
Freshly ground pepper

SOUR CREAM AND ONION LAYER:
1 cup sour cream
¼ cup minced onion

1 4-ounce jar black caviar
Fresh lemon juice

Freshly chopped parsley
Orange slices
Thinly sliced pumpernickle bread

In a small bowl soften gelatin in water and set aside. This gelatin mixture will be divided and used in all the layers. In the bowl of a food processor prepare mayonnaise by combining egg, lemon juice, vinegar, mustard, salt, pepper and 3 tablespoons of the oil. Mix for 5 seconds. With machine running, gradually begin to add oil in a thin stream until mayonnaise thickens. Add remaining oil more quickly. Taste and adjust seasoning if desired; set aside.

Line the bottom of a 1-quart soufflé dish with foil, extending the foil up four inches beyond the rim on two sides. Grease lightly with mayonnaise and set aside. Soften the gelatin by setting the bowl in a pan of hot water or in the microwave for about 20 seconds at the lowest setting. Prepare layers beginning with egg layer.

Egg layer: Combine all ingredients with 1 tablespoon of gelatin mixture.

continued

continued

Taste and adjust seasonings. Neatly spread egg mixture into prepared dish with a spatula, smoothing top. Wipe any egg mixture from foil with a paper towel. Set aside and prepare avocado layer.

Avocado layer: Combine all ingredients with 1 tablespoon gelatin mixture. Taste and adjust seasonings. Spread over egg layer as described previously. Set aside and prepare sour cream layer.

Sour cream layer: Combine all ingredients with the remaining gelatin mixture. Spread carefully over avocado layer. Cover dish tightly with plastic wrap and refrigerate overnight.

Just before serving place caviar in fine sieve and rinse gently under cold water. Sprinkle with lemon juice and drain well. Lift mold out of dish using foil extensions as handles. Transfer mold to serving dish with a wide spatula. Spread caviar over top. Garnish with parsley and orange slices. Serve with thin slices of dark pumpernickle bread.

CRAB MOUSSE

Yield: 8-10 servings
Assemble: 30 minutes
Chill: 6 hours

1 10¾-ounce can cream of mushroom soup
8 ounces cream cheese
1 envelope gelatin
¼ cup cold water
½ cup finely chopped celery
½ cup finely chopped green onions
1 cup mayonnaise
6 ounces crabmeat
¼ teaspoon curry powder

Crackers

In a small-size saucepan heat soup and cream cheese, stirring until smooth; set aside. In a small dish add gelatin to cold water and soften for 5 minutes. Fold gelatin mixture into soup. Add remaining ingredients; let rest for a few minutes, then mix well. Pour into a lightly greased 4-cup mold. Chill 6 hours or overnight. Unmold and serve with crackers.

PATÉ MAISON

Yield: 8 servings
Assemble: 1 hour
Chill: 8 hours

1 cup butter, divided
1 pound chicken livers
½ cup finely chopped yellow onions
2 tablespoons shallots, chopped
¼ cup chopped tart peeled apples
¼ cup shelled pine nuts
¼ cup brandy
3 tablespoons heavy cream
1 tablespoon lemon juice
1 teaspoon salt
¼ teaspoon pepper

3 midget sweet gherkin pickles
Black bread or crackers

Place 10 tablespoons butter in a small bowl and set aside to soften. Rinse the chicken livers and dry with paper towels. Cut livers in half. In a large skillet sauté onions in 3 tablespoons of butter for 5 minutes; add shallots and apples and cook gently until the apples are tender. Remove to bowl of a food processor fitted with metal blade.

Sauté chicken livers in same skillet, using remaining 3 tablespoons of butter. Cook for 4 minutes. Add brandy and cook for an additional 2 minutes. Place chicken livers in the processor. Add the cream and blend until smooth; cool in processor bowl.

Place the 10 tablespoons of softened butter into the cooled liver mixture. Blend on high until paté is smooth. Fold in lemon juice, nuts, salt and pepper. Pour into a lightly greased 4-cup loaf-shaped mold. Cover tightly and refrigerate until firm. Unmold and decorate with very thinly sliced sweet gherkins (sliced to base of pickle then "fanned" out) in a line down the center of the paté. Serve with black bread or crackers.

EASY BAVARIAN PATÉ

QUICK
& EASY

Yield: 4-6 servings
Assemble: 10 minutes
Chill: 50 minutes

4 inches liverwurst roll
3 ounces cream cheese, softened
4 ounces sour cream
Touch of sherry or brandy
½ cup chopped pistachios

Buttered toasted cocktail bread rounds

Blend first four ingredients in bowl of food processor with metal blade or blender until smooth. Fold in pistachios and spoon into serving dish. Chill until ready to serve.

ITALIAN SHRIMP DIP

Yield: 6-8 servings
Assemble: 10 minutes
Chill: 24 hours

8 ounces cream cheese, softened
1 pint sour cream
1 package dry Italian dressing mix
1 teaspoon lemon juice
1 tablespoon finely chopped green pepper (optional)
8 ounces tiny fresh shrimp, cooked

1 red cabbage or round loaf rye bread
Vegetable crudites or chips

Combine softened cream cheese, sour cream, dressing mix, lemon juice and green pepper. Mix with beater. Fold shrimp into mixture by hand so as not to break up shrimp. Refrigerate 24 hours. Serve in a red cabbage which has been hollowed out or in a country round loaf of rye or pumpernickle bread. Use vegetable crudites or chips as dippers.

FIVE ALLS RESTAURANT SUMMER DILL DIP

QUICK
& EASY

Yield: 2½ cups
Assemble: 10 minutes
Chill: 50 minutes

1 cup sour cream
1 cup mayonnaise
4 tablespoons finely chopped fresh parsley
4 tablespoons chopped green onions
2 tablespoons dried dill weed
½ teaspoon salt
2 teaspoons Worcestershire sauce
Dash of pepper
Firm squeeze of lemon

Combine all ingredients. Chill for flavors to blend.

CUCUMBER SANDWICH CANAPES

QUICK
& EASY

Yield: 48 appetizers
Assemble: 30 minutes

1 loaf Hollywood bread
8 ounces cream cheese, softened
1 long English cucumber or 2 regular cucumbers,
   scored down the sides and sliced into ¼-inch rounds

Dill Dip (recipe above)
Schilling Salad Supreme

Trim crusts from bread and spread slices with softened cream cheese. Cut each slice into 4 square pieces. Top with a cucumber slice. Add dollop of Dill Dip and sprinkle with Schilling Salad Supreme for color. (If these are not to be served immediately, add all but dip and Salad Supreme and cover with plastic wrap. May be made the night before.)

SHRIMP STUFFED WITH FETA AND DILL (Pictured)

Yield: 25-30 shrimp
Assemble: 1 hour
Chill: 1 hour

4 ounces cream cheese, softened
4 ounces feta cheese
2 tablespoons lemon juice
2 tablespoons snipped fresh dill weed or 2 teaspoons dried
dill weed
Pinch of salt
Pinch of cayenne pepper
⅛ teaspoon coarsely ground pepper

1½ pounds large shrimp
Parsley for garnish
Fresh dill weed for garnish

In a food processor fitted with metal blade or blender, mix cream cheese and feta until smooth. Add lemon juice, dill, salt, cayenne and pepper. Blend the mixture until well combined. Cover and chill for 1 hour or until firm.

Shell the shrimp, leaving the tail and first joint of the shell intact. Cut a deep slit down the length of the outside curve of each shrimp and devein. Place the shrimp into a large saucepan of rapidly boiling salted water and cover for about 60-90 seconds or until they turn pink and are cooked inside. Drain shrimp in colander, refresh under cold running water and pat dry.

Transfer the cheese mixture to a pastry bag and pipe mixture into slit of each shrimp. Arrange on platter and chill for 1 hour or until filling is firm. Garnish with parsley and fresh dill weed.

WILD RICE IN CHERRY TOMATOES (Pictured)

Yield: 40 tomatoes
Assemble: 1½ hours

1 6-ounce package wild rice
8 ounces hot sausage, cooked, drained and crumbled
½ cup finely diced celery
¼ cup chopped green onion
1 tablespoon chopped fresh parsley
⅓ cup mayonnaise
1 tablespoon lemon juice

2 pounds cherry tomatoes
Parsley for garnish

Prepare wild rice as directed on package. Cook and drain sausage. Add to rice. Add celery, green onion, parsley, mayonnaise and lemon juice. Mix well and chill.

Wash and dry cherry tomatoes. Cut around the stem, remove and hollow out tomato. Stuff tomatoes with rice mixture and place a tiny parsley sprig on top.

SHRIMP STUFFED WITH FETA AND DILL
CRAB-FILLED PEA POD BOATS
WILD RICE IN CHERRY TOMATOES

CRAB-FILLED PEA POD BOATS (Pictured)

QUICK & EASY

Yield: 6 servings
Assemble: 30 minutes

½ pound select fresh snow peas
1 pound crabmeat
⅓ cup mayonnaise
2 tablespoons Dijon mustard
2 tablespoons capers, drained
Small peas reserved from pods

Red leaf lettuce

Wash snow peas, pick off stem end. Make a slit through the vein that runs along the top to form a boat. Remove peas from inside and set aside to be added to crab mixture. Blanch pea pods very slightly (10 seconds in boiling water). Immerse in cold water to stop cooking process. Pea pods should still be crisp. Remove, drain and pat dry.

Mix crab, mayonnaise, mustard, capers and reserved peas. Fill pea pods with crab mixture. Arrange on a bed of red leaf lettuce on a decorative tray.

ROSEMARY FILLET OF BEEF ON FRENCH BREAD

Yield: 10-12 servings
Assemble: 50 minutes
Bake: 25-30 minutes

1 3-pound beef tenderloin, room temperature
Salt
Freshly ground pepper
Sprigs of fresh or dried rosemary
1 large loaf of French bread
Watercress for garnish

HERB BUTTER:
1 cup unsalted butter, softened
2 tablespoons finely chopped fresh parsley
2 tablespoons finely chopped dill, chervil or tarragon

Preheat over to 450°. Rub tenderloin with salt, pepper and rosemary and place in a shallow metal baking pan. Bake for approximately 25-30 minutes. Let meat stand for 20 minutes before slicing. (Meat can be cooked several hours early, chilled, and hors d'oeuvre assembled before serving.)

Make herb butter by chopping all herbs in food processor fitted with a metal blade, adding softened butter and mixing well. To serve as a hot appetizer slice French bread into ¼-inch slices, spread one side with herb butter and broil 6 inches away from heat until toasty. Pile thinly sliced hot beef on top and garnish with watercress sprigs.

To serve cold, slice bread as directed above, spread with herb butter and top with the cold thinly sliced beef and a watercress sprig.

BRUNCHES & BREADS

 Sun's up, and so are the hot air balloons dotting the azure sky with an unlimited spectrum of vivid technicolor and pattern. It's Autumn Aloft, an annual balloon festival, hosted by Park City, a nineteenth-century silver boom town turned twentieth-century resort. Adept navigators maneuver their colorful vessels leisurely through the bracing September air while spectators admire the display and enjoy a carefully-selected brunch of fresh Orange Crescent Rolls, Rainbow Pasta Salad, Almond Ambrosia Spread and autumn-crisped fruits.

HAM AND ASPARAGUS CASSEROLE

Yield: 6 servings
Assemble: 30 minutes
Bake: 25-30 minutes

1 pound asparagus, cleaned and trimmed or
1 10-ounce package frozen asparagus
2 cups cubed cooked ham
½ cup grated mild Cheddar cheese
2 tablespoons quick-cooking tapioca
2 tablespoons chopped green pepper
2 tablespoons chopped onion
1 tablespoon minced fresh parsley
1 tablespoon lemon juice
4 hard-boiled eggs, sliced
½ cup light cream
1 10¾-ounce can cream of mushroom soup
½ cup seasoned bread crumbs
2 tablespoons butter, melted

Steam asparagus for 2 minutes; drain. Place asparagus in the bottom of a greased 1½-quart casserole dish. Preheat oven to 350°. In a medium-size bowl combine the ham, cheese, tapioca, green pepper, onion, parsley and lemon juice. Place alternate layers of ham mixture and egg slices on top of the asparagus.

In a small bowl stir the cream into the mushroom soup. Mix until smooth. Pour over casserole. Mix the bread crumbs with butter and sprinkle over top. Bake for 25-30 minutes.

SWISS AND MUSHROOM CUSTARD

Yield: 4 servings
Assemble: 30 minutes
Bake: 30 minutes

4 slices white bread
2½ cups grated Swiss cheese
3 eggs
1 cup heavy cream
⅓ cup milk
⅓ teaspoon Dijon mustard
⅓ teaspoon salt
2½ cups sliced fresh mushrooms
⅓ cup chopped green onions with stems
2 tablespoons butter
¼ teaspoon garlic salt
⅛ teaspoon white pepper
¼ teaspoon thyme
1 tablespoon sliced pimiento

Trim crusts from bread and place one slice in each of four buttered ramekins. Sprinkle cheese over bread. Beat eggs until frothy; add cream, milk, mustard and salt. Mix and set aside. Melt butter in a skillet and add mushrooms and green onion, sauteing until slightly tender. Add garlic salt, pepper, thyme and pimiento. Pour egg mixture evenly over bread and cheese in ramekins. Top by spooning mushroom mixture over all. Bake at 350° for 30 minutes, until set. Serve at once.

STUFFED EGGS MORNAY

Yield: 12 servings
Assemble: 45 minutes
Bake: 30 minutes

½ cup butter, divided
1 teaspoon salt
½ cup flour
Pinch of cayenne pepper
¼ teaspoon white pepper
3 cups hot milk, divided
4 ounces Swiss cheese, grated
6 tablespoons grated Parmesan cheese
12 hard-boiled eggs
½ pound fresh mushrooms, minced
2 tablespoons chopped fresh parsley
½ teaspoon crumbled tarragon leaves
1 cup seasoned bread crumbs
2 tablespoons butter, melted

Place 4 tablespoons of butter in a blender. Add salt, flour, cayenne, pepper and 2 cups of hot milk; cover and whirl 30 seconds. Pour mixture into a large saucepan; add remaining hot milk and cook over heat until thickened, stirring constantly (about 2 minutes). Add Swiss cheese and 4 tablespoons Parmesan. Cook, stirring continuously until cheese melts. Remove from heat; cover and set aside.

Shell eggs and cut in half lengthwise. Place yolks in a small bowl, reserving the white part. Heat 4 more tablespoons butter and saute' minced mushrooms. Stir in tarragon and parsley. Mash yolks with ½ cup cheese sauce and add mushroom mixture. Fill the white sections with yolk mixture. Preheat oven to 350°.

Spread a thin layer of cheese sauce in 9 x 13-inch pan and arrange stuffed eggs, stuffed side up, on top. Spoon on the remaining sauce. Toss remaining 2 tablespoons butter with bread crumbs and Parmesan. Sprinkle evenly over eggs; cover. Casserole may be refrigerated at this point. Bake for 30 minutes before serving.

EASY COTTAGE SOUFFLE'

QUICK
& EASY

Yield: 6 servings
Assemble: 10 minutes
Bake: 45-60 minutes

6 eggs
16 ounces small-curd cottage cheese
1 pound Monterey Jack cheese, grated
1 cup biscuit mix
½ cup melted butter, divided

Preheat oven to 350°. Beat eggs in a medium-size bowl. Add cottage cheese and cheese; blend well. Stir in biscuit mix and ¼ cup melted butter. Place ¼ cup butter in souffle' dish then add the souffle' mixture. Bake for 45-60 minutes.

CRUSTLESS CRAB QUICHE

QUICK
& EASY

Yield: 6 servings
Assemble: 15 minutes
Bake: 45 minutes

4 eggs
1½ cups sour cream
½ cup grated Parmesan cheese
½ cup flour
⅛ teaspoon salt
4 drops Tabasco sauce
1 6½-ounce can crabmeat, drained
2 tablespoons butter
2 shallots, minced
1 cup chopped fresh mushrooms
2 cups grated Swiss cheese

Preheat oven to 350°. Combine eggs, sour cream, Parmesan cheese, flour, salt and Tabasco sauce in a large bowl; beat with a whisk until smooth. Stir in crabmeat and Swiss cheese. Saute' mushrooms and shallots in butter until soft and add to mixture. Pour into ungreased 10-inch pie plate. Bake for 45 minutes or until knife inserted near center comes out clean. Cool 5 minutes before serving.

FESTIVE FRUIT COMPOTE

QUICK
& EASY

Yield: 12 cups
Assemble: 30 minutes
Cook: 20 minutes

1 pound dried apricots
2 cups white wine (Chablis)
⅔ cup sugar
¼ teaspoon salt
1 tablespoon freshly grated lemon peel
1 tablespoon freshly grated orange peel
3 tablespoons fresh lemon juice
⅓ cup fresh orange juice
1½ cups halved pitted prunes
1 29-ounce can sliced peaches, drained
1 8-ounce can pineapple chunks, in unsweetened juice, undrained
1-2 cups seedless green grapes
½ cup slivered blanched almonds
2 tablespoons grated or finely chopped candied ginger (optional)
½ cup rum or orange flavored liqueur
1-2 cups sliced fresh strawberries (optional)

In a 3-4 quart saucepan combine apricots, wine, sugar, salt, lemon and orange peels and juices. Bring to a boil and simmer for 10 minutes. Add prunes and cook 5-10 minues longer, until fruit is tender; remove from heat. Gently stir in peaches, pineapple with juice, grapes, almonds, ginger and liqueur. Stir in strawberries and serve warm. Compote can be refrigerated at this point if strawberries and almonds are omitted. It can be saved up to 1 week; then stir in strawberries and almonds and serve cold or reheat gradually until warm.

MAKE-AHEAD SHERRIED EGGS

Yield: 16-18 servings
Assemble: 30 minutes
Chill: overnight
Bake: 30-45 minutes

1 pound hot ground sausage
3 dozen eggs
½ cup milk
½ cup sliced green onions
¼ cup butter or margarine
2 10¾-ounce cans cream of mushroom soup
½ cup sherry
1 pound fresh mushrooms, thinly sliced (optional)
2 tablespoons butter (optional)
1 cup grated Cheddar cheese
1 cup grated Swiss cheese
1 cup grated Monterey Jack cheese

Butter a 9 x 13-inch pan. Brown sausage in a large skillet and drain on paper towels; crumble. In a medium-size bowl combine eggs, milk and green onions. Melt ¼ cup butter in a large skillet. Add egg mixture and scramble eggs until soft-set. Heat soup and sherry together in a small saucepan. Saute' mushrooms in 2 tablespoons butter (if desired). Layer in prepared pan the eggs, sausage, soup, mushrooms, cheese; repeat ending with cheese. Cover pan with foil and refrigerate overnight. Next day, heat at 325° for 30-45 mintues or until hot throughout. Serve with sweet rolls and fresh melon wedges.

CLASSIC FRENCH QUICHE

Yield: 6 servings
Assemble: 30 minutes
Bake: 45 minutes

1 10-inch pie crust, unbaked
8-10 pieces bacon, fried crisply and drained
½ pound broccoli, cut into flowerettes or equal amount
**   of spinach or cauliflower**
1½ cups grated Gruyère cheese
1 pound Emmentauer cheese, grated
1 cup heavy cream
2 eggs
½ teaspoon salt
¼ pound cooked ham, thinly sliced

Preheat oven to 350°. Break bacon into small pieces and form bottom layer in pie crust. Steam vegetables of choice for 2 minutes until crisp-tender; drain. Layer vegetables and cheeses; reserve 1 cup cheese for topping.

In a small bowl whip cream, eggs and salt together for 2 minutes. Pour evenly over vegetable-cheese layers; then top with the remaining cheese. Garnish with ham. Bake for 45 minutes. Quiche is cooked when a knife inserted into the middle comes out clean. Allow to stand for 15 minutes to set up before serving.

BAKED CHILI RELLENO PUFF

Yield: 6 servings
Assemble: 30 minutes
Bake: 40 minutes
Cool: 10 minutes

Note: Try Baked Chili Relleno Puff for a different dinner entree.

3 7-ounce cans whole green chilies, cut into strips
5 corn tortillas, cut into strips
1 pound Monterey Jack cheese, grated
1 cup thick green salsa
8 eggs, beaten
½ cup milk
½ teaspoon ground cumin
½ teaspoon garlic powder
½ teaspoon onion salt
½ teaspoon freshly ground pepper
Paprika, for garnish

Generously grease a 9 x 13-inch baking pan. Layer half of the chilies over the bottom of the pan. Top chilies with ½ of the tortilla strips. Top the strips with half of the cheese, then all of the salsa. Repeat layers of chilies, tortillas and cheese.

Preheat oven to 350°. In a medium-size bowl beat eggs, milk, cumin, garlic powder, onion salt and pepper. Pour over layers in pan. Color garnish with paprika. Bake uncovered for 40-45 minutes, until light and puffy. Let stand for 10 minutes, then slice.

CHERRY CLAFOUTI

QUICK & EASY

Yield: 4-6 servings
Assemble: 10 minutes
Bake: 45 minutes

1 tablespoon sugar
2 cups pitted sweet cherries (fresh or canned), drained
¾ cup milk
¾ cup light cream
¾ cup flour
2 eggs
1 egg yolk
⅛ teaspoon salt
¼ cup sugar
1 teaspoon vanilla extract

Preheat oven to 375°. Generously butter a 10-inch pie plate; sprinkle with 1 tablespoon sugar. Distribute cherries over sugar; set aside.

Combine milk, cream, flour, eggs, egg yolk and salt for 2 minutes in a blender. Add ¼ cup sugar and vanilla; blend. Pour mixture over cherries. Bake for 45 minutes or until puffed and golden. Dust with sifted powdered sugar and serve warm. Puffs high like a Dutch pancake.

CHEESY MUSHROOM-CRUST QUICHE

Yield: 6 servings
Assemble: 20 minutes
Bake: 25-30 minutes

½ pound fresh mushrooms, coarsely chopped
5 tablespoons butter, divided
¾ cup finely crushed soda crackers
¾ cup chopped green onions
2 cups grated Monterey Jack or Swiss cheese
1 cup small curd cottage cheese
3 eggs
¼ teaspoon cayenne pepper
2 tablespoons finely chopped fresh parsley
¼ teaspoon paprika

In a medium-size skillet saute' chopped mushrooms over medium heat in 3 tablespoons butter until limp. Stir in the crushed crackers and place into a well-greased 9-inch pie pan. Press mixture evenly over bottom and up sides to form crust. Preheat oven to 350°.

Using the same skillet melt remaining 2 tablespoons butter, add onions and saute' until limp. Spread onions over crust; sprinkle evenly with grated cheese. In a blender whirl the cottage cheese, eggs and cayenne until smooth. Stir parsley into egg mixture. Pour into crust and sprinkle with paprika. Bake 25-30 minutes or until knife inserted in the center comes out clean. Allow to stand 5-10 minutes before cutting.

HAM ROLLS

Yield: 12 servings
Assemble: 20 minutes
Bake: 20 minutes

1 10-ounce package frozen chopped spinach,
**   cooked and well drained**
1 pint dried curd cottage cheese
**   (or 1 pint regular cottage cheese, drained)**
½ cup chopped green onions
½ teaspoon dry mustard
Salt to taste
2 eggs, slightly beaten
1 cup sour cream
24 boiled ham slices

CREAMY SAUCE:
1 10¾-ounce can cream of mushroom soup
½ cup sour cream

Mix drained spinach, cottage cheese, onion, mustard, salt, eggs and sour cream together in a large bowl. Place a large tablespoonful of mixture on ham slice and roll up. Place rolls in a 9 x 13-inch baking dish. Mix sauce ingredients together in a small bowl. Pour sauce over ham rolls. Bake at 325° for 15-20 minutes.

ALMOND AMBROSIA SPREAD

Yield: 6-8 servings
Assemble: 20 minutes
Chill: 6 hours

Note: Your brunch buffet is not complete without Almond Ambrosia Spread. Watch out for rave reviews!

12 ounces cream cheese, softened
½ cup butter, softened
½ cup sour cream
½ cup sugar
1 tablespoon finely grated lemon rind
1 tablespoon finely grated orange rind
1 envelope unflavored gelatin
¼ cup cold water
½ cup golden raisins
½ cup currants
½ cup slivered almonds, toasted
½ cup coarsely chopped pecans
4 ounces sliced almonds, toasted, for garnish

Table water-style crackers
Apple and pear slices

In a large bowl combine cream cheese, butter, sour cream and sugar. Add the grated citrus rinds; set aside. Soften gelatin in ¼ cup cold water and dissolve in a double boiler. Add gelatin to cream cheese mixture. Fold in raisins, currants and nuts. Pour into a 1-quart mold (greased liberally with mayonnaise). Refrigerate for at least 6 hours. Unmold and garnish with toasted almonds. Serve with crackers and/or apple and pear slices (treated with lemon juice as not to darken).

LIGHT LEMON SOUFFLE'

Yield: 12 servings
Assemble: 5 minutes
Chill: 2 hours

Note: Who would guess this lucious souffle' would be so easy? It also makes a great dessert after a spicy meal.

2 cups boiling water
1 6-ounce package lemon gelatin
14 ounces lemon-lime soda
1 lemon rind, grated
Juice of 1 lemon
2 cups heavy cream, whipped
Fresh strawberries, raspberries, lemon slices
   and mint leaves for garnish

Pour boiling water over gelatin and stir until dissolved. Add carbonated soda, lemon rind and lemon juice. Chill until slightly thickened, then beat until foamy. Fold in whipped cream. Turn into a 2-quart souffle' dish or individual goblets and chill until firm. Serve with fresh berries or garnish with lemon slices or mint sprigs. To cut calories use sugar-free gelatin and sugar-free soda.

MEXICAN BREAKFAST

Yield: 4-6 servings
Assemble: 30 minutes
Bake: 30-45 minutes

1 cup sour cream
1 10¾-ounce can cream of mushroom soup
1 4-ounce can chopped green chilies
1 7-ounce can green chili salsa
¼ teaspoon ground cumin
¼ teaspoon ground coriander
1 pound spicy ground sausage
2 tablespoons butter
6 eggs, slightly beaten
¼ cup cottage cheese
1 tablespoon chopped fresh parsley
¼ cup finely chopped green onions (green stems only)
8 12-inch flour tortillas, buttered
1 cup grated mild Cheddar cheese
1 cup grated Monterey Jack cheese

Whisk sour cream, soup, green chilies, salsa, cumin and coriander together in a mixing bowl. Saute' sausage; drain on paper towels and crumble. Melt butter in skillet; add eggs and cottage cheese and blend. Add parsley and onions and cook until lightly set. Add 2 tablespoons sauce and the sausage. Remove from heat when set. Preheat oven to 325°.

Divide filling and roll into the eight tortillas. Place a small amount of sauce into a buttered 9 x 13-inch pan. Arrange tortillas in a single layer; top with remaining sauce. Cover with cheeses. Bake for 30-45 minutes or until cheeses are bubbly.

CHILLED SPICED PEACHES

Yield: 6-8 servings
Assemble: 5 minutes
Cook: 10 minutes
Chill: 4 hours

1 29-ounce can cling peach halves
¾ cup firmly packed brown sugar
½ cup cider vinegar
2 3-inch sticks cinnamon
1 teaspoon whole cloves
1 teaspoon whole allspice

Drain peaches; reserve syrup. Place syrup into a medium-size saucepan. Add sugar, vinegar and spices; boil for 5 minutes. Add peach halves and simmer for 5 more minutes. Allow fruit to chill in spiced syrup for several hours or overnight.

ARTICHOKE HEART QUICHE

Yield: 6-8 servings
Assemble: 25 minutes
Bake: 35-40 minutes

CREAM CHEESE CRUST:
3 ounces cream cheese, chilled
½ cup butter, chilled
1 cup flour

FILLING:
½ cup green onions and tops, chopped
2 tablespoons butter
½ pound mild ground sausage (optional)
1 14-ounce can artichoke hearts, drained
  and cut in fourths
3 eggs
1¼ cups heavy cream
Pinch of nutmeg
⅛ teaspoon white pepper
½ teaspoon salt
Pinch of cayenne pepper
½ cup grated Swiss or Cheddar cheese

Preheat oven to 375°. Cut cream cheese and butter together with a pastry cutter or use a food processor. Add flour, cut together and form ball. Roll out dough and fit into a 10-inch pie plate; flute edges.

In a medium-size skillet saute' onions in butter. Remove from skillet; set aside. In the same pan cook sausage, drain and crumble.

Beat eggs, cream and seasonings in a bowl. Stir in onions, sausage and artichoke hearts. Pour into the pie shell and sprinkle with cheese. Bake in the upper third of oven for 35-40 minutes or until firm.

CHEESE BLINTZES

Yield: 4 servings
Assemble: 5 minutes
Cook: 5 minutes

4 eggs
1 cup cottage cheese
1 cup sour cream
1 tablespoon sugar
1 teaspoon salt
1 cup flour

TOPPING:
Cottage cheese
Strawberry jam
Whipped cream

In a medium-size bowl beat eggs with a fork. Add cottage cheese and sour cream; blend well. Add dry ingredients and mix until blended. Cook like pancakes, center should remain cheesy. Serve hot topped with a spoonful each of cottage cheese, strawberry jam and whipped cream.

CREAMY HOTCAKES

Yield: 4 servings
Assemble: 10 minutes
Cook: 5 minutes

2 eggs, separated
1 cup heavy cream
½ cup milk
1 tablespoon sugar
½ teaspoon salt
2 tablespoons baking powder
1 cup flour
1 teaspoon vegetable oil

Using an egg beater, whip egg yolks with sugar. Add cream and milk. Sift together flour, baking powder and salt. Fold dry ingredients into egg-cream mixture (do not beat). Whip egg whites until frothy (not dry) and fold into complete mixture; add oil. Heat griddle to desired temperature before dropping on batter.

WHOLE WHEAT PANCAKES

Yield: 6 servings
Assemble: 10 minutes
Cook: 5 minutes

1 cup whole wheat (kernals of wheat, not whole wheat flour)
1½ cups milk or buttermilk, divided
2 eggs
½ teaspoon salt
¼ cup vegetable oil
2 teaspoons baking powder (4 teaspoons if using sweet milk)
1 teaspoon baking soda
3 tablespoons brown sugar

Blend wheat and 1 cup milk in blender on high for 4 minutes. Add remaining ingredients and blend. Cook on preheated griddle. Serve with Honey Strawberry Syrup.

HONEY STRAWBERRY SYRUP

Yield: 2 cups
Assemble: 10 minutes

¼ cup butter, softened
½ cup honey
1 10-ounce package frozen strawberries, thawed and drained or
1 pint fresh strawberries, cleaned and sliced

Combine butter and honey in a blender or a food processor fitted with a metal blade. Add strawberries and blend until all ingredients are smooth, about 30 seconds. Scrape into a ceramic crock and refrigerate. This is the perfect accompaniment to waffles, pancakes, muffins or oven hot scones.

STORY WAFFLES ROMANOFF

Yield: 8 waffles
Assemble: 20 minutes
Cook: 5 minutes

WAFFLES:
3 eggs, separated
3 tablespoons sugar
2 cups milk or buttermilk
1½ cups flour
2 tablespoons butter, melted
½ teaspoon salt
2 teaspoons baking powder (with buttermilk use 1
  teaspoon baking soda in place of baking powder)

TOPPING:
Strawberries or other fresh fruits
Sour cream
Brown sugar

In a medium-size bowl beat the egg whites until still peaks form. Add sugar and beat 30 seconds longer; set aside. Beat egg yolks and milk together in a large bowl. Add flour, melted butter, salt and baking powder or soda; mix well. Gently fold the egg whites into the flour mixture. Cook in a preheated waffle iron (Belgium waffle iron works nicely, too) at a high setting. Iron should be treated with vegetable spray before heating. Top with fresh strawberries, dollops of sour cream and a sprinkle of brown sugar.

FRENCH DOUGHNUTS

Yield: 36 doughnuts
Assemble: 45 minutes
Cook: 10 minutes

Note: French doughnuts are scone-like sans the hole. Dough can be rolled out without chilling or may be conveniently chilled overnight.

2½-3 cups flour
1 package active dry yeast
½ teaspoon ground nutmeg
1 cup milk
¼ cup sugar
¼ cup vegetable oil
¾ teaspoon salt
1 egg
Vegetable oil for deep-frying
Powdered sugar

In a large mixing bowl or bread mixer combine 1¾ cup flour, yeast and nutmeg. In a saucepan heat the milk, sugar, oil and salt just until warm, stirring occasionally (this can be done in a microwave). Add the liquid and egg to the flour mixture. Beat with an electric beater on low speed for 30 seconds and scrape sides of bowl. Beat three minutes at high speed. By hand, stir in enough of the remaining flour to make a soft dough. (If using a bread mixer—do the same.) Turn into greased bowl; cover and chill. Turn dough onto a floured board and roll to an 18 x 12-inch rectangle. Cut like scones, into 3 x 2-inch pieces; cover and let rise 30 minutes. Deep-fry a few at a time in hot oil (375°), turn over and fry until golden. Drain on paper towels and sprinkle with powdered sugar.

SOURDOUGH STARTER

Yield: 2 cups
Assemble: 20 minutes
Ferment: 5-10 days

1 package active dry yeast
½ cup warm water
2 cups warm water
2 cups flour, sifted
1 tablespoon sugar

Dissolve yeast in ½ cup warm water in a large bowl; let stand for 10 mintues. Stir in remaining ingredients with a wooden spoon until smooth. Cover loosely and let stand at room temperature for 5 to 10 days; stir down 2 or 3 times per day. Time required to ferment will depend on room temperature. When ready, starter will have a yeasty sourdough smell. Place in a covered container and refrigerate until ready to use.

TO KEEP STARTER GOING:
1 cup sourdough starter
¾ cup water
¾ cup flour
1 teaspoon sugar

Stir all ingredients together and allow to stand at room temperature until bubbly and well fermented (at least 1 day). Refrigerate. If not used within 10 days, stir in 1 teaspoon sugar.

TANGY SOURDOUGH ENGLISH MUFFINS

Yield: 12-14 muffins
Assemble: 15 minutes
Rise: 2¼ hours
Bake: 20 minutes

1 package active dry yeast
¼ cup warm water (about 110°)
1 cup warm milk (about 100°)
½ cup sourdough starter
1 tablespoon sugar
¾ teaspoon salt
3¾ cups flour, sifted
¼ cup yellow cornmeal

Soften yeast in water. Stir in milk, starter, sugar, salt and enough of the flour (start with 3½ cups) to form a stiff dough. Knead about 3 minutes on a floured board. Let rise in a greased bowl until double (about 1½ hours). Punch down; roll out on a board lightly sprinkled with cornmeal, until about ¼ to ½ inch thick. Cut with a 3-inch cookie cutter and place about 2 inches apart on cookie sheet that has been lightly sprinkled with cornmeal; let rise about 45 minutes. Bake muffins in a lightly greased electric fry pan (preheated to 275°), or on stove on medium-low heat. Cook 10 minutes on each side.

For a change-of-pace, whole wheat cinnamon raisin muffin, use half whole wheat flour, ½ cup raisins and cinnamon to taste.

STRAWBERRIES DIVINE (Pictured)

Yield: 1 quart
Assemble: 40 minutes

**1 quart fresh strawberries, washed and dried
(do not remove stem)
8 ounces cream cheese, softened
3 tablespoons powdered sugar
2 tablespoons orange juice
Strawberry or mint leaves, for garnish**

Beat cream cheese until fluffy. Add powdered sugar and orange juice. Fill a cake decorator tube with mixture. From the point, slit each berry into quarters (do not cut through the bottom of the berry). Pipe cream cheese mixture into each berry. Arrange on a serving tray and garnish with strawberry or mint leaves.

CHOCOLATE ALMOND ZUCCHINI BREAD

Yield: 2 loaves
Assemble: 20 minutes
Bake: 50-60 minutes

**3 eggs
1 cup sugar
1 cup firmly packed brown sugar
1 cup vegetable oil
1 teaspoon vanilla or ½ teaspoon almond extract
2 cups grated zucchini
2 cups flour
2 ounces unsweetened chocolate squares
1 teaspoon salt
1 teaspoon cinnamon
½ teaspoon baking powder
1 teaspoon baking soda
1 cup slivered or sliced almonds**

In a large bowl beat 3 eggs until smooth and lemon colored. Beat in sugars and oil. Melt chocolate; cool slightly. Add zucchini and flavoring to the egg mixture; add chocolate. Preheat oven to 350°. Sift all dry ingredients and stir into zucchini mixture. Fold in almonds. Bake in 2 well-greased 9 x 5-inch loaf pans or a single bundt pan for 50-60 minutes. Cool in pan 15-20 minutes, remove from pan and cool on rack.

CHEESY CORN MUFFINS

Yield: 18 muffins
Assemble: 30 minutes
Bake: 25 minutes

Note: A natural accompaniment to soups and stews.

**1 17-ounce can of corn
¼ cup melted butter
2 cups biscuit mix
⅓ cup dry nonfat milk
3 tablespoons sugar
1 cup grated Cheddar cheese
1 egg, beaten
2 tablespoons chopped onion
¼ teaspoon dill weed**

Drain corn reserving liquid and add to melted butter to measure ⅔ cup liquid. Combine biscuit mix, dry milk and sugar in a large bowl. Stir in corn, cheese, liquid ingredients, egg, onion and dill weed; blend lightly. Fill paper muffin cups or greased muffin pan ⅔ full. Bake at 400° for 25 minutes.

PINEAPPLE MUFFINS

Yield: 12 large muffins
Assemble: 20 minutes
Bake: 18-20 minutes

Note: These muffins
taste great and are
also high in fiber and
low in sugar and fat.

1 8-ounce can crushed pineapple (in its own juice), drained
¾ cup flour
¾ cup whole wheat flour
⅔ cup toasted wheat germ
½ cup sugar
½ cup flaked coconut
½ cup chopped nuts (optional)
1½ teaspoons baking soda
½ teaspoon salt
1 cup plain yogurt
2 eggs
¼ cup vegetable oil

Combine flours, wheat germ, sugar, coconut, nuts, baking soda and salt in a large bowl. In a separate bowl combine drained pineapple, yogurt, eggs and oil; mix well. Add wet ingredients to dry mixture; stir lightly, just until all of dry mixture is moistened. Spoon into greased or paper-lined muffin pans, filling ¾ full. Bake 18-20 minutes in 400° oven. Delicious with Paska (recipe below), yet note that Paska recipe makes enough for 4-5 dozen Pineapple Muffins.

MORNING MUFFINS

Yield: 12 muffins
Assemble: 10 minutes
Bake: 15 minutes

1 egg, beaten
4 tablespoons vegetable oil
¾ cup milk
¾ cup hot cereal (Zoom, Ralston, Orowheat, etc.), uncooked
1¼ cups flour
½ cup sugar
3 teaspoons baking powder
½ teaspoon salt

In a large bowl mix all ingredients in order. Preheat oven to 400°. Fill greased muffin cups to ½ full. Bake for 15 mintues.

PASKA

Yield: 2 pounds
Assemble: 20 minutes
Chill: 24 hours

32 ounces cream cheese, softened
½ cup butter, softened
2 cups powdered sugar
3 egg yolks
1 tablespoon brandy or 1 tablespoon lemon juice
1⅓ cups dates, chopped
1 cup almond slivers

Mix cream cheese, butter, sugar and egg yolks. Add all remaining ingredients and mix well. Line a bowl with a cotton towel and place mixture in the bowl; pack tightly. Cover with another towel and refrigerate 1 day. Serve with fruit breads or Pineapple Muffins.

POPPY SEED BREAD

Yield: 2 loaves
Assemble: 20 minutes
Bake: 1 hour

3 cups flour, sifted
2½ cups sugar
1½ teaspoons salt
1½ teaspoons baking powder
3 eggs
1½ cups milk
1⅛ cups vegetable oil
1½ teaspoons poppy seeds
1½ teaspoons vanilla extract
1½ teaspoons almond extract
1½ teaspoons butter flavoring

GLAZE:
¾ cup sugar
¼ cup orange juice
½ teaspoon vanilla extract
½ teaspoon almond extract
½ teaspoon butter flavoring

Grease and lightly flour two 9 x 5-inch loaf pans. Preheat oven to 350°. Mix all bread ingredients together, then beat for 2 minutes. Pour into pans and bake for 1 hour. Mix glaze ingredients together in a small bowl and pour over hot bread in pans. Let cool before removing from pans.

PUMPKIN BREAD

Yield: 4 loaves
Assemble: 30 minutes
Bake: 30-45 minutes

Note: Equally luscious with chocolate chips or with sugared date and pecan option.

5 eggs, well beaten
3 cups sugar
2½ cups canned pumpkin
2 cups corn oil
4½ cups flour
1½ teaspoons salt
1½ teaspoons baking soda
4½ teaspoons cinnamon
1½ teaspoons nutmeg
1½ teaspoons cloves
1 teaspoon ginger
1¼ cups milk chocolate chips
1 cup sugared dates, chopped (optional)
½ cup chopped pecans (optional)

Preheat oven to 350°. Grease and flour four 9 x 5-inch loaf pans or 24 miniature loaf pans. Cream eggs and sugar. Add pumpkin and oil, mixing slightly. Sift dry ingredients together and add to pumpkin mixture; combine thoroughly. Fold in chips or dates and nuts. Pour into loaf pans and bake large loaves for 45 minutes, or bake miniature loaves for 30 minutes.

CREAM CHEESE BRAIDS

Yield: 4 loaves
Assemble: 1 hour
Chill: 8 hours
Rise: 2 hours
Bake: 15-20 minutes

½ cup sour cream, scalded
½ cup sugar
½ cup butter, melted
1 teaspoon salt
2 packages active dry yeast
½ cup warm water
2 eggs, beaten
4 cups flour

FILLING:
16 ounces cream cheese, softened
¾ cup sugar
1 egg beaten
⅛ teaspoon salt
2 teaspoons vanilla extract
2 teaspoons lemon peel (optional)

GLAZE:
¼ cup butter
½ teaspoon vanilla extract
1½ cups powdered sugar
1 tablespoon heavy cream
2 teaspoons lemon peel (optional)

Combine scalded sour cream, sugar, butter and salt. Mix well; let cool to lukewarm. Dissolve yeast in water; stir in cream mixture and eggs. Gradually add flour (soft dough). Cover and chill overnight. Divide dough into 4 equal parts; turn out onto a floured board and knead 4 or 5 times. Roll each into a 12" x 8" rectangle.

Blend all filling ingredients together and spread ¼ of filling on each rectangle, leaving ½" margin. Roll jelly roll fashion; pinch edges and ends to seal. Place on greased baking sheets and make 6 equally spaced X-shaped cuts on each loaf. Cover and let rise in warm place until double. Bake at 375° for 15-20 minutes.

Combine glaze ingredients and spread on braids while they are still warm.

FROZEN BANANAS

QUICK
& EASY

Yield: 12 bananas
Assemble: 10 minutes
Freeze: 50 minutes

12 bananas
1 cup heavy cream, whipped
2 cups flaked coconut

Whip cream but do not allow to get too stiff. Peel bananas and cut into 2-inch slices. Dip into cream, cover all surfaces and roll in coconut. Freeze on a waxed paper-lined cookie sheet; cover with waxed paper. Before using allow to thaw for 15-20 minutes. Makes a delightful addition to a fruit tray.

CHEESE-GLAZED COFFEE CAKE

Yield: 10 servings
Assemble: 40 minutes
Bake: 45 minutes

1 cup butter, chilled and divided
2 cups flour, divided
1 cup plus 2-3 tablespoons water
4 eggs
¾ teaspoon almond extract

GLAZE:
3 ounces cream cheese
¾ cup powdered sugar
1 teaspoon grated orange peel
1 tablespoon orange juice

TOPPING:
½ cup sliced almonds

Crumble ½ cup butter and 1 cup flour using fingers or pastry blender to make fine crumbs; sprinkle with 2-3 tablespoons water. Stir with fork until pastry holds together. On a 10″ x 15″ baking sheet or pizza pan, pat dough out into 10″ circle.

In a medium-size saucepan combine 1 cup water and remaining ½ cup butter (cut into pieces); bring to a boil. Add remaining 1 cup flour and stir until dough pulls from pan sides. Remove from heat. With a wooden spoon beat in eggs, one at a time, until well-mixed; add almond extract. Spread evenly to cover pastry. Preheat oven to 400°. Bake for 45 minutes or until cake is puffed, brown and looks crisp. Cool 10 minutes.

While cake cools, blend all glaze ingredients together. Drizzle over cake and top with almonds. Cut cake into wedges and serve.

CHOCOLATE CHIP COFFEE CAKE

Yield: 12 servings
Assemble: 30 minutes
Bake: 45-60 minutes

1 cup butter
1 cup sugar
2 eggs
1 cup sour cream
1 teaspoon baking powder
1 teaspoon salt
1 teaspoon baking soda
2 teaspoons vanilla extract
2 cups sifted flour

TOPPING:
¼ cup sugar
⅓ cup firmly packed brown sugar
1 teaspoon cinnamon
1 cup chopped pecans or walnuts
1 6-ounce package chocolate chips

In a large bowl cream butter and sugar together until smooth. Add eggs, sour cream, baking powder, salt, soda and vanilla. Gradually add flour and mix well. Preheat oven to 350°.

Mix topping ingredients together in a small bowl. Sprinkle a greased tube pan with ¼ of the topping. Alternate layers of topping and batter. There should be 4 layers of topping and 3 layers of batter. Bake for 45-60 minutes or until knife comes out clean.

ORANGE GLAZED CRESCENT ROLLS

Yield: 12 large rolls
Assemble: 3 hours
Rise: 1½ hours
Bake: 20 minutes

Note: A great gift for a new neighbor.

DOUGH:
1 package active dry yeast
½ cup warm water
½ cup sugar
2 eggs
½ cup sour cream
6 tablespoons melted butter
½ teaspoon salt
3½ cups flour

ORANGE FILLING:
2 tablespoons melted butter
½ cup sugar
2 tablespoons orange rind

ORANGE GLAZE:
½ cup sour cream
¾ cup sugar
2 tablespoons orange juice

In a large bowl dissolve the yeast in water. Add all other ingredients except flour. Add 2 cups of flour, then knead in the rest. Cover and let rise until double in bulk (about 1 hour). Punch down and knead 25 times. Roll out into a 12-inch circle and brush with filling. Cut into pie-shaped wedges and roll into crescents (begin at large end and end with point). Let rise again until double.

Preheat oven to 350°. Bake for 20 minutes or until golden. Mix glaze ingredients in a small saucepan and boil for 3 minutes, stirring constantly. Spread glaze, as desired, over hot rolls.

SWEET PETALS

Yield: 12 servings
Assemble: 1 hour
Rise: 1¾ hours
Bake: 25 minutes

1 package rapid-rise yeast
¼ cup warm water
¾ cup scalded milk
3 tablespoons vegetable shortening
2 tablespoons sugar
1½ teaspoons salt
3-4 cups flour
½ cup butter, melted
¾ cup sugar
¼ cup firmly packed brown sugar
2 teaspoons cinnamon

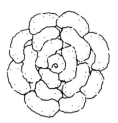

Mix yeast in water and set aside. In a large bowl add hot milk to shortening, sugar and salt. When milk mixture reaches room temperature, add yeast, and mix well. Gradually beat in 3 to 4 cups flour until a stiff dough is formed. Knead 3 to 5 minutes and let rise 1 hour (or until doubled in bulk). Place a sheet of foil on a pizza pan; butter foil. Melt butter and set aside. Combine sugar, brown sugar and cinnamon. Pull off a small piece of dough and roll it into a cigar shape. Dip the dough in butter and roll in the sugar mixture. Roll up the piece of dough and place in the center of the pan. Continue this procedure with the rest of the dough, placing each piece around the center roll to form "petals" (see diagram). Let rise again for ¾ to 1 hour. Bake in a preheated 350° oven for 25 minutes.

VERSATILE REFRIGERATOR ROLLS

Yield: 24-36 servings
Assemble: 1 hour
Rise: 2 hours
Bake: 15-20 minutes

Note: Delicious basic dough with the convenience of making ahead. Equally good as sweet roll cake, breadsticks or Parker House rolls.

BASIC DOUGH:
2 packages active dry yeast
½ cup warm water
2 cups warm milk (scalded then cooled)
⅓ cup sugar
⅓ cup vegetable oil
1 tablespoon baking powder
2 teaspoons salt
1 egg
⅛ teaspoon coconut extract (optional)
5-6 cups flour
¼ to ½ cup butter, softened
½ cup sugar and 2 tablespoons cinnamon, mixed (optional)

SWEET ROLL CAKE ICING:
1 cup powdered sugar
2 tablespoons butter
½ teaspoon vanilla extract
Pinch of salt
2 tablespoons evaporated milk
½ cup chopped nuts for topping

To make basic dough, dissolve yeast in warm water in a large bowl. After yeast bubbles, add next 6 ingredients; add coconut extract if making sweet roll cake. Slowly mix in half the flour, stirring until smooth. At this point, if using bread mixer, mix at high speed for 8-10 minutes; then slowly add the rest of the flour until mixture holds together and pulls from sides of mixing bowl. If mixing by hand, add the rest of the flour until it is a good consistency for kneading. Knead until smooth and elastic (approximately 10-15 minutes). Place dough in a greased bowl. Cover and let rise until double (approximately 1½ hours). May be refrigerated, covered, at this point for 12-48 hours (no longer).

For sweet roll cake, punch down dough, turn over and let rise again for 30 minutes. Divide dough in half and roll each into a 12" circle. Spread each with softened butter and sprinkle with cinnamon sugar mixture. Fold circle in half two times, then roll out again into a large circle. Place each on a greased pizza pan and cut **nearly** to the center with a pizza cutter-wheel or knife, making 16 wedge-shaped pieces. Twist each piece over once all the same direction.

To bake, let sweet roll cake dough rise, covered, in a warm place until doubled in volume (time will depend on whether dough has been refrigerated). Bake in a preheated 350° oven for 15-20 minutes or until brown on top. Combine icing ingredients and drip over top while cake is warm; sprinkle with nuts.

Breadsticks or Parker House rolls may be made by preparing basic dough (omitting coconut extract). For easy pan breadsticks, punch dough down and divide in half. Roll each half into a 9x13-inch rectangle, cut into sticks with a knife and place in a 9x13-inch greased pan. Brush with melted butter or melted herb butter (page 139). Let rise until doubled. Bake in a preheated 350° oven for 20 minutes.

For Parker House rolls, punch dough down and roll into two large rectangles. Spread with softened butter and cut into 3-inch circles. Fold each circle over and place on greased cookie sheets. Butter tops, let rise until doubled. Bake in a preheated 350° oven for 20 minutes.

COUNTRY CINNAMON ROLLS

Yield: 24 large rolls
Assemble: 1 hour
Rise: 1½ hours
Bake: 10-15 minutes

ROLLS:
2 packages active dry yeast
2¾ cups warm water
½ cup powdered milk
2 tablespoons sugar
1 tablespoon salt
⅓ cup vegetable oil
7-7½ cups flour

APPLE FILLING:
½ cup butter, melted
¾ cup sugar and 2 tablespoons cinnamon, mixed
3-4 finely chopped and peeled Golden Delicious or Granny Smith apples
¾ cup chopped pecans or walnuts
½ cup raisins (optional)

OPTIONAL FILLINGS:

ALMOND FILLING:
¼ cup butter, softened
¾ cup sugar
⅓ cup raisins
½ teaspoon cinnamon
2 teaspoons almond extract

COCONUT FILLING:
⅔ cup sugar
½ cup flaked coconut
½ cup pecans, chopped
⅓ cup butter, softened
2 tablespoons evaporated milk
1 teaspoon vanilla extract
½ teaspoon cinnamon

FROSTING:
1¾ cups powdered sugar
1 tablespoon butter
1 tablespoon vegetable shortening
2-3 tablespoons milk
1 teaspoon vanilla extract

In a large bowl sprinkle yeast in lukewarm water. Stir to dissolve. Add milk, sugar, salt, oil and 3 cups flour. Beat until smooth (about 3 minutes). Gradually add the rest of the flour until it pulls away from the sides of the bowl. Knead about 10-15 minutes on low speed or by hand; let dough sit for 15 minutes. Place dough on a lightly floured surface and punch down. Place in a greased bowl, let rise, covered, until double in bulk. Roll dough out into a large rectangle, ¼-inch thick.* Spread melted butter generously over entire surface. Sprinkle sugar and cinnamon mixture over butter. Distribute apples, nuts and/or raisins evenly. Roll up lengthwise and cut rolls with a knife or string about ¾-inch thick or thicker, if desired. Place on 2 greased jelly roll pans, cover and let rise (about 1 hour). Bake in preheated 400° oven until light brown (10-15 minutes). Mix frosting ingredients and frost rolls while they are warm.
*If using an optional filling, combine filling ingredients of choice together and proceed as directed.

APPLE STREUSEL BARS

Yield: 2 dozen bars
Assemble: 30 minutes
Bake: 40 minutes

Note: Apple Streusel Bars are a delicious addition to a morning meeting.

2 cups flour
½ cup sugar
½ teaspoon baking powder
½ teaspoon salt
1 cup butter, softened
1 egg, beaten

APPLE FILLING:
½ cup sugar
¼ cup flour
1 teaspoon cinnamon
4 cups sliced, pared baking apples

GLAZE:
2 cups powdered sugar
Light cream
1 teaspoon vanilla extract

In a medium-size bowl combine flour, sugar, baking powder and salt; cut in butter. Stir in egg to moisten. Mixture will be fairly dry. Divide mixture in half. Press half in the bottom of a lightly greased 9 x 13-inch pan. Preheat oven to 350°. Combine sugar, flour and cinnamon in a large bowl. Stir in apples and arrange over bottom crust. Crumble remaining dough over apples. Bake for 40 minutes and cool.

In a small bowl combine powdered sugar, vanilla and enough cream to make a thin glaze. Drizzle across top and cut into 2 x 2-inch squares.

CHALLAH

Yield: 2 loaves
Assemble: 45 minutes
Rise: 4 hours
Bake: 45-55 minutes

Note: The traditional braided bread used to celebrate the Sabbath and important Jewish holidays.

2 packages active dry yeast
⅔ cup plus 2 teaspoons brown sugar, divided
8 cups unbleached flour, divided
2¼ cups warm water, divided
2 tablespoons salt, preferably Kosher
3 eggs (1 reserved for brushing top)
½ cup vegetable oil
1 tablespoon poppy seeds for garnish

Combine yeast, 2 teaspoons brown sugar, 2 tablespoons flour in a small bowl with ¾ cup warm water. Set aside until volume is double.

In a large bowl measure 4 cups flour, ⅔ cup brown sugar and add 1½ cups warm water, salt, 2 eggs and mix thoroughly with electric mixer or bread mixer. Add yeast mixture and beat one minute. Add oil and mix for 2 or 3 minutes.

Add remaining 4 cups flour and knead until smooth and elastic. Place in greased mixing bowl, cover; let rise in a warm place until double in bulk (about 1½-2 hours).

Punch down (adding more flour if dough is sticky) and knead again for 2 minutes. Let rise again (about 1 hour).

Divide dough in half. Divide each half into thirds and roll each third into ropes. Braid ropes into loaf on a greased baking sheet (repeat with other half) and let rise for 1 hour more.

Preheat oven to 350°. Brush tops with beaten reserved egg and sprinkle with poppy seeds. Bake for 45-55 minutes.

SWEDISH TEA RINGS

Yield: 2 tea rings
Assemble: 1 hour
Chill: 2 hours
Rise: 1½ hours
Bake: 25-30 minutes

Note: Swedish Tea Rings make lovely gifts or a beautiful addition to a brunch buffet.

1 package active dry yeast
½ cup lukewarm water
¾ cup milk, scalded
½ cup margarine
⅓ cup sugar
2 teaspoons salt
1 egg
4 cups sifted flour, divided

ORANGE RAISIN FILLING:
2 tablespoons butter, melted
½ cup sugar
2 teaspoons cinnamon
2 teaspoons grated orange peel
½ cup raisins
½ cup chopped walnuts

BUTTER FROSTING:
2 tablespoons butter, softened
2 cups powdered sugar
1-2 tablespoons heavy cream
½ teaspoon vanilla extract

Optional decorations: maraschino cherries, walnuts, colored sprinkles, silver dragees.

Dissolve yeast in ½ cup water. In a large bowl combine scalded milk, margarine, sugar and salt; cool to lukewarm. Blend in yeast mixture, egg and 2 cups of the flour. Mix until well blended. Add remaining flour; combine well. Place dough in a greased bowl. Cover and place in the refrigerator for at least 2 hours, but no more than 2 days.

Combine filling ingredients in a small bowl; set aside. Divide dough into 2 balls. Cover and let dough rest for 10 minutes. Roll each half into a 9 x 13-inch (¼-inch thick) rectangle on a lightly floured surface. Spread the filling over each half and roll up jelly roll fashion; seal long edge. On 2 greased baking sheets, shape each roll into a ring, seam-side down. Seal edges of ring and snip with scissors ⅔ of the way to the center at 1½-inch intervals. Turn each section slightly to one side. Cover and let rise until double in bulk (about 1½ hours). Bake in a preheated 350° oven for 25-30 minutes. Combine frosting ingredients in a small bowl. Spread warm rings with frosting and decorate, if desired.

MAPLE-CREAM LOGS

Yield: 20 rolls
Assemble: 30 minutes
Bake: 25 minutes

1 cup firmly packed brown sugar
½ cup chopped walnuts
⅓ cup maple syrup
¼ cup butter, melted
8 ounces cream cheese, softened
⅓ cup powdered sugar
2 tablespoons butter, softened
2 cans refrigerated biscuits (10 per can)

Combine brown sugar, nuts, syrup and melted butter in a 9 x 13-inch pan. Blend cream cheese, powdered sugar and butter until smooth. Preheat oven to 350°. Separate biscuits into 20 pieces. Roll each into a 4-inch circle. Spoon 1 tablespoon of the cream cheese mixture into the middle of each biscuit circle. Fold the sides over the filling; pinch ends to seal. Place in pan and bake for 25 minutes.

PORTUGUESE SWEET BREAD

Yield: 2 round loaves
Assemble: 30 minutes
Rise: 1½ hours
Bake: 45 minutes

2 cakes yeast
2 cups warm milk
1 cup mashed potatoes
½ cup butter, melted
Pinch of salt
8 cups flour
6 eggs, slightly beaten
2 cups sugar
1 egg white

In a large bowl dissolve yeast in a small amount of the warm milk. Mix mashed potatoes in when yeast has dissolved. Add all other ingredients, except egg whites, and knead. Place in a greased bowl, cover with a heavy cloth and set in a warm place to let double in size. Preheat oven to 375°. Divide dough in half; shape into a ball and put into two greased 9-inch round cake pans. Let rise, covered lightly until double. Brush tops with egg whites. Bake for 45 minutes.

APRICOT BUTTER

Yield: 5-7 pints
Assemble: 30 minutes
Cook: 30 minutes

1½ quarts (6 cups) pureed fresh apricots
3 cups sugar
3 tablespoons fresh lemon juice

In a medium-size saucepan bring the apricot puree, sugar and lemon juice to a boil. Continue cooking over medium heat for 30 minutes, stirring occasionally. Pour the mixture into clean pint jars; seal. Place jars in a kettle of boiling water and process for 10 minutes. Tighten lids.

BOSTON BROWN BREAD

Yield: 4 loaves
Assemble: 20 minutes
Cook: 3 hours

Note: One tester, a Boston Brown Bread aficionado, claimed this to be the best Boston Brown ever, "sweet, heavy, dense and very moist."

1 cup sifted flour
1 teaspoon baking powder
1 teaspoon baking soda
1 teaspoon salt
1 cup yellow cornmeal
1 cup whole wheat flour
¾ cup dark molasses
2 cups buttermilk
1 cup raisins

Sift flour with baking powder, soda and salt; stir in cornmeal and whole wheat flour. Add remaining ingredients; beat well. Divide batter among 4 greased and floured 1-pound coffee cans. Cover tightly with foil.

Place on rack in deep kettle; pour in boiling water to 1-inch depth. Cover kettle; steam 3 hours, adding more boiling water if needed. Uncover cans; place in very hot preheated oven (450°) for 5 minutes. Remove bread from cans. Cool on rack. Wrap and store overnight before serving.

IRISH SODA BREAD

QUICK
& EASY

Yield: 2 loaves
Assemble: 20 minutes
Bake: 30 minutes

Note: Perfect accompaniment to soups and stews.

4 cups flour
½ teaspoon baking soda
1 teaspoon baking powder
½ teaspoon salt
4 tablespoons sugar
2-3 teaspoons caraway seeds
1½ cups golden raisins
2 cups buttermilk

Preheat oven to 400°. Sift together flour, baking soda, baking powder, salt and sugar. Add caraway seeds, raisins and buttermilk. Knead dough to soften. Bake in two 8-inch round greased pie or cake pans for 30 minutes.

GOUGERE

QUICK
& EASY

Yield: 8 servings
Assemble: 10 minutes
Bake: 50-60 minutes

Note: This is a cheese-flecked ring, thought to have originated in France along the Loire River Valley. It resembles a popover in texture.

1 cup milk
1 cup butter or margarine
1 cup flour
4 eggs, slightly beaten
1 cup grated Gruyère cheese (about 3 ounces), divided

Preheat oven to 400°. Heat milk and butter to rolling boil in a 2-quart saucepan. Stir in flour. Stir vigorously over low heat until mixture forms a ball, about one minute; remove from heat. Beat in 4 eggs all at once; continue beating until smooth. Fold in ⅔ cup of cheese. Drop dough by tablespoonsful onto greased cookie sheet to form an 8-inch ring; smooth drops together with spatula. Sprinkle with remaining cheese. Bake until puffed and golden (about 50 to 60 minutes). Serve hot, warm or cold, as an appetizer or main dish bread.

ONION CORN BREAD

Yield: 12 servings
Assemble: 30 minutes
Bake: 25-30 minutes

Note: Onion Corn
Bread is heavy and
cheesy. It's a natural
served with Jess's
Chili (page 87).

1 large onion, sliced
¼ cup butter
1 14-ounce package corn muffin mix
1 egg, beaten
⅓ cup milk
1 cup cream-style corn
2 drops Tabasco sauce
1 cup sour cream
¼ teaspoon salt
1 teaspoon dill weed
1 cup grated sharp Cheddar cheese, divided

Sauté onion slowly in butter; set aside. Preheat oven to 425°. Combine muffin mix, egg, milk, corn and Tabasco in a large bowl. Mix well and turn into a greased 9 x 13-inch pan. Add sour cream, salt, dill weed and ½ cup of cheese to onions. Stir until mixed and spread over batter. Sprinkle remaining cheese over top. Bake for 25-30 minutes; cut into squares and serve warm.

SPINACH HERB TWISTS

Yield: 24 twists
Assemble: 1 hour
Rise: 2 hours
Bake: 12-15 minutes

Note: Spinach Herb
Twists are fantastic
with leg of lamb.

1 13¾-ounce package hot roll mix
½ pound fresh spinach or 10 ounces frozen spinach,
**   thawed and well drained**
2 small green onions, thinly sliced
1 clove garlic, minced
1 tablespoon butter
¼ cup grated Parmesan cheese
½ teaspoon dried oregano, crushed
½ teaspoon dried basil, crushed
2 tablespoons butter, melted

Prepare hot roll mix as directed through first rising. Tear fresh spinach leaves into bite-size pieces; steam spinach 4 minutes or until just limp. Drain well and set aside. In a small skillet cook green onions and garlic in butter until tender, not brown.

In a mixing bowl combine spinach and onion mixture, Parmesan cheese, oregano and basil; mix well.

Divide dough in half on lightly floured surface. Roll one-half dough into a 10 x 12-inch rectangle. Brush dough with half of melted butter. Spread half of spinach filling over dough. Fold dough in half lengthwise to make 5 x 10-inch rectangle. Press edges well to seal.

Cut twelve 1-inch wide strips. Place strips on a greased baking sheet. Secure one end of strip on baking sheet with fingers; twist strip at other end to form a spiral. Repeat, twisting remaining strips. Roll out remaining dough; repeat as directed above. Cover and let rise in warm place for about 25 minutes. Bake in a preheated 375° oven for 12-15 minutes or until golden brown. Lightly brush with melted butter just after removing from oven.

BEST HARD ROLLS

Yield: 16 rolls
Assemble: 35 minutes
Rise: 3 hours
Bake: 20 minutes

1 package active dry yeast
¼ cup lukewarm water
½ teaspoon sugar
1 cup lukewarm water
1 tablespoon sugar
2 tablespoons margarine or shortening
1 teaspoon salt
4 cups flour
2 egg whites, stiffly beaten
1 egg yolk
1 teaspoon water
Sesame seeds

Dissolve yeast in the ¼ cup water with ½ teaspoon sugar added. In large mixing bowl combine 1 cup water, 1 tablespoon sugar, margarine and salt with 2 cups of the flour. Add softened yeast and beat mixture until smooth.

In a separate bowl beat egg whites until stiff. Fold into yeast mixture, blending thoroughly. Add remaining flour to make moderately stiff dough. Knead until smooth and satiny, about 10 minutes. Cover and let rise until doubled in bulk. Punch down; let rise again, covered, until doubled in bulk.

Divide dough into 16 portions for rolls; cover and let rest 10 minutes. Shape into rolls and place 2½ inches apart on greased and cornmeal-dusted baking sheet. Cover and let rise until almost doubled. Preheat oven to 425°. Combine egg yolk with 1 teaspoon water and carefully brush on rolls; sprinkle with sesame seeds. Place small pan of boiling water on rack in oven. Bake for 15-18 minutes.

CHEESY MONKEY BREAD

Yield: 8 servings
Assemble: 10 minutes
Rise: 6 hours
Bake: 30 minutes

36 frozen bake and serve rolls
½ cup butter, melted
1 4-ounce package crumbled blue cheese

Generously grease a bundt pan with butter. Dip each frozen roll in melted butter, then place 20 rolls on bottom of pan. Sprinkle with half of crumbled cheese. Place the rest of the rolls on top and sprinkle with the remaining cheese. Loosely cover with plastic wrap and let rise until approximately 1-inch above the rim of the pan. (Time varies with room temperature. Allow about 6 hours in winter.) Bake in a preheated 350° oven for 30 minutes. Invert onto a serving platter.

CORN POPOVERS

QUICK
& EASY

Yield: 6 servings
Assemble: 20 minutes
Bake: 40 minutes

Note: Clam or sea-food chowder will never seem as good without Corn Pop-overs.

⅓ cup fresh or frozen corn kernals, thawed
⅓ cup water (or more)
2 eggs, beaten
½ cup milk
1 tablespoon vegetable oil
1 teaspoon sugar
½ teaspoon salt
Pinch freshly ground pepper
1 cup flour

Preheat oven to 425°. Generously grease six 6-ounce custard cups or popover pan. Mince corn with water in blender or food processor. Drain corn through sieve into measuring cup. Add water, if necessary, to make ½ cup liquid; reserve corn. In a medium-size bowl mix corn liquid, eggs, milk, oil, sugar, salt and pepper. Whisk in flour until smooth. Stir in corn. Place custard cups on baking sheet. Heat in oven 4 minutes. Remove and ladle ⅓ cup batter into each custard cup. Bake 15 minutes. Reduce oven temperature to 400° and continue baking until brown and firm (about 20 minutes). Carefully remove from cups; pierce with knife; turn popovers on sides; place on baking sheet. Bake about 5 minutes more until dry and crisp. Serve hot.

THIRTY-MINUTE BREADSTICKS

QUICK
& EASY

Yield: 24 breadsticks
Assemble: 20 minutes
Bake: 10-15 minutes

Note: So easy to bake ahead and transport.

1 package active dry yeast
1 tablespoon honey
1½ cups warm water (115°)
1 teaspoon salt
3-4½ cups flour
1 egg, beaten

Optional seasonings: sesame seeds, poppy seeds, Parmesan cheese, Salad Supreme

In large mixing bowl soften yeast and honey in warm water. Add salt; blend. Add flour gradually, blending in until dough pulls away from sides of bowl and forms a ball. Divide dough into 24 pieces. Roll each piece between hands to make sticks about 10 inches long (about ½-inch in diameter). Place crosswise on 2 large greased baking sheets, not touching so sides will be crisper. (Dough can be divided into 12 pieces and placed on one pan to make thicker and softer sticks.) Brush with beaten egg; sprinkle with desired seasonings. Allow to rise 10-15 minutes, if desired, but not necessary. Bake in a preheated 400° oven for 10-15 minutes until browned.

HERBED TOMATO BREAD

Yield: 12 servings
Assemble: 30 minutes
Bake: 20-25 minutes

⅔ cup milk
2 cups biscuit mix
1 large onion, minced
3 tablespoons butter
¾ cup sour cream
⅓ cup mayonnaise
½ teaspoon salt
¼ teaspoon coarsely ground pepper
¼ teaspoon dried oregano leaves
⅛ teaspoon rubbed sage
1 cup grated sharp Cheddar cheese
3 medium tomatoes, peeled and sliced ¼-inch thick
Paprika for garnish

Blend milk and biscuit mix together in a medium-size bowl. Turn onto a well-floured board and knead lightly (10-12 strokes). Grease a 9 x 13-inch baking dish and pat dough over the bottom and up the sides of pan to form a rim; set aside. Preheat oven to 400°.

Saute' onion in butter until limp. Combine onion with sour cream, mayonnaise, salt, pepper, oregano, sage and cheese in a medium-size bowl. Layer tomato slices over dough and top with sour cream mixture. Sprinkle with paprika and bake for 20-25 minutes. Let stand for 10 minutes before cutting.

WHOLE WHEAT BUTTERMILK BREAD

Yield: 2 loaves
Assemble: 30 minutes
Rise: 2 hours
Bake: 40 minutes

2 cups buttermilk
½ cup vegetable shortening
1 tablespoon salt
¼ cup sugar
3 packages active dry yeast
1 tablespoon sugar
½ cup warm water
3 cups whole wheat flour
½ teaspoon baking soda
3 cups white flour

Heat first 4 ingredients until shortening melts. Mix yeast, 1 tablespoon sugar and water in a small bowl. Blend whole wheat flour and baking soda together in a large bowl. Add buttermilk and yeast mixture to whole wheat and soda; beat until smooth. Sift the remaining 3 cups white flour into dough; beat or knead 10 minutes. Place in a greased bowl and let rise until double. Shape into two loaves and place in greased 9 x 5-inch loaf tins; let rise. Bake in a preheated 425° oven for 10 minutes; reduce temperature to 350° and continue baking for 30 minutes.

CRUSTY FRENCH BREAD

Yield: 2 loaves
Assemble: 30 minutes
Rise: 4 hours
Bake: 45-50 minutes

1 package active dry yeast
¼ cup warm water
1 cup boiling water
1 tablespoon vegetable shortening
2 teaspoons salt
1 tablespoon sugar
¾ cup cold water
5-6 cups flour
1 egg white

Sprinkle dry yeast into ¼ cup warm water. Let stand for a few minutes; stir until dissolved. Pour boiling water over shortening, salt and sugar in large mixing bowl. Add ¾ cup cold water and cool to lukewarm. Add yeast and gradually beat in enough of the flour to form a moderately stiff dough. Turn out on floured board or pastry cloth and knead until smooth and satiny (15 minutes by hand or 10 minutes in a bread mixer). Place in a greased bowl, turn once, cover and let rise until doubled (1 to 1½ hours). Punch down and let rise until doubled again (30 to 45 minutes). Turn out onto lightly floured surface and divide into 2 portions. Cover and let rest for 10 minutes. Roll each portion into a rectangle. Roll up tightly, beginning at long side, seal well while rolling.

Place each loaf seam side down on a greased baking sheet (or sprinkle with cornmeal). Cover and let rise until double (1 to 1¼ hours). Do not skimp on the rising time; it is essential for a **light** bread. Beat egg white until foamy, then add 1 tablespoon water. Brush over tops and sides of loaves. (For a crisper crust, brush with water only.) With a sharp knife or single-edged razor blade, make three slashes across the top of each loaf. Bake in a preheated 375° oven for 45 to 50 minutes until loaves are brown and sound hollow when tapped.

RYE POULSBO BREAD

Yield: 2 loaves
Assemble: 45 minutes
Rise: 2½ hours
Bake: 35-45 minutes

2 cups warm water, divided
2 packages active dry yeast
2 teaspoons sugar
2 cups rye flour
5-6 cups white flour
½ cup firmly packed dark brown sugar
2 teaspoons salt
½ cup honey
1 cup vegetable shortening
½ cup sunflower seeds
1 cup very finely chopped walnuts
1 egg, beaten lightly with 1 tablespoon milk (optional)

Dissolve yeast in ½ cup warm water and 2 teaspoons of sugar in a small bowl; let sit until bubbles appear. In a large bowl or bread mixer, place rye flour, 4 cups of white flour, brown sugar and salt; add yeast mixture, the remaining 1½ cups warm water, honey and shortening, sunflower seeds and nuts. Stir or mix, adding more flour until a smooth non-sticky dough results. (If mixing by hand, this will have to be accomplished by kneading dough on a floured board.) Continue kneading or mixing for about 10 minutes until dough is smooth and elastic.

continued

continued

Place dough in a greased bowl and cover with a damp cloth to prevent drying. Allow dough to rise until double (1 to 1½ hours). Grease two 9 x 5-inch loaf pans. Divide dough into two equal parts and form into two loaves. Place in pans and allow to rise until double.

Preheat oven to 375°. Brush loaves with egg-milk mixture if a shiny surface is desired. Bake for 35 minutes. To test for doneness, turn loaves out and tap with knuckles. The loaves should sound hollow; if not return to oven for 5-10 minutes. Cool on wire rack.

RAISIN BREAD

Yield: 4 loaves
Assemble: 45 minutes
Rise: 3 hours
Bake: 25-30 minutes

5 packages active dry yeast
1 cup warm water
3½ cups warm water
6 tablespoons sugar
1 tablespoon salt
4 tablespoons vegetable oil
12-14 cups flour (if using electric mixer, 11-12 cups)
4 cups raisins
4 tablespoons water
4 tablespoons sugar and 4 teaspoons cinnamon, combined
Unsalted margarine or butter (optional)

In a large bowl dissolve yeast in 1 cup warm water. Add 3½ cups warm water, sugar, salt, oil and 7 cups of flour. Beat until smooth. Add raisins now if kneading by hand; wait until last 3 minutes if using electric mixer. Mix in enough of remaining flour (5-7 cups) to make a pliable dough. Turn out onto floured board and knead until smooth and elastic (10 minutes) or knead with mixer. Place in greased bowl; turn greased side up. Cover and let rise in warm place until double (about 40 minutes).

Punch dough down; let rest 10 minutes. Divide into 4 equal portions. Roll each portion into 9 x 18-inch rectangle. Sprinkle each rectangle with 1 tablespoon water then ¼ of the cinnamon-sugar mixture. Roll up, beginning at short end, seal edges. Place in 4 greased 9 x 5-inch loaf pans. Brush loaves with unsalted butter, if desired. Let rise until doubled (about 25 minutes). Bake in a preheated 425° oven for 25-30 minutes. Turn out of pans and cool on wire rack. May be glazed if desired.

SOUPS & STEWS

Eleven major ski resorts are each within an hour's drive of Salt Lake City. Granite peaks draped in winter's luxurious white cape provide "The Greatest Snow on Earth," for the greatest skiing on earth. Whether the skier has schussed the mountainside or tracked winter meadows cross-country, requirements for the après-ski celebration include a bubbling hot tub, a vigorous fire and generous portions of Pork Onion and Apple Stew, Tossed Winter Salad with Poppy Seed Dressing, Crusty French Bread and Pumpkin Pie Squares for dessert.

SOPA DA AGUACATA CON JAIBAS (AVOCADO AND CRAB SOUP)

QUICK & EASY

Yield: 6-8 servings
Assemble: 30 minutes
Cook: 30 minutes

¼ **cup butter**
1 small white onion, minced
1 clove garlic, minced
4 tablespoons flour
1 quart chicken broth
4 ripe avocados, peeled and mashed
9 ounces crab meat, drained and flaked
2 cups heavy cream
Salt and pepper to taste

Melt the butter in a large saucepan. Add onion and garlic and cook until tender. Stir in flour and cook until thick. Gradually add chicken broth and stir until thickened and smooth (can be prepared ahead to here). Reduce heat and add cream and crab; simmer 5 minutes. Be careful not to let soup boil after this point. Stir in mashed avocado and season to taste with salt and pepper. Allow to heat for 5 more minutes and serve.

TOMATO ONION SOUP

Yield: 8-10 servings
Assemble: 1½ hours
Cook: 3½ hours

Note: Terrific served with a souffle' on a cold winter evening.

½ **cup butter**
2 pounds yellow onions, sliced
5 unpeeled tomatoes, diced
2 cloves garlic, minced
1 cup dry white wine
2 quarts beef bouillon
4 tablespoons flour
6 tablespoons olive oil
½ **cup heavy cream**
4 egg yolks
¼ **cup grated Gruyère cheese**
3 slices French bread, cubed and toasted

In a large skillet saute' sliced onions in butter over medium heat until golden (about 8-10 minutes). Meanwhile, combine diced tomatoes and garlic with wine in a large mixing bowl. Add saute'ed onions to this mixture; set aside. Heat bouillon in a medium-size saucepan. In a large stockpot make roux of flour and olive oil. Cook roux 2 minutes. Slowly add 2 cups of the heated bouillon. Gradually add remaining bouillon, stirring until smooth. Add onion and tomato mixture and simmer on stove for 3 hours.

In a medium-size bowl whisk egg yolks until lemon colored. Add 1 cup of hot soup and mix well. Then stir into soup. Before serving add cream to soup. Sprinkle top of soup with toasted bread cubes, then grated cheese.

BROCCOLI CHEESE POTAGE

Yield: 6 servings
Assemble: 45 minutes
Cook: 40 minutes

1½ pounds fresh broccoli
1 medium onion, chopped
2 tablespoons butter or margarine
1 potato, pared and diced
2 14½-ounce cans chicken broth
½ teaspoon salt
Pinch of cayenne pepper
1 cup light cream
⅛ teaspoon nutmeg
1½ cups grated medium Cheddar cheese

Trim outer leaves and tough ends from the broccoli. Separate stalks and cut into 2 or 3 shorter lengths. Parboil in boiling salted water in a large saucepan for 5 minutes; drain well. In a large saucepan sauté onion in butter until soft but not brown (approximately 5 minutes). Add potato, chicken broth, salt and cayenne pepper. Heat to a boil, reduce heat and simmer for 15 minutes. Add broccoli, reserving a few flowerettes for garnish; simmer 5 minutes longer or until vegetables are tender.

Pour mixture half at a time into a blender or food processor fitted with a metal blade; whirl until smooth. Return mixture to saucepan and add cream, cheese and nutmeg. If too thick, add more cream or milk. Taste and adjust seasonings if needed. Garnish with flowerettes.

CRÈME VICHYSSOISE

Yield: 6 servings
Assemble: 30 minutes
Cook: 60 minutes
Chill: 4 hours

4 medium leeks
3 cups pared and sliced potatoes
3 cups boiling water
4 chicken bouillon cubes
3 tablespoons butter or margarine
1 cup heavy cream
1 cup milk
1 teaspoon salt
¼ teaspoon pepper
2 tablespoons snipped chives
¼ teaspoon paprika

Wash leeks well. Cut into small pieces and include 3 inches of the green tops. Cook with potatoes in boiling water, covered, until very tender (about 40 minutes). Press, without draining, through a fine sieve into a double boiler (or puree in a blender). Add bouillon cubes, butter, cream, milk, salt and pepper. Mix well and slowly reheat; do not boil. Heat just until butter melts, then chill thoroughly. Serve very cold, topped with chives and paprika.

FRENCH ONION SOUP

Yield: 6 servings
Assemble: 1 hour
Cook: 4 hours

2 beef neckbones
1 beef bone-in shank
1 tablespoon vegetable oil
Flour
Garlic salt
Pepper

BOUQUET GARNI:
1 carrot, unpared and sliced in strips
1 celery stalk, sliced in strips
1 garlic clove, peeled and cut in half
1 bay leaf
15 peppercorns
5 sprigs fresh parsley

STOCK:
2 teaspoons catsup
½ teaspoon Worcestershire
½ teaspoon crushed thyme leaves
2 tablespoons beef bouillon granules
2 quarts water, divided
5 large yellow onions, sliced
1 tablespoons olive oil
1 tablespoon butter
¼ teaspoon salt
¼ teaspoon coarsely ground pepper
2 teaspoons sugar
¼ teaspoon crushed thyme leaves
¼ cup Marsala or sherry
1 tablespoon fresh parsley, chopped

2 cups grated Swiss cheese
1 cup grated Parmesan cheese
6 3-inch rounds of toast

Coat beef bones with flour, season with garlic salt and pepper. In a large stockpot brown meaty bones in oil. Add 2 cups of the 2 quarts of water to loosen praticles, bring to a boil. Add the bouquet garni, catsup, Worcestershire, thyme, bouillon granules and remaining water. Simmer for 3 hours (remove the bay leaf after 1 hour).

Saute' sliced onions in the olive oil and butter. Season with salt, pepper, sugar and thyme. Onions should become opaque and begin to brown. Strain soup stock and cut meat off bones. Place stock, meat, onions, Marsala and parsley back into pot and continue to simmer for 30 minutes.

Preheat oven to 350°. In 6 oven-proof soup bowls place Swiss cheese on bottom and 1 round of toast. Ladle in soup and sprinkle Parmesan cheese on top. Bake for 10 to 15 minutes.

MUSHROOM SOUP

Yield: 4 servings
Assemble: 20 minutes
Cook: 30 minutes

1 clove garlic, peeled and left whole
¼ cup vegetable oil
¼ cup butter
1 onion, very thinly sliced
3 tablespoons tomato paste
1 pound fresh mushrooms, cleaned, stems
removed and sliced
¼ cup dry vermouth
3 cups chicken stock
3 egg yolks
⅓ cup grated fresh Parmesan cheese
2 tablespoons chopped fresh parsley

Homemade croutons

In a large saucepan cook garlic and onions in butter, oil and tomato paste until onions become slightly transparent; remove garlic. Stir mushrooms into paste mixture, add vermouth and chicken stock. Cook until mushrooms are soft. In a large bowl whisk together egg yolks, Parmesan cheese and parsley. Add hot soup to egg mixture by spoonfuls, until over half the broth is stirred into eggs; add back to soup. Do not boil again. Sprinkle with croutons.

SOUP IN A PUMPKIN

Yield: 8-10 servings
Assemble: 30 minutes
Bake: 1½ hours

1 10-pound pumpkin
Butter, softened
2½ cups fresh white bread crumbs
2 cups minced onion
½ cup butter
1½ cups grated Swiss cheese
2 quarts chicken stock
½ teaspoon sage
Salt and pepper to taste
1 cup heavy cream
¼ cup chopped fresh parsley

Cut lid out of pumpkin, remove seeds. Rub inside flesh of pumpkin and lid with soft butter.

Press bread crumbs onto a cookie sheet, allow to dry out in a 350° oven for 15 minutes. In a large skillet saute' onions in butter until tender. Stir crumbs into onion mixture, cook 3 minutes. Place crumb mixture into pumpkin. Stir in cheese and add chicken stock. Season with sage, salt and pepper.

Place pumpkin with lid on a large pizza pan. Bake at 400° for 1½ hours or until pumpkin has softened. Do not overcook or pumpkin will collapse. Keep in 175° oven until ready to serve. Just before serving heat cream in a saucepan to simmer. Add parsley and place into pumpkin. Mix contents well. To serve, scrape bits of pumpkin from inside as soup is ladled into heated bowls.

SIMPLY ZUCCHINI SOUP

Yield: 6-8 servings
Assemble: 30 minutes
Cook: 20 minutes

8 small zucchini (about 8 inches each), unpared and cut
**   into 1-inch pieces**
1 large onion, chopped
½ cup butter or margarine
2 10¾-ounce cans chicken broth
1¼ cups evaporated lowfat milk
⅛ teaspoon cayenne pepper
Pinch of salt
Freshly ground nutmeg (optional)

In a medium-size stockpot cook zucchini and onion in butter until transparent (no liquid). Puree zucchini and onions in a blender or food processor until smooth. Return to pan and add chicken broth, evaporated lowfat milk and pepper. Heat thoroughly; adjust seasonings. Sprinkle with freshly ground nutmeg when served.

STRAWBERRY SOUP

Yield: 6-8 servings
Assemble: 20 minutes
Chill: 2 hours

Note: Lovely soup to begin an elegant dinner.

1 quart fresh strawberries, cleaned and hulled or
**   1 16-ounce package frozen whole strawberries (thawed)**
1 cup sour cream
1 cup light cream
¼ cup sugar
2 tablespoons light rum or 1 teaspoon rum flavoring

Blend strawberries in blender or food processor. Add remaining ingredients and continue blending until smooth. Chill several hours or overnight. Garnish with fresh strawberry slices.

BORSCH A' LA EASY

Yield: 4 servings
Assemble: 5 minutes
Chill: 30 minutes

Note: A light, low-cal and refreshing chilled soup.

1 16-ounce can sliced beets, undrained
1 10½-ounce can beef consomme'
9 ounces unflavored yogurt
Juice of 1 lemon

TOPPINGS:
Grated hard-boiled eggs
Sour cream
Croutons
Yogurt
Sliced green onions

Puree beets, consomme', yogurt and lemon juice in blender or food processor. Chill until ready to serve. Garnish with desired toppings.

SPANISH SEAFOOD STEW

Yield: 6 servings
Assemble: 30 minutes
Cook: 45 minutes

¼ cup olive oil or vegetable oil
¼ cup flour
2 medium celery stalks, diced
1 medium green pepper, diced
1 medium onion, diced
1 clove garlic, minced
1 tablespoon curry powder
1 28-ounce can tomatoes, undrained
¼ cup water
2½ teaspoons sugar
1½ teaspoons salt
1 pound flounder or sole
1 pound uncooked medium or large shrimp, shelled and deveined

Heat oil in a large saucepan over medium heat. Stir in flour; cook, stirring constantly until flour is dark brown (mixture will be thick). Add celery, green pepper, onion and garlic. Cook until vegetables are lightly browned and tender, stirring occasionally. Stir in curry powder; cook 1 minute. Add tomatoes and their liquid, water, sugar and salt. Heat to a boil, then reduce heat to low; keep warm. Preheat oven to 350°. With sharp knife, cut fish fillets into bite-size chunks. Pour sauce into 2-quart casserole, arrange fish and shrimp in sauce. Bake casserole, uncovered, 30-35 minutes until fish flakes when tested with a fork and shrimp are opaque and tender.

VEGETABLE CHEESE SOUP

Yield: 6 servings
Assemble: 30 minutes
Cook: 50 minutes

2 cups diced potatoes
1½ onions, diced
1 cup diced carrots
1 cup diced celery
¼ cup butter
2 10¾-ounce cans chicken broth
2 teaspoons or 2 cubes chicken bouillon
2 cups milk
½ cup flour
3 cups grated Cheddar cheese
1 teaspoon dry mustard
⅛ teaspoon cayenne pepper

In a large saucepan combine diced vegetables, butter, bouillon and broth together. Simmer for 30 minutes or until vegetables are tender. In a medium bowl gradually mix milk with flour; blend until smooth. Gradually add milk mixture to vegetables, stirring constantly. Add grated cheese, dry mustard and cayenne pepper. Simmer and stir until cheese melts.

CREAM MARY STUART

Yield: 6-8 servings
Assemble: 1 hour
Cook: 1½ hours

1½ cups chopped onions
1 cup chopped celery
½ cup chopped carrots
½ cup butter
½ cup flour
2 quarts chicken stock, warmed
1 whole chicken breast, cooked, meat diced
1 bay leaf
2 cups hot milk
1 cup hot light cream
Salt and pepper to taste
½ cup barley
1 cup coarsely chopped carrots
1 cup coarsely chopped celery
1 cup coarsely chopped leeks
Chicken stock to cover vegetables
Fresh dill to taste and for garnish

Prepare basic chicken soup by saute'ing vegetables in butter in a stockpot until tender. Add flour to make roux. Cook, stirring continuously 5-8 minutes, but do not brown. Add stock gradually, stirring until slightly thickened and smooth. Add bay leaf and simmer for 30 minutes; remove bay leaf. Puree vegetable broth mixture in a food processor or blender. Pour back into pot and add chicken meat, heated milk and cream; adjust seasonings.

Meanwhile, cook barley according to package directions. In a large saucepan cook remaining vegetables in chicken stock until tender. Add barley and vegetables with broth to chicken mixture and season to taste. Stir in dill. Serve in heated cups, with a light sprinkling of additional dill.

MAGIC TOMATO SOUP

QUICK
& EASY

Yield: 4 servings
Assemble: 15 minutes
Cook: 15 minutes

2 cups whole milk
3 cups tomato juice
¼ teaspoon baking soda
1 teaspoon onion powder
1 tablespoon butter
Freshly ground pepper
Salt to taste

Parmesan cheese

In a large saucepan heat milk until almost boiling. In a smaller saucepan (and at the same time) heat tomato juice until almost boiling. Remove both pans from the heat. Add baking soda to juice and mix thoroughly (the juice will be foamy). Pour juice into milk, sprinkle in onion powder. Add butter and season with salt and pepper. Stir mixture, then let soup stand for 5 minutes before serving. Top with Parmesan cheese.

SKINNY SOUP

QUICK
& EASY

Yield: 6 servings
Assemble: 30 minutes
Cook: 30 minutes

Note: Leftover
chicken or ham may
be added for variety.

½ cup chopped celery
½ cup shredded cabbage
½ cup chopped green beans
1 cup peeled and chopped tomatoes
½ cup chopped carrots
½ cup chopped onions
½ chopped cauliflower
1 16-ounce can tomato sauce
4 cups water
3 beef bouillon cubes
1 teaspoon basil
2 teaspoons Worcestershire sauce
¼ teaspoon thyme
¼ teaspoon marjoram
¼ teaspoon oregano
Black pepper to taste
8 ounces spaghetti pasta, uncooked

Combine all ingredients in a medium stockpot and simmer 30 minutes.

COUNTRY LENTIL SOUP

Yield: 6 servings
Assemble: 30 minutes
Cook: 2 hours

2 cups lentils, rinsed
3 bratwurst (knockwurst for a spicier taste)
3 slices bacon
1 medium onion, chopped
1 carrot, chopped
1 clove garlic, minced
1 stalk celery, chopped
4 cups water
1 beef bouillon cube
2 tablespoons minced fresh parsley
1 teaspoon salt
Pinch of pepper
¼ teaspoon thyme
1 bay leaf
1 28-ounce can tomatoes, with juice

In a large stockpot cover lentils with cold water, bring to a boil for 2 minutes. Remove from heat; cover and let stand for 1 hour. Meanwhile, cover bratwurst with water in a large saucepan, cover, and boil for 30 minutes. Fry bacon in a medium skillet and reserve the drippings. Saute' the onion in the bacon drippings. Add carrot, garlic, celery and parsley.

Add 4 cups water to lentils, (may include the liquid used to cook the bratwurst in this amount). Add crumbled bacon, bouillon cube, salt, pepper, thyme, bay leaf, sliced bratwurst and saute'ed vegetables. Cook soup 1 hour; remove bay leaf. Add tomatoes and cook 30 minutes longer.

SEAFOOD CHOWDER

Yield: 4-6 servings
Assemble: 20 minutes
Cook: 40 minutes

4 tablespoons butter (no substitutes)
1 onion, chopped
1½ cups chopped celery
1 cup chopped carrots
4 cups chicken stock
½ teaspoon crushed thyme leaves
2 bay leaves
2 cups diced potatoes
2 teaspoons cornstarch
2 tablespoons water
1 quart heavy cream
3-4 dashes Tabasco sauce
¼ teaspoon paprika
½ teaspoon dry mustard
2 egg yolks
1 cup sour cream
3 tablespoons white wine
1 very generous cup cooked tiny bay shrimp
1 very generous cup crab
Salt and white pepper to taste
Fresh parsley for garnish

In a medium stockpot saute' onions in butter until translucent. Add celery and cook until soft. Add carrots and simmer for 3-4 minutes. Add chicken stock, thyme, bay leaves and potatoes. Simmer for 20 minutes, uncovered. Mix cornstarch and 2 tablespoons water to form paste. Thicken soup with cornstarch paste adding a little at a time until it reaches the desired consistency. Add cream, Tabasco, paprika and mustard. Add more cornstarch paste if desired. DO NOT BOIL—mixture will curdle.

In a medium bowl mix sour cream and egg yolks with whisk until smooth. Heat this with a few spoonsful of the hot chowder and then add warmed sour cream-egg mixture to the pot of chowder. Remove bay leaves. Add seafood and season to taste with salt and pepper. Serve in warm chowder bowls and garnish with parsley.

PORK ONION AND APPLE STEW

Yield: 8 servings
Assemble: 30 minutes
Cook: 1¼ hours

2 pounds lean pork shoulder, cut into 1-inch cubes
  (trim all excess fat)
2 tablespoons flour
1 teaspoon salt
1 teaspoon ground cumin
½ teaspoon pepper
2 tablespoons vegetable oil
2 large onions, cut into eighths
¾ cup hot water
2 large tart apples, cored, peeled if desired, and cut into eighths

continued

continued

Dredge pork in mixture of flour, salt, cumin and pepper. In a large Dutch oven heat oil until hot and brown pork well. Add onions and mix well with pork and pan drippings until onions are tender. Stir in ¾ cup hot water, cover pan and simmer for 40 minutes. Add more water as necessary. Add apples, simmer 10 to 15 minutes until meat is tender and apples still hold their shape.

SUPERB VENISON STEW

Yield: 4-6 servings
Assemble: 30 minutes
Cook: 2½ hours

2 pounds venison
Pinch of salt
Pepper to taste
3 slices bacon
2 tablespoons butter
¾ cup finely chopped onions
½ cup finely chopped carrots
1 clove garlic, minced
1 bay leaf
Pinch thyme leaves
2 tablespoons flour
⅔ cup dry red wine or golden sherry
1 10½-ounce can beef broth
1 4-ounce can sliced mushrooms, undrained
1 tablespoon lemon juice

Mashed potatoes, rice or pasta

Tenderize venison by pounding or using a Jaccard tenderizer, then cut into 1½-inch squares. Season with salt and pepper. In a heavy skillet fry bacon until crisp; remove, crumble and set aside. Slowly brown venison in bacon drippings on all sides. Add chopped onion, carrot and garlic and cook 5 minutes longer. Add bay leaf, flour and thyme; mix well. Place in buttered 2½-quart casserole and pour wine and bouillon over top. Bake covered at 300° for 2 hours or until tender.

Remove cover, stir in mushrooms and lemon juice; bake 30 minutes longer. Remove from oven and garnish with crumbled bacon. Serve hot over mashed potatoes, rice or pasta.

A crockpot may be used to prepare stew. Cook 10 hours on low heat or 8 hours on high.

CLAM CHOWDER, SALT LAKE-STYLE

Yield: 8 servings
Assemble: 45 minutes
Cook: 1 hour

4 large potatoes, peeled and cubed
4 large carrots, cut into 1½-inch julienne strips
½ pound bacon, sliced into small strips
1 large onion, sliced
3 stalks celery, sliced, leafy tops included
1 red pepper, sliced into thin rings
1 10-ounce package frozen corn
3 6½-ounce cans chopped clams, juice reserved
½ teaspoon coarsely ground pepper
½ teaspoon seasoned salt
½ teaspoon Old Bay Seasoning (optional)
2 10¾-ounce cans cream of potato soup
1 quart whole milk
2-3 tablespoons fresh parsley, chopped

2 cups grated mild Cheddar cheese

In a large stockpot boil cubed potatoes and carrot strips in water to cover for 20-30 minutes. Drain and return to pot. Saute' bacon in medium skillet until done but not crisp. Remove bacon and saute' onions and celery until limp. Place onions and celery into the stockpot with the vegetables. Add bacon, red pepper, corn, clam juice and seasonings; simmer for 15 minutes. Add potato soup and milk; simmer for 15 minutes more. Add clams and parsley 5 minutes prior to serving. Allow to heat thoroughly. Serve in warmed bowls with a generous sprinkling of Cheddar cheese on top.

TACO BEEF SOUP

QUICK
& EASY

Yield: 6 servings
Assemble: 30 minutes
Cook: 30 minutes

Note: A quick and easy taco in a bowl!

1 pound ground beef
½ cup chopped onions
3 cups water
2 26-ounce cans stewed tomatoes, undrained
2 16-ounce cans kidney beans, undrained
1 16-ounce can tomato sauce
1 1⅝-ounce envelope taco seasoning mix
2 small avocados, peeled, seeded and chopped

Grated Cheddar cheese
Corn chips
Sour cream

In large saucepan cook ground beef and onion until meat is browned, drain off excess fat. Add the water, tomatoes, kidney beans, tomato sauce and taco seasoning mix. Simmer the soup, covered, for 15 minutes. Add avocado just before serving. Pass cheese, corn chips and sour cream to top each serving.

CROCKED KIELBASA

Yield: 4-6 servings
Assemble: 30 minutes
Cook: 6-10 hours

½ pound lean ground beef
1 pound Kielbasa sausage, sliced
1 28-ounce can whole tomatoes, undrained
1 9-ounce package frozen French-cut green beans
1 6-ounce can pitted black olives, drained and left whole
½ cup red wine
2 cloves garlic, minced
1 medium onion, sliced into thin rings
1 medium green pepper, chopped
1 teaspoon dried sweet basil, crushed
1 teaspoon dried oregano, crushed
½ teaspoon dried thyme, crushed
¼ teaspoon coarsely ground pepper
1 pound fusilli or rotelli pasta

4 ounces fresh Parmesan cheese, grated

In a medium skillet saute' ground beef. When browned transfer to crockpot. Add all other ingredients (except pasta and Parmesan) and simmer on low for 6-10 hours. Cook pasta according to package directions. Ladle crocked Kielbasa over pasta in large bowls. Pass the Parmesan cheese to garnish.

HEARTY STEW

Yield: 12 servings
Assemble: 30 minutes
Cook: 5½ hours

2½ pounds ground beef
2 cups slivered onions
2½ cups diced celery with leaves
1 32-ounce can tomatoes, undrained and mashed
1 46-ounce can tomato juice
½ cup barley
1½ teaspoon salt
½ teaspoon pepper
½ teaspoon Italian seasoning
2 cups water
2 10-ounce packages frozen mixed vegetables
2 potatoes, peeled and diced

In a large stockpot brown ground beef with onions; drain. Add remaining ingredients except mixed vegetables. Simmer for 4 hours or more, stir often as barley will stick. Add mixed vegetables 1½ hours before serving, continue to stir often.

This may be made in a crockpot. Simmer stew on low for 6-8 hours.

SPINACH LAMB STEW WITH BLACK-EYED PEAS

Yield: 4-6 servings
Assemble: 45 minutes
Cook: 1 to 1½ hours

½ cup dried black-eyed peas
6 cups water, divided
2 teaspoons salt, divided
½ cup lentils
1 pound ground lamb (may use beef)
1 large onion, grated
½ teaspoon salt
½ teaspoon pepper
2 tablespoons flour
1-2 tablespoons butter or margarine
2 pounds fresh spinach

1 cup unflavored yogurt
Paprika
3 cups hot cooked white rice (optional)

In a large stockpot cook black-eyed peas in 3 cups water and 1 teaspoon salt for 30 minutes or until tender; drain. In a medium saucepan cook lentils in 3 cups water and 1 teaspoon salt for 20 minutes or until tender; drain.

Meanwhile, combine meat, onion, salt, pepper and flour in a large bowl. Form into meatballs the size of hazelnuts and brown on all sides in butter or margarine. Drain meatballs and set aside.

In the large stockpot combine the drained black-eyed peas, drained lentils, meatballs and spinach. Simmer for 20 minutes. Transfer this mixture to a soup tureen. In a small bowl whisk yogurt to make it smooth; pipe or decorate the top of meat and bean mixture. Sprinkle with paprika. Stew may be served over rice, if desired.

ONION STEW

Yield: 4 servings
Assemble: 5 minutes
Cook: 60 minutes

1 pound beef stew meat
2 tablespoons vegetable oil or butter
¼ cup red wine
1 cup water, divided
1 teaspoon allspice
¼ teaspoon thyme leaves
2 bay leaves
½ cup tomato sauce
½ teaspoon salt
¼ to ½ teaspoon pepper
Pinch of garlic powder
3 tablespoons wine vinegar
4 medium onions, quartered

In a large saucepan brown meat in oil or butter. Add wine and simmer 10 minutes. Add ½ cup water, allspice, thyme, bay leaves and tomato sauce; simmer 15 minutes. Add salt, pepper, garlic powder, vinegar, onions and ½ cup water. Cook until onions are tender, about 30 minutes.

CHICKEN AND PORK ADOBO

Yield: 6-8 servings
Assemble: 1 hour
Cook: 1 hour

Note: This Chicken and Pork Adobo recipe came from the chef on a ship in the South Pacific during World War II.

1 3-pound stewing hen, cut into pieces
1 pound lean pork meat, cut into bite-size cubes
1½ teaspoons whole peppercorns
4 cloves garlic, lightly crushed
4 bay leaves
1 cup cider vinegar
2½ cups water
½ cup soy sauce
2 teaspoons paprika
1-2 tablespoons cornstarch for thickening
½ cup water

4 cups hot cooked white rice
Chutney, spiced apples and fresh peaches

Combine chicken, pork and next seven ingredients in a large stockpot. Bring to a boil, stew over low heat until juice is like syrup, or until the meat is tender. Strain the mixture through a colander into a large bowl. Remove peppercorns, garlic, and bay leaves. Remove skin and bones from chicken and cut chicken into bite-size pieces. Place adobo (meat, chicken and drippings) back into pot and add cornstarch mixed with water to thicken, if necessary. Serve over rice accompanied by chutney, spiced apples and fresh peaches.

MAGICALLY EASY STEW

Yield: 6 servings
Assemble: 25 minutes
Cook: 3 to 4 hours

2 pounds beef stew meat, cubed
2 onions, chopped
2 stalks celery, diced
1 green pepper, coarsely chopped
6 carrots, cut into 2-inch pieces
3 large potatoes, peeled and cut into large chunks
2 teaspoons salt
¼ teaspoon ground pepper
1 teaspoon sugar
1 bay leaf or oregano to taste
2 tablespoons chopped fresh parsley
3 tablespoons Minute Tapioca
2 cups tomato juice or V-8

Place beef in a large heavy casserole with a tight fitting lid. (Don't brown meat first!) Add onions, celery, green pepper, carrots and potatoes. Combine the salt, pepper, sugar, seasoning, parsley and tapioca with the 2 cups of tomato juice. Pour this mixture over the vegetables and meat. Do not stir. Cover tightly and cook 3 hours at 325° or 4 hours at 275°. Do not peek!

KERRY'S "GET THE RED OUT" CHILI

Yield: 14-16 servings
Assemble: 1 hour
Cook: 5-8 hours

Note: "Get the Red Out" is the University of Utah football fans' war cry. Bedecked in red clothing, the fans fire up before the game with a tailgate party of hot chili and "suds."

4½ pounds lean chuck (coarse grind)
48 ounces whole tomatoes, juice included
1-4 tablespoons finely ground red hot chilies
3-4 tablespoons finely ground mild red chilies
2 cloves garlic, finely chopped
1¼ teaspoons salt
⅛-¼ teaspoon cayenne pepper
1¼ teaspoon oregano leaves, crushed
2 teaspoons cumin
3-5 teaspoons chili powder
1-2 chopped jalapeño peppers, seeds removed
1-2 cans beer
1 8-ounce can thick tomato sauce
2 16-ounce cans pinto beans
¼-½ cup maza flour

TOPPINGS: chopped raw onions, chopped green chilies, grated Monterey Jack cheese and sour cream

In a large Dutch oven brown the chuck. Add the next 9 ingredients. Bring mixture to a boil and cook for 15 minutes. Lower heat until the mixture just brings large bubbles to the surface (like the mud pots at Yellowstone). Once the chili has cooked for about 30 minutes, taste to check for hotness. At this point, add one or two chopped jalapeño peppers. NEVER COVER THE CHILI, BUT STIR OFTEN.

As chili cooks, use beer to maintain the consistency. Continue tasting and use additional cumin (gives that "chili" taste), cayenne pepper (adds the "hot") and chili powder. These three spices maintain the hotness and flavor. About 2 hours before serving, add the tomato sauce, pinto beans and maza flour. Seasoning may need to be adjusted to taste at this point. Continue cooking until time to serve.

It is wise to have lots of liquid available for your guests to help put out the "fire" when eating this chili! Also, if you make it too hot, try adding an additional pound of ground chuck and more tomato sauce.

CUBAN BLACK BEANS

Yield: 6 servings
Assemble: 20 minutes
Soak: Overnight
Cook: 6-8 hours

1 pound black beans
2 quarts water
1 large onion, chopped
1 green pepper, chopped
2 cloves garlic, minced
½ cup vegetable oil
1 ham bone or ½ pound bacon
½ cup vinegar

3 cups hot cooked white rice
GARNISHES: Grated Cheddar cheese, onions, chopped hard-boiled eggs

Wash beans, place in a large bowl, add water and soak overnight. (Use same water for cooking.) In a large stockpot saute' onions, pepper and garlic in oil. Add ham bone and beans with liquid. Simmer over very low heat until beans are mushy and liquid is thick (6-8 hours). Remove ham bone and dice meat. Add meat and vinegar to beans. Serve over rice and garnish.

SOUTHERN RED BEANS AND RICE

Yield: 8 servings
Assemble: 20 minutes
Soak: Overnight
Cook: 3-4 hours

1 pound red beans
1 large ham bone
3 large onions, sliced
2 cloves garlic, minced
Salt and pepper to taste
2 stalks celery, sliced
2 tablespoons vegetable oil

4 cups hot cooked white rice
6 green onion stalks, chopped

Wash beans and soak overnight in a large bowl with water to the rim of bowl. The next day place all ingredients (except rice) in a large, heavy metal pot. Add enough water to cover 1-inch over top of ingredients and cook, covered, over low heat for 3-4 hours. Remove ham bone and dice meat. Place back into beans. When beans are tender, mash some of the beans against the side of the pot to make the gravy.

To serve, form individual molds of rice from small ramekins. Place on a plate, pour beans over and garnish with chopped green onions on top.

JESS'S CHILI

Yield: 8 servings
Assemble: 30 minutes
Cook: 3 hours

2 pounds extra lean sirloin, chopped
1 pound round steak, cut into 1-inch cubes
2-4 tablespoons bacon grease
1 large onion, chopped
1 16-ounce can tomato sauce
4 tablespoons Worcestershire sauce
1 red Mexican pepper pod, cut into strips
1 green pepper, chopped
1 tablespoon cumin
1½ tablespoons garlic powder
4 tablespoons chili powder
2 cups water
Salt to taste
4 ounces jalapeño pepper, chopped
6-8 dashes Tabasco sauce
1 16-ounce can kidney beans
½ pound Velveeta cheese, cut into small cubes

In a large Dutch oven brown meat in bacon grease; add onions and reduce heat. Add the next nine ingredients. Cover and simmer over low heat for 3 hours.

One hour before serving add jalapeño peppers, Tabasco and beans. Add Velveeta and allow to melt before serving. If too hot add more cheese. Serve with corn chips and beer.

SALADS

Sheer natural majesty awaits Salt Lakers with a southward journey to a pair of Utah's grand canyons: Bryce with its intricate maze of giant, red spindles; and Zion with its monolithic masses soaring skyward. The visitor is awestruck by the diverse forces of nature which not only eroded Bryce's sandstone plateaus as artfully as a sculptor chisels, but also thrust enormous stone monuments far above Zion's canyon floor. A picnic lunch of Pineapple Chicken Salad piled high on bagels, fresh vegetable crudités and a duo of Sliced Spiced Nut Cookies and Best-in-the-World Oatmeal Raisin Cookies gives renewed vigor to the canyon explorers.

SUMMER SALAD

Yield: 6-8 servings
Assemble: 20 minutes

2 heads butter lettuce, torn into bite-size pieces
1 medium Bermuda onion, sliced into rings and separated
½ pound fresh mushrooms, sliced
3 kiwi fruit, peeled and sliced
½ pound red grapes
1 large avocado, sliced
1 6-ounce jar marinated artichoke hearts, drained
1 orange, segmented
1 cup mild Italian dressing, red wine vinegar dressing
**   or Caesar dressing**
1 cup croutons
½ cup chopped pecans

In a large bowl combine all ingredients except the croutons and dressing. Before serving add the croutons and the dressing of choice. Toss thoroughly and serve. If preparing ahead of time, put the sliced avocados on the bottom of the salad bowl and brush with lemon juice. Add the rest of the ingredients and toss just prior to serving.

GREEN SALAD WITH ALMONDS AND ORANGE DRESSING

Yield: 8 servings
Assemble: 30 minutes
Chill: 30 minutes

1 large head red leaf lettuce, washed, dried and chilled
1 medium Bermuda onion, sliced into rings
2 oranges peeled and thinly sliced, or
**   1 11-ounce can mandarin oranges, drained**
1 small jicama peeled and cut into julienne strips
4 ounces sliced almonds
3 tablespoons sugar

ORANGE DRESSING:
½ teaspoon grated orange peel
⅓ cup fresh orange juice
2 tablespoons red wine vinegar
½ cup vegetable oil
2 tablespoons sugar
1 tablespoon Good Seasons dry Italian dressing mix

Place first 4 ingredients in a salad bowl; chill. In a small skillet sprinkle 3 tablespoons sugar over the almonds and cook over medium heat until almonds are coated and sugar has dissolved. (They brown quickly; do not burn.) Place in a small bowl and allow to cool.

Mix dressing in a shaker jar; chill. Pour salad dressing over chilled salad and sprinkle sugared almonds over all. Toss and serve.

GREEN SALAD WITH BANANAS

Yield: 12-16 servings
Assemble: 20 minutes

4 cups salad greens, torn into bite-size pieces
2 bananas, peeled and sliced
1 11-ounce can mandarin orange segments, drained
  and chilled
1 sliced green pepper
1 Bermuda onion, thinly sliced

BACON DRESSING:
½ cup vegetable oil
2 tablespoons wine vinegar
2 slices bacon, fried and crumbled
2 teaspoons sugar
1 teaspoon dry mustard
¼ teaspoon salt

Just before serving, arrange the greens, orange segments, bananas, green pepper and onion in a salad bowl. Prepare the dressing by combining the oil, vinegar, bacon, sugar, mustard and salt. Pour dressing over greens, toss and serve.

TOSSED WINTER SALAD WITH POPPY SEED DRESSING

Yield: 8 servings
Assemble: 30 minutes
Chill: 2 hours

Note: Poppy Seed Dressing is scrumptious over greens, avocado slices, fruit or shrimp.

½ head iceberg lettuce
½ head red leaf lettuce
3 pink grapefruit, segmented with membrane removed
1 fresh pear, thinly sliced
1 avocado, sliced
6 green onions (green tops only), cut into 2-inch
  matchstick-size strips

POPPY SEED DRESSING:
1 clove garlic
1-2 green onions or shallots
1 tablespoon Dijon mustard
1 tablespoon poppy seeds
1 scant tablespoon brown sugar
½ teaspoon Worcestershire sauce
1 teaspoon salt
Dash of Tabasco sauce
⅓ cup vinegar (red or white wine vinegar)
½ cup olive oil
½ cup vegetable oil

Prepare dressing first to allow to chill. Chop onions (or shallots) and garlic in a food processor. Add the remaining dressing ingredients and process quickly. Transfer dressing to a covered jar and refrigerate several hours before serving.
Break lettuce into bite-size pieces and place on 8 plates (or place in a large salad bowl). Assemble fruit over lettuce. Place green onion shreds on top. Add just enough dressing to salad to moisten slightly.

"LET US ENTERTAIN YOU" SALAD

Yield: 12-16 servings
Assemble: 1 hour
Chill: 24 hours

Note: Such a versatile salad! The Relish may be used over greens for smaller salads. Ham and/or chicken and cheeses cut into julienne strips may be added to make this a unique chef's salad. Looks great layered in a straight-sided glass bowl.

2 large heads iceberg lettuce, washed, drained
  and torn into bite-size pieces
1 Relish recipe, prepared 24 hours in advance
1 Feta Dressing recipe, prepared 24 hours in advance
3 large fresh tomatoes, peeled and cut into
  wedges (optional)

RELISH:
1 6-ounce can pitted ripe olives, drained and sliced
1 16-ounce can French-style green beans, drained
1 17-ounce can LeSueur peas, drained
1 12-ounce can shoe-peg corn (or tender
  young corn) drained
1 medium-size Bermuda onion, sliced into thin rings
1 medium-size red or golden pepper, sliced into
  thin rings
1 cup thinly sliced celery
½ cup vegetable oil
¼ cup tarragon vinegar
½ cup sugar
2 teaspoons water
½ teaspoon coarsely ground pepper

FETA DRESSING:
1 cup mayonnaise
¼ cup sour cream
2 cups buttermilk
1 1.4-ounce package Good Seasons Buttermilk
  Farm-Style dressing (with buttermilk in the mix)
4 ounces crumbled feta cheese

To prepare Relish, toss the first 7 Relish ingredients in a large mixing bowl suitable for marinating. Combine the next 5 ingredients in a jar and shake well. Pour over Relish and allow to marinate, refrigerated, for 24 hours.

To prepare Feta Dressing whisk the first 4 dressing ingredients together in a wide-mouthed quart jar. Add the feta cheese and refrigerate for 24 hours.

Assemble the salad in layers beginning with a layer of iceberg lettuce, then drained Relish, tomato (optional) and dollops of Feta Dressing.

MARINATED VEGETABLE AND PASTA SALAD

Yield: 12 servings
Assemble: 45 minutes
Marinate: 10 hours

1 pound large shell pasta (conchiglie rigate)
1 Bermuda onion, thinly sliced into rings
1 large yellow bell pepper, thinly sliced into rings
2 carrots, thinly sliced
1 head cauliflower, separated into small flowerettes
2 small zucchini, thinly sliced
2 cups broccoli flowerettes
½ pound fresh mushrooms, halved
2 tomatoes, peeled and diced
1 6-ounce can pitted black olives, drained
1 .07-ounce package Good Seasons Italian dressing mix
1 16-ounce Bernstein's Cheese and Garlic Italian dressing

continued

continued

Cook pasta according to package directions; immerse in cold water, drain and set aside.

Wash and cut vegetables; place in a large container suitable for marinating. Add pasta and sprinkle with dry Italian dressing. Pour bottled dressing over all, toss and refrigerate for 10 to 24 hours.

SUMMERTIME PASTA

QUICK
& EASY

Yield: 4-6 servings
Assemble: 20 minutes
Chill: 40 minutes

1 pound linguine pasta
2-3 large tomatoes, chopped
½ cup chopped green onions
1 cucumber, pared and diced
1 6-ounce jar marinated artichoke hearts, drained
½ cup grated fresh Parmesan cheese

BALSAMIC DRESSING:
½ cup olive oil
3 tablespoons Balsamic vinegar
1 tablespoon fresh parsley
½ teaspoon basil
1 clove garlic, pressed
Pinch of salt
Pepper to taste

Prepare pasta according to package directions. Drain and rinse with cold water. In a large bowl combine the tomatoes, green onion, cucumber, artichoke hearts and Parmesan cheese. Toss to blend well.

In a shaker jar with lid combine oil, vinegar, parsley, basil and garlic. Shake well and pour over tomato mixture. Allow to stand for 15 minutes, then add the pasta, salt and pepper. Toss well; chill and serve.

COLD TORTELLINI SALAD

Yield: 8-10 servings
Assemble: 45 minutes
Marinate: 6 hours

8 ounces spinach tortellini (cheese-filled spinach pasta)
Broccoli flowerettes (optional)
4 ounces Parmesan cheese, grated
1 6-ounce jar marinated artichoke hearts (optional)
1 6-ounce can pitted black olives, drained (optional)
1 8-ounce can garbanzo beans, rinsed and drained (optional)
1 8-ounce can kidney beans, rinsed and drained (optional)
1 8-ounce can lima beans, rinsed and drained (optional)
1 Bermuda onion, sliced (optional)
16 ounces creamy Italian dressing
1 avocado, sliced
24 cherry tomatoes, halved
¼ pound sliced salami

In a large saucepan cook tortellini in boiling salted water for 15-20 minutes. Drain well; cover with cold water to cool, and drain again. Add any of the optional ingredients as desired. Marinate in a creamy Italian dressing for at least 6 hours. Just prior to serving, add the avocado, tomatoes and salami.

RAINBOW PASTA SALAD

Yield: 6-8 servings
Assemble: 1¼ hours

1 pound fresh pasta (below), cooked, drained and chilled (use spinach pasta or tomato pasta or a combination of both, one half pound of each)
1 cup grated Asiago cheese (may substitute grated fresh Romano or Parmesan cheese)
1 cup cubed smoked turkey or ham
1 cup julienne sliced carrots, blanched
1 cup cauliflower flowerettes, cooked crisp-tender
½ cup stuffed green olives, sliced

VINAIGRETTE DRESSING:
1 clove garlic, crushed
¼ teaspoon salt
½ cup olive oil
¼ cup red wine vinegar
1 teaspoon Dijon mustard
½ teaspoon freshly ground pepper
½ teaspoon dried oregano, crumbled

PASTA:
Spinach Pasta (yields one pound):
  2½ cups flour
  2 tablespoons cooked and pureed fresh spinach
  3 eggs
Tomato Pasta (yields one pound):
  2½ cups flour
  2 tablespoons tomato paste
  3 eggs

To make either spinach or tomato pasta, place desired ingredients in bowl of food processor fitted with a metal blade. Process until mixture forms a ball. Let dough rest covered for 30 minutes. Use pasta maker and cut into fettuccine.

In an 8-quart stockpot cook pasta in 5 quarts of boiling water until al dente' (5 minutes). Immerse in cold water to stop cooking and drain well; set aside.

To prepare vinaigrette dressing, crush garlic and salt with a mortar and pestle, blender or food processor. Transfer to a small bowl. Add oil, vinegar, mustard, pepper and oregano; set aside.

In a large bowl combine the pasta, cheese, turkey, ham, carrots, cauliflower and olives. Pour dressing over mixture and toss to mix well.

SALMON PASTA SALAD WITH HERB DRESSING

Yield: 6-8 servings
Assemble: 1½ hours
Chill: 1 hour

1-2 pounds sockeye salmon, fresh or frozen

FETTUCCINE (yields one pound):
1¾ cups flour
2 eggs
3 tablespoon water
1 teaspoon olive oil

continued

continued

COURT BOUILLON:
1 quart water
2 bay leaves
1 teaspoon rosemary
2 cloves garlic, halved
2 whole green onions
2 sprigs fresh parsley
4 lemon slices
1 teaspoon black peppercorns
½ teaspoon salt

1 pound fresh spinach, washed and cut into strips, chilled
½ cup slivered almonds
2 tablespoons butter
1 cup green onions (green tops only), finely sliced
4 ounces fresh Parmesan cheese, grated
2 tablespoons finely chopped fresh parsley

HERB DRESSING:
1 clove garlic
1 tablespoon sweet basil
2 eggs
1 tablespoon tarragon vinegar
⅓ cup lemon juice
2 teaspoons sugar
½ cup olive oil
½ cup vegetable oil
1½ teaspoons dry mustard
1 teaspoon salt
1 teaspoon coarsly ground pepper
1 teaspoon dill weed
2 teaspoons crushed rosemary
1 teaspoon lemon peel

Prepare fettuccine first by mixing flour, eggs, water and olive oil in the bowl of a food processor fitted with a metal blade. Process until mixture forms a ball. Let dough rest covered for 30 minutes. Use pasta maker and cut into fettuccine. Cook until al dente' (5 minutes). Rinse with cold water and drain; chill.

Poach salmon in the Court Bouillon until cooked throughout (approximately 5-10 minutes). Remove fish from Court Bouillon and chunk into 1-inch pieces into a large salad bowl; add fettuccine and chill. In a medium-size skillet toast almonds in 2 tablespoons butter; cool. Add almonds to pasta and salmon.

Prepare dressing by mincing the garlic and basil in the bowl of a food processor or blender; remove and set aside. Whirl the eggs in the processor and add vinegar, lemon and sugar. Dribble salad oils into egg mixture with processor running. Then stir in mustard, salt, pepper, dill weed, rosemary, lemon peel, basil and garlic.

Pour dressing over pasta and salmon. Add green onions, Parmesan cheese, spinach and parsley. Toss well and chill until ready to serve.

CHINESE NOODLES AND SLAW

Yield: 8-10 servings
Assemble: 20 minutes
Chill: 2 hours

Note: Fun salad to serve at a barbecue or tailgate party.

**2 packages chicken-flavored ramen noodles, spice
  packs reserved**
1 cup slivered almonds
1 tablespoon butter
1 medium-size head cabbage, finely shredded
1 red bell pepper, thinly sliced
2 tablespoons sesame seeds
1 bunch green onions, chopped
¾ cup vegetable oil
4 teaspoons sugar
½ cup cider vinegar
Spice packs from noodles
Pinch of salt
Pepper to taste

Boil noodles according to package directions, but do not add spice packs. Drain and rinse with cold water to stop cooking; drain again.

Toast almonds in butter. Combine the noodles, toasted almonds, finely shredded cabbage, pepper, sesame seeds and green onions.

Prepare dressing by combining the oil, sugar, vinegar, spice packs from noodles, salt and pepper. Pour the dressing over salad and allow to chill several hours before serving.

COLD CAULIFLOWER SALAD PLATTER

Yield: 8-10 servings
Assemble: 30 minutes
Chill: 12 hours

1 cauliflower, approximately 2 pounds
Pinch of salt
4 lemon slices
2 tablespoons lemon juice
½ teaspoon salt
Pinch of pepper
½ cup mayonnaise
⅓ cup brown mustard (grainy-type works well)
2 tablespoons sour cream
Romaine lettuce leaves
2 large tomatoes
2 tablespoons chopped fresh parsley
½ cup frozen peas, thawed (optional)
¼ cup honey-roasted peanuts (optional)

One day ahead, prepare the cauliflower by cutting into flowerettes. In a large saucepan cook cauliflower in boiling salted water with lemon slices added for about 8-10 minutes until crisp-tender. Drain and cool in ice water; drain again.

To prepare dressing, combine the lemon juice, salt, pepper, mayonnaise, mustard and sour cream; mix well and refrigerate overnight.

To serve, assemble salad by lining a serving platter with romaine. Arrange sliced tomatoes over lettuce around edges of platter. Toss cauliflower with desired optional ingredients and mound in the center; cover with dressing, sprinkle with parsley and serve.

RICE AND SHRIMP SALAD

Yield: 4 servings
Assemble: 20 minutes
Chill: 24 hours

Note: Make ahead and transport to tomorrow's meeting.

1 cup cooked converted rice, chilled
½ cup chopped celery
2 tablespoons minced onion
2 4½-ounce cans tiny shrimp, rinsed and drained
1 8-ounce package frozen peas, partially cooked
3 carrots, grated
½ cup mayonnaise
½ cup salad dressing (Miracle Whip-type)

Combine all ingredients together and chill at least 24 hours before serving.

CHILLED RICE AND ARTICHOKES

Yield: 6 servings
Assemble: 30 minutes
Chill: 12 hours

Note: Wonderful alternative to a pasta or potato salad. Great with barbecued ribs.

1 8-ounce package chicken flavored Rice-a-Roni
2 green onions (green tops only), chopped
12 large pimiento-stuffed green olives, sliced
½ medium green pepper, diced
2 6-ounce jars marinated artichokes, cut into bite-size pieces; reserve marinade
¼ cup mayonnaise
¼ teaspoon curry powder
1 small tomato, diced (optional)
1 8-ounce can sliced water chestnuts (optional)
½ cup slivered almonds (optional)

Prepare Rice-a-Roni according to package directions, reducing amount of water by ¼ cup. Do not over cook. The Rice-a-Roni should be tender-firm; chill.

To prepare dressing, drain the marinade from the artichoke hearts and combine it with mayonnaise and curry powder.

In a large bowl combine the Rice-a-Roni, onion, olives, green pepper and artichokes. Add optional ingredients, if desired. Toss with dressing and refrigerate several hours before serving. (Salad is best when made one day before serving.)

PICKLED COLESLAW

Yield: 8 servings
Assemble: 15 minutes
Marinate: 24 hours

1 3-pound head cabbage, shredded
1 medium red or white onion, chopped
1 green pepper, chopped
2 cups water
2 cups sugar
2 cups vinegar
2 tablespoons mustard seed
Pinch of salt

Combine shredded cabbage, onion and green pepper; mix well. Boil the water with sugar, vinegar, mustard seed and salt. Pour liquid over cabbage mixture and allow to stand refrigerated, for 24 hours. Stays fresh, refrigerated, for up to 2 weeks.

PEA POD SALAD WITH SOY GINGER DRESSING

Yield: 4 servings
Assemble: 20 minutes

12 ounces Chinese pea pods, cleaned
1 8-ounce can sliced water chestnuts, drained
6 green onions, cut into 3-inch lengths
1 head romaine lettuce, washed and torn into bite-size pieces
¼ cup chopped salted peanuts
Pinch of salt
Pepper to taste
Lemon juice to taste

SOY GINGER DRESSING:
1½ tablespoons vegetable oil
½ teaspoon minced fresh gingerroot
2 green onions, minced
⅓ cup chicken broth
1 tablespoon cider vinegar
2 teaspoons soy sauce

Blanch pea pods in boiling water for 30 seconds. Drain and run cold water over to stop cooking; drain again. Combine pea pods, water chestnuts, green onions and lettuce in a large serving bowl. Chill until ready to serve.

Prepare dressing by heating oil in a small saucepan over medium-high heat. Add the gingerroot and cook, stirring until just brown. Add the minced green onion. Stir in broth, vinegar and soy sauce. Set aside and keep warm.

Before serving, bring dressing to a boil. Stir in the salt, pepper and lemon juice. Toss with the salad, sprinkle with peanuts and serve at once.

CAULIFLOWER AND OLIVE SALAD

Yield: 4-6 servings
Assemble: 15 minutes
Marinate: 30 minutes

1 Bermuda onion, sliced
½ small head cauliflower, flowerettes sliced
½ cup sliced pimiento-stuffed green olives
1 head bibb lettuce
½ cup blue cheese, crumbled

LEMON DRESSING:
½ cup olive oil
½ cup lemon juice
½ teaspoon basil
Pepper to taste

Prepare dressing first by combining oil, lemon juice, basil and pepper in a large bowl. Slice onion, cauliflower and olives. Add to dressing mixture and marinate for at least 30 minutes.

Tear the lettuce and add to cauliflower mixture. Sprinkle with blue cheese. Toss and serve.

ELEGANT SLAW-STUFFED TOMATOES

Yield: 6 servings
Assemble: 30 minutes
Chill: 30 minutes

Note: Delicious with grilled meats, fresh corn and Cheesy Monkey Bread (page 65).

6 large fresh tomatoes, peeled and chilled
1 teaspoon sugar
1 tablespoon red wine vinegar
⅓ cup mayonnaise
⅓ cup sour cream
½ teaspoon celery seed
2 teaspoons Dijon mustard
1 teaspoon prepared mustard
5 cups shredded green cabbage
1 2-ounce jar pimiento-stuffed green olives, sliced
Red leaf lettuce

To peel tomatoes, plunge them in to boiling water for 10 seconds and then slip off the peel. Core and chill.

To prepare dressing, dissolve the sugar in the vinegar in a large mixing bowl. Add mayonnaise, sour cream, celery seed and mustards; whisk until smooth. Add the cabbage and olives to dressing; mix well. Chill until ready to assemble stuffed tomatoes.

Cut each tomato into 6 wedges, but do not cut through bottom, so that tomato forms a "cup." Place on a leaf of lettuce and spoon the slaw into the center of each tomato.

MARINATED MUSHROOM SALAD

Yield: 8-12 servings
Assemble: 20 minutes
Marinate: 1 hour

Note: Unusual salad to include on a buffet table.

1 cup vegetable oil
2 teaspoons salt
2½ teaspoons dry basil
2½ teaspoons Dijon mustard
½ teaspoon pepper
½ teaspoon paprika
5 tablespoons white wine vinegar
4 teaspoons lemon juice
2 pounds fresh mushrooms, sliced
1½ cups thinly sliced green onions (green tops included)
1 quart cherry tomatoes, washed and stems removed

In large bowl suitable for marinating, combine oil, salt, basil, mustard, pepper, paprika, vinegar and lemon juice. Beat with a fork until well blended. Mix in mushrooms and green onions. Cover and marinate at room temperature, stirring occasionally, for about 1 hour or until serving time. Prior to serving, fold in tomatoes.

CURRIED SPINACH SALAD (Pictured)

Yield: 6-8 servings
Assemble: 20 minutes

Note: Curried Spinach Salad is delicious served with pork.

2 pounds fresh spinach or romaine lettuce, cleaned
3 unpared apples, thinly sliced
½ cup golden raisins
¼ cup thinly sliced green onions
⅔ cup honey-roasted peanuts
1 orange, segmented with membrane removed
2 tablespoons sesame seeds

CURRY DRESSING:
½ cup white wine vinegar
⅔ cup vegetable oil
1 tablespoon finely chopped chutney
1 teaspoon curry powder
1 teaspoon salt
1 teaspoon dry mustard
1-2 drops Tabasco sauce

Prepare dressing first to allow flavors to blend. Combine vinegar, oil, chutney, curry powder, salt, dry mustard and Tabasco sauce in a jar and shake until blended well. For best flavor, allow dressing to stand for 2 hours at room temperature before serving.

Combine spinach or romaine lettuce, apples, raisins, green onions, peanuts, oranges and sesame seeds. Toss with Curry Dressing.

ORIENTAL SPINACH SALAD

Yield: 8-10 servings
Assemble: 20 minutes

Note: The secret of the salad is the dressing. Use your imagination to create other combinations.

2 pounds fresh spinach, washed, dried and stems removed
1 8-ounce can sliced water chestnuts, drained
2 carrots, grated
3 cups bean sprouts
1 11-ounce can mandarin oranges, drained
1 Bermuda onion, sliced into rings (optional)

PAPRIKA DRESSING:
½ cup sugar
¼ cup tarragon vinegar
½ cup lemon juice
2 tablespoons grated onion
½ cup vegetable oil
1 teaspoon salt
1 teaspoon paprika
2 tablespoons sesame seeds browned in
  1 tablespoon butter

Tear spinach into bite-size pieces and place into a large salad bowl. Add water chestnuts, carrots and bean sprouts; set aside.

Prepare the dressing by combining all ingredients, except sesame seeds, in a blender. Mix well. Then **stir** in the sesame seeds. Pour the dressing over the salad just before serving.

CURRIED SPINACH SALAD

WARM SPINACH SALAD WITH CHEESES

Yield: 6-8 servings
Assemble: 30 minutes

2 pounds fresh spinach, washed, dried, and stems removed
4 green onions (green tops included), thinly sliced
2 tablespoons butter, divided
¼ cup sunflower seeds
¼ teaspoon Beau Monde seasoning
½ pound fresh mushrooms, sliced
½ pound bacon
½ cup finely grated fresh Parmesan cheese
½ cup finely grated feta cheese

FRAGRANT DRESSING:
⅔ vegetable oil
¼ cup red wine vinegar
2 tablespoons white wine
2 teaspoons soy sauce
1 teaspoon sugar
1 teaspoon dry mustard
½ teaspoon curry powder
½ teaspoon coarsely ground pepper
1 clove garlic, crushed

Prepare dressing in pint-size jar with lid. Shake vigorously to combine. Refrigerate and allow flavors to blend.

. Tear spinach into a large salad bowl. Add onion and set aside. In a large skillet toast sunflower seeds in 1 tablespoon of the butter. Sprinkle with Beau Monde. Remove toasted seeds and set aside. In the same skillet saute' mushrooms in 1 tablespoon butter until golden. Remove and set aside. Add bacon to skillet; fry until crisp. Drain bacon on paper towels; crumble. Pour bacon grease out of skillet, but do not wash pan.

Add sunflower seeds, mushrooms, bacon and cheeses to the spinach; toss lightly. Heat dressing in skillet until it almost reaches a boil. Pour over salad, toss and serve immediately. This salad is also delicious chilled, but do not cook mushrooms or heat dressing.

DILLED SOUR CREAM CUCUMBERS

Yield: 4-6 servings
Assemble: 15 minutes
Chill: 2 hours

2 medium cucumbers, peeled and sliced
1 cup sour cream
1 teaspoon salt
1 tablespoon lemon juice
1 tablespoon chopped onion
2 tablespoons chopped dill pickles
½ teaspoon sugar
Pinch of pepper
Fresh parsley for garnish

Combine all ingredients and refrigerate several hours before serving. May be served as a vegetable or salad.

LAYERED SHRIMP AND CRAB ASPIC

Yield: 12 servings
Assemble: 45 minutes
Chill: 4 hours

1 6-ounce package lemon gelatin
3½ cups tomato juice, heated
¼ cup vinegar
¼ cup lemon juice
3 4½-ounce cans shrimp, rinsed and drained
  (or 1 pound cooked bay shrimp)
1 2-ounce jar pimiento-stuffed green olives, coarsely chopped
1 cup chopped celery
¼ cup chopped green pepper
2 tablespoons minced onion
Pinch of salt
Pepper to taste
2 hard-boiled eggs, chopped
6 ounces cream cheese, softened
1 cup heavy cream, whipped
1 cup chopped pecans or almonds
1 4½-ounce can crab, rinsed and drained
1 cup mayonnaise
1 teaspoon horseradish (optional)
Onion salt to taste
Lemon juice to taste

In a large bowl dissolve gelatin in heated tomato juice. Add vinegar and lemon juice. Chill until the mixture has thickened slightly. Add the shrimp, olives, celery, green pepper, onion and cooked eggs. Add salt and pepper to taste. Chill until slightly thickened.

Mix together cream cheese, whipped cream and nuts. Place half of the tomato mixture in a 9 x 13-inch pan. Top with the cream cheese mixture and then top with remaining tomato mixture. Refrigerate until set.

Combine crab, mayonnaise, horseradish, onion salt and lemon juice. Spread over salad just prior to serving.

OVERNIGHT LAYERED CHICKEN SALAD

Yield: 10-12 servings
Assemble: 30 minutes
Chill: 12 hours

1 head iceberg lettuce, shredded
¼ pound fresh bean sprouts
1 8-ounce can sliced water chestnuts, drained
½ cup sliced green onions
1 medium cucumber, sliced
2 whole chicken breasts, cooked, chilled and cut into
  bite-size pieces
2 pounds frozen peas, thawed
2 cups mayonnaise
2 teaspoons curry powder
½ teaspoon powdered ginger
½ cup raw, unsalted Spanish peanuts
12-18 cherry tomatoes, cut in half

In a 4-quart serving dish layer lettuce, bean sprouts, water chestnuts, onion, cucumber and chicken. Pat peas dry and arrange on top.

Mix the mayonnaise, curry powder and ginger; spread over the peas. Refrigerate 24 hours. Garnish with Spanish peanuts and tomato halves.

HOT TACO SALAD

Yield: 8-10 servings
Assemble: 15 minutes
Cook: 20 minutes

Note: A quick-fix main dish salad the whole family will love!

2½ pounds lean ground beef
1 package taco seasoning mix
1 cup canned tomatoes, with juice
1¾ cups catsup
1½ teaspoons chili powder
¼ cup taco sauce
1 10¾-ounce can tomato soup
1 large head lettuce, shredded
1 8-ounce package Fritos corn chips
2 tomatoes, diced
1 pound Cheddar cheese, grated
1 pint sour cream
1 6-ounce can black olives, sliced

In a large skillet brown beef and spoon off excess grease. Add taco seasoning, canned tomatoes, catsup, chili powder, taco sauce and tomato soup. Simmer for 20 minutes

On individual plates arrange a bed of shredded lettuce and corn chips. Spoon the sauce over the chips and top with diced tomatoes, cheese, dollops of sour cream and olives.

RUSSIAN VEAL SALAD

Yield: 6-8 servings
Assemble: 45 minutes
Chill: 2 hours

3½ cups cooked, diced veal
1½ cups boiled and diced new potatoes
1½ cups diced, peeled and seeded cucumbers
1½ cups diced, unpared tart red apples
⅔ cup diced Kosher dill pickle

CREAMY HERB DRESSING:
2 hard-boiled eggs, sieved
1 teaspoon salt
1 teaspoon dry mustard
1 teaspoon sugar
½ teaspoon white pepper
Dash Tabasco sauce
1½ cups sour cream
3 tablespoons vegetable oil
1 tablespoon vinegar
1 teaspoon lemon juice
1 teaspoon tarragon
1 teaspoon fresh parsley
1 teaspoon chervil
Red leaf lettuce

In a large bowl combine the veal, potatoes, cucumbers, apples and pickle; chill. In a medium-size bowl make a paste of the eggs, salt, mustard, sugar, pepper and Tabasco. Gradually add the sour cream, then whisk in oil briskly. Blend in the remaining ingredients. Chill before using.

To serve, toss veal and potato mixture with dressing and mound on a red lettuce leaf; accompany with hard rolls.

CHICKEN SALAD HABANERA

Yield: 6-8 servings
Assemble: 30 minutes
Chill: 3 hours

**1½ cups cooked chicken breasts, cut into strips
  and chilled**
1 cup sliced black olives
1 avocado, cut into strips
⅓ cup green pepper, cut into strips
¼ cup finely chopped Bermuda onion
2-3 tablespoons pimiento strips
4 cups shredded lettuce

HABANERA DRESSING:
⅓ cup vegetable oil
¼ cup red wine vinegar
¼ cup lemon juice
1 tablespoon sugar
1 teaspoon salt
½ teaspoon pepper
⅛ teaspoon minced fresh garlic

Combine chicken, olives, green pepper, onion and pimiento; chill. Prepare dressing by combining oil, vinegar, lemon juice, sugar, salt, pepper and garlic. Just prior to serving, add avocado to salad ingredients. Toss salad with dressing and serve on bed of shredded lettuce.

PINEAPPLE CHICKEN SALAD IN MELON

QUICK
& EASY

Yield: 6 servings
Assemble: 45 minutes

Note: Bake a few extra chicken breasts with tonight's dinner and enjoy this luscious, cool salad tomorrow.

1 fresh pineapple
3 cups diced cooked chicken, chilled
1 cup diced celery
1 cup sliced banana
½ cup salted cashews
1 cup mayonnaise
2 tablespoons chutney
1 teaspoon curry powder
½ cup shredded coconut
Pinch of salt
Pepper to taste
3 small cantaloupes, halved

Cut pineapple in half lengthwise. Scoop fruit from the halves and dice. In a large bowl blend mayonnaise, curry powder, salt, pepper and chutney. Add pineapple pieces, chicken, celery, banana and cashews; toss. Pile into cantaloupe halves and garnish with shredded coconut.

COBB SALAD WITH CHIVE DRESSING

QUICK
& EASY

Yield: 4 servings
Assemble: 45 minutes

1 medium-size head iceberg lettuce, shredded
1 large tomato, chopped
1½ cups diced cooked chicken
**1 large avocado, peeled, diced and sprinkled
  with lemon juice**
1 pound sliced bacon, cooked, drained and crumbled
2 hard-boiled eggs, chopped
4 ounces blue cheese, crumbled

continued

continued

CHIVE DRESSING:
6 tablespoons white wine vinegar
½ teaspoon salt
¼ teaspoon garlic powder
¼ teaspoon pepper
3 tablespoons chopped chives
½ cup vegetable oil

Place shredded lettuce in a large salad bowl. Prepare dressing by combining salt, garlic powder, pepper, chives and the oil in a jar and shake well. Pour the dressing over the lettuce and toss. Arrange the tomato, chicken, avocado, bacon and eggs on top of the lettuce. Place crumbled cheese in the center of the salad. Toss at the table.

RUSTY PELICAN SALAD WITH HONEY DRESSING

QUICK
& EASY

Yield: 6 servings
Assemble: 40 minutes

Note: Honey Dressing
is great on greens of
all kinds or as a sauce
to accompany cold
chicken.

Iceberg lettuce
Romaine lettuce
Escarole
Chickory
Watercress
6 cups finely sliced fresh mushrooms
2 tomatoes, cut into wedges
2 hard-boiled eggs, finely chopped
1 pound small shrimp, shelled and deveined
1 bay leaf
Pinch of salt
Juice of ½ lemon

HONEY DRESSING:
1¼ cups mayonnaise
½ cup vegetable oil
¼ cup honey
¼ cup prepared mustard
¼ cup finely chopped onion
1 teaspoon finely chopped fresh parsley
Juice of ½ lemon
Pinch of salt
Pinch of Accent

Cut assorted salad greens into 1-inch pieces to measure a total of 6 cups. Place in large salad bowl; chill.

In a large saucepan poach shrimp for 2-3 minutes in boiling water seasoned with 1 bay leaf, a pinch of salt and juice of ½ lemon. Remove from heat, run cold water over, drain and set aside in refrigerator.

Prepare dressing by combining the mayonnaise, oil, honey, mustard, onion, parsley, lemon juice, salt and Accent. The dressing may be kept in a glass jar, refrigerated, for up to 7 days.

To serve, combine salad greens, shrimp, mushrooms, tomatoes and eggs. Toss with dressing and serve.

BAKED PEAR SALAD

Yield: 6 servings
Assemble: 10 minutes
Bake: 25 minutes
Chill: 4 hours

3 firm ripe Bartlett pears
1 teaspoon grated orange rind
¾ cup orange juice
⅓ cup orange syrup (reserved from baked pears)
¾ cup mayonnaise
1 teaspoon grated orange rind
1 tablespoon sugar
Lettuce leaves

Halve, core and peel pears. Place cut side down in a 1½-quart buttered, glass baking dish. Combine 1 teaspoon orange rind with orange juice and pour over the pears. Bake for 25 minutes at 350°, basting occasionally. Remove pears, reserve juice and chill separately.

Arrange chilled pears on lettuce-lined plates and serve with dressing made by blending ⅓ cup reserved orange syrup with mayonnaise, grated orange rind and sugar.

CRANBERRY CHEESE RIBBON

Yield: 12 servings
Assemble: 30 minutes
Chill: 4 hours

1 envelope unflavored gelatin
1 cup cold water
1 3-ounce package strawberry gelatin
¾ cup boiling water
1 12-ounce package fresh cranberries
1 small orange, cut into wedges
¾ cup sugar
¼ cup lemon juice
8 ounces cream cheese, softened
1 4½-ounce container frozen whipped topping, thawed
Lettuce leaves
Orange slices for garnish

In a small saucepan sprinkle unflavored gelatin over cold water to soften. Heat and stir until gelatin dissolves. Remove from heat and set aside. Dissolve the strawberry gelatin in boiling water.

In a food processor fitted with a metal blade, combine cranberries, orange and sugar and process until ingredients are evenly chopped. Stir the cranberry mixture into strawberry gelatin and add 2 tablespoons lemon juice. Pour into a 1½-quart oiled mold and chill until slightly thickened.

In a large mixing bowl beat the cream cheese with remaining 2 tablespoons lemon juice until fluffy. Blend in whipped topping. Add unflavored gelatin mixture and mix well. Spoon this mixture evenly over the cranberry mixture into the mold. Chill approximately 4 hours or until set.

Unmold and garnish with lettuce leaves and orange slices.

REFRESHING LOW-CAL APPLE SET SALAD

Yield: 6-8 servings
Assemble: 20 minutes
Chill: 4 hours

1 3-ounce package sugar-free orange gelatin
1 3-ounce package sugar-free pineapple gelatin
2 cups boiling water
1 cup cold water
Juice and finely grated rind of 1 medium orange
1 15¼-ounce can crushed pineapple (packed in
  its own juice), undrained
1 medium apple, peeled and coarsely grated

Dissolve gelatin in boiling water and add cold water. Add orange juice and grated orange rind. Chill and allow to set to syrupy stage. Add crushed pineapple, with juice, and refrigerate again. When mixture thickens, add apple and mix well. Refrigerate and allow to set completely.

FROSTY FRUIT SALAD

Yield: 8 servings
Assemble: 20 minutes
Freeze: 12 hours

1 pint sour cream
3 tablespoons lemon juice
¾ cup sugar
⅛ teaspoon salt
⅔ cup crushed pineapple, well drained
¼ cup chopped maraschino cherries
¼ cup chopped pecans
1 large banana, sliced (optional)

Lettuce leaves

Combine all ingredients and place in a 9 x 9-inch square pan. Freeze overnight. Remove from freezer approximately 10 minutes before serving. Cut into squares and serve on lettuce leaves.

CELERY SEED DRESSING

QUICK
& EASY

Yield: 1½ cups
Assemble: 10 minutes

½ cup sugar
1 teaspoon dry mustard
1 teaspoon salt
1½ teaspoon celery seed
2 tablespoons grated onion
1 cup vegetable oil
⅓ cup vinegar

Mix all ingredients in a blender for 30 seconds. Serve over green salad, avocado slices, mandarin orange segments or fresh fruit.

LEMON DRESSING FOR FRUIT

Yield: 1 pint
Assemble: 20 minutes
Chill: 1 hour

⅓ cup sugar
1 tablespoon flour
½ teaspoon finely shredded lemon peel
¼ cup lemon juice
1 egg, well beaten
1 cup miniature marshmallows
1 cup mayonnaise

In a saucepan combine sugar and flour. Stir in lemon peel, lemon juice, egg and marshmallows. Cook and stir over low heat until the mixture thickens slightly and marshmallows melt (approximately 10 minutes). Cool slightly and fold in mayonnaise; cover and chill.

Serve approximately 1 tablespoon of dressing, or to taste, over each fresh fruit serving.

CREAMY LEMON BLUE CHEESE DRESSING

Yield: 1 pint
Assemble: 10 minutes
Chill: 3 hours

¼ pound blue cheese (do not substitute Roquefort)
¾ cup vegetable oil
1 teaspoon grated lemon peel
¼ cup lemon juice
1 cup sour cream
1 medium clove garlic, minced
1 teaspoon salt
¼ teaspoon Accent (optional)

Break up cheese with a fork or electric mixer. Slowly blend with oil, beating until smooth. Add grated lemon peel, lemon juice, sour cream, garlic, salt and Accent; mix well. Cover and chill several hours. Bring to room temperature before serving.

VINAIGRETTE DRESSING

QUICK
& EASY

Yield: 1½ cups
Assemble: 10 minutes

⅔ cup olive oil
½ cup vinegar
½ teaspoon salt
½ teaspoon pepper
3 cloves garlic, crushed
1 tablespoon oregano
1 tablespoon basil

In jar with lid combine the olive oil, vinegar, salt, pepper, garlic, oregano and basil. Pour over fresh pasta, greens, avocados, fresh tomatoes, hot or cold vegetables.

GORGONZOLA WALNUT DRESSING

QUICK & EASY

Yield: 1 cup
Assemble: 10 minutes

¼ cup raspberry or red wine vinegar
½ cup olive oil
1 medium clove garlic, coarsely chopped
2 ounces Gorgonzola cheese
Pinch of salt
Pepper to taste
Pinch of sugar
¼ cup walnuts

In a blender or food processor fitted with a metal blade blend vinegar, oil and garlic for 15 seconds. Add Gorgonzola cheese, salt, pepper, walnuts and a pinch of sugar. Blend another 15 seconds or until walnuts are chopped, but not pureed. (They should remain slightly chunky.) Pour dressing over a simple green salad. It is especially good over romaine or spinach leaves.

FRENCH SALAD DRESSING

QUICK & EASY

Yield: 3 cups
Assemble: 10 minutes
Chill: 50 minutes

1 cup vegetable oil
⅔ cup catsup
⅔ cup brown sugar
½ chopped onion
¼ cup vinegar
2 teaspoons salt
2 tablespoons lemon juice
½ teaspoon dry mustard
Pinch of pepper
Pinch of paprika

Combine all ingredients in a blender and mix until thickened; chill. Dressing will keep several weeks refrigerated. Delicious over greens, fruit or taco salad.

ROQUEFORT DRESSING

QUICK & EASY

Yield: 1 quart
Assemble: 15 minutes
Chill: 45 minutes

⅓ cup crumbled Roquefort cheese
2 cups buttermilk
2 cups mayonnaise
1 tablespoon garlic salt
1 scant tablespoon coarsely ground pepper
8 ounces cream cheese, softened
1 tablespoon celery salt (optional)
Pinch of onion powder
1 tablespoon chopped fresh chives (optional)
1 tablespoon chopped fresh parsley (optional)

Combine all ingredients together in a large bowl and mix well with a beater; chill.

VEGETABLES & SIDE DISHES

 June skies boast an array of vibrant banners welcoming spectators to the heart of Salt Lake City for the annual Utah Festival of the Arts. Festival enthusiasts stroll among a generous sampling of artisans' wares—pottery, jewelry, clothing, oils, watercolors, carvings—mingled with food vendors enticing visitors with succulent aromas and palate-pleasing specialties. In the heat of late afternoon, the browsers might relax to the drifting lilt of a lazy-tempoed jazz troupe before heading home to entertain fellow art patrons with an assembled-ahead dinner. Tomato and Zucchini Ratatouille, Marinated Mushroom Salad, Bulgogi, Cheesy Monkey Bread and Creamy Berry Ice Cream reward the sun-toasted shoppers.

ORIENTAL ASPARAGUS (Pictured)

Yield: 4 servings
Assemble: 10 minutes
Cook: 10 minutes

1 pound asparagus, trimmed
1 tablespoon sesame seeds
1 teaspoon butter
¼ teaspoon sesame oil
1 teaspoon soy sauce
2 tablespoons butter
Optional garnishes: enoki mushrooms, red pepper strips,
   lemon zest

Steam or stir-fry asparagus until crisp-tender (2 minutes). Drain and set aside. Place sesame seeds and 1 teaspoon butter in a large skillet and toast over medium heat until golden. Combine remaining ingredients in skillet, add asparagus. Stir-fry just to coat. Garnish with enoki mushrooms, red pepper strips and lemon zest.

CHILLED ASPARAGUS WITH MUSTARD DRESSING

Yield: 4 servings
Assemble: 20 minutes
Chill: 1 hour

1 pound tender young asparagus

MUSTARD DRESSING:
3 egg yolks, room temperature
¼ cup Dijon mustard
2 tablespoons fresh lemon juice
½ cup olive oil
Pinch of salt
Freshly ground pepper

Cut off the base of the asparagus spears and pare or peel as necessary. Cook the asparagus in boiling, lightly salted water, about 3 minutes. Remove the asparagus gently with tongs to a colander. Run cold water over to stop cooking process. Drain and refrigerate, covered with plastic wrap, until ready to serve.

Place egg yolks, mustard and lemon juice in bowl of a food processor or blender. Process until the mixture is pale yellow and foamy, about 1 minute. While blending, add oil in a steady stream just until the mixture is blended and has the consistency of thin mayonnaise. Add salt and pepper to taste. Chill before serving over asparagus.

ALMOND GREEN BEAN SAUTE'

Yield: 4-6 servings
Assemble: 10 minutes
Cook: 20 minutes

1 pound fresh green beans (about 4 cups), trimmed
2 tablespoons butter
1 medium stalk celery, sliced
¼ cup slivered almonds
10 whole fresh mushrooms
Salt to taste
Pinch of freshly ground pepper

In a medium saucepan cook beans in boiling water until crisp-tender (about 6-7 minutes). Drain and run cold water over to stop cooking process. Saute' celery, almonds and mushrooms in the same pan until mushrooms are tender (about 10 minutes). Add beans, salt and pepper; toss lightly. Heat thoroughly.

GREEN BEANS WITH TOMATO MUSHROOM SAUCE

Yield: 8-10 servings
Assemble: 45 minutes
Cook: 30 minutes

2 tablespoons dried wild (boletus) mushrooms
½ cup hot water
2 pounds fresh green beans, trimmed and halved diagonally
(frozen may be used)
3 tablespoons light-bodied olive oil
1 medium onion, minced
2 large cloves garlic, minced
1 16-ounce can plum tomatoes, seeded, drained and crushed
¼ cup tomato paste
¼ cup chicken broth or stock
2½ teaspoons dried basil
2 teaspoons sugar
Pinch of salt
Freshly ground pepper to taste

Rinse mushrooms quickly under cold running water; drain well. Crumble into a small bowl. Add hot water and let stand for 30 minutes.

In a large saucepan steam green beans until crisp-tender (about 10 minutes). Rinse under cold running water to stop cooking process and retain color. Drain well and set aside.

Pour oil into large non-aluminum skillet. Place over high heat until hot. Add onion and brown quickly. Add garlic and saute' several seconds; do not burn. Add mushrooms and their liquid, tomatoes, tomato paste, broth and basil; blend well. Boil until thickened, about 5 minutes. Remove from heat and stir in sugar, salt and pepper.

Transfer beans to tomato sauce tossing to coat. Allow beans and sauce to heat thoroughly over low heat.

VEGETABLES IN A CLOUD

Yield: 12 servings
Assemble: 30 minutes
Bake: 40 minutes

2 tablespoons butter
1 cup chopped onions
3-4 cups cut broccoli
6-8 carrots, cut into 3-inch julienne strips
1 8-ounce can sliced water chestnuts, drained
1 cup heavy cream
½ cup grated Cheddar cheese
½ cup mayonnaise
¼ cup Parmesan cheese

Saute' onion in butter in a small skillet. Cook the vegetables in a small amount of water until crisp-tender (about 5 minutes). Layer the vegetables, onions and water chestnuts in a 2-quart baking dish. Preheat oven to 350°. Whip cream in a medium-size bowl. Fold cheeses and mayonnaise into cream and spread on top of the vegetables. Bake uncovered for 30-40 minutes.

BROCCOLI-TOPPED TOMATOES

Yield: 12 servings
Assemble: 30 minutes
Bake: 10 minutes

6 tomatoes, sliced ½-inch thick
3 10-ounce packages frozen chopped broccoli
3 tablespoons grated onion
1 egg
½ teaspoon salt
½ teaspoon pepper
3 cups grated Swiss cheese
Lemon pepper to taste

Cook broccoli according to package directions and drain well; cool. Slice tomatoes and place on a baking sheet. In a large bowl combine the broccoli, grated onion, beaten egg, salt, pepper and Swiss cheese. Using an ice cream scoop, place a scoop of the broccoli mixture on top of each tomato slice. Bake at 350° for 10 minutes, or broil for 5 minutes.

BROCCOLI AND SWISS

Yield: 4-6 servings
Assemble: 30 minutes
Bake: 20 minutes

2 pounds fresh broccoli, trimmed and cut into flowerettes
(or 2 10-ounce packages of frozen broccoli)
1 cup grated Swiss cheese
⅓ cup mayonnaise
2 tablespoons finely chopped green onion
¼ teaspoon salt
⅛ teaspoon pepper
½ teaspoon prepared mustard (a spicy mustard works well)

In a large saucepan bring a quart of water to boil. Cook broccoli for 5 minutes until crisp-tender; drain. Arrange in a shallow 2-quart baking dish. Combine remaining ingredients together in a small bowl and spoon evenly over broccoli. Bake uncovered at 350° for 20 minutes until cheese sauce is melted.

TANGY RED CABBAGE AND APPLES

Yield: 8 servings
Assemble: 15 minutes
Cook: 1 hour

¼ cup butter or margarine
2 medium cooking apples, peeled, cored and thinly sliced
1 medium onion, diced
1 medium red cabbage, shredded (about 8 cups)
1 cup water
½ cup red wine vinegar
⅓ cup sugar
1½ teaspoons salt
⅛ teaspoon pepper
1 bay leaf

In a 4-quart saucepan heat butter or margarine over medium heat until hot, but not brown. Add apples and onion; cook until tender (about 10 minutes). Add cabbage and remaining ingredients; heat to boiling. Reduce to low, cover and simmer 40 minutes or until cabbage is very tender. Stir occasionally. Discard bay leaf and serve.

APRICOT-GLAZED CARROTS

QUICK & EASY

Yield: 6-8 servings
Assemble: 20 minutes
Cook: 10 minutes

4 cups carrots, sliced
3 tablespoons butter
⅓ cup apricot preserves
¼ teaspoon salt
Pinch of nutmeg
¼ teaspoon freshly grated lemon peel
2 teaspoons lemon juice

In a medium-size saucepan cook carrots until crisp-tender (about 8 minutes). Drain and set aside. Melt butter in a skillet; stir in preserves. Add all other ingredients, except carrots, and cook briefly. Toss in carrots and cook just long enough to heat thoroughly.

SWEET CARROTS AND GREEN GRAPES

QUICK & EASY

Yield: 6 servings
Assemble: 10 minutes
Cook: 15 minutes

½ cup butter
4 cups carrots, cut into 2-inch julienne strips
1 cup seedless green grapes
2 tablespoons honey
1 tablespoon lemon juice
Pinch of salt
3-4 mint leaves, finely chopped

Melt the butter in a heavy skillet. Add carrots and stir until well coated. Cover and cook until almost tender (about 10 minutes). Add grapes, honey and lemon juice and cook slowly for 5 minutes. Add salt and scatter the mint leaves over the top just before serving.

CASHEW MANDARIN VEGETABLES

QUICK & EASY

Yield: 4-6 servings
Assemble: 30 minutes
Cook: 10 minutes

1 cup thinly sliced carrots
1 cup thinly sliced green beans
2 tablespoons vegetable oil
1 cup thinly sliced cauliflower
½ cup sliced green onions
1 cup water
2 teaspoons chicken stock base
2 teaspoons cornstarch
½ cup unblanched whole cashews
Pinch of garlic powder

Stir-fry carrots and beans with oil in a large skillet over medium heat for 2 minutes. Add cauliflower and onion; cook 1 minute longer. Combine water, chicken stock base, cornstarch and garlic powder in small dish. Add to vegetables. Stir over medium heat until thickened. Vegetables should be crisp and tender. If further cooking is needed, reduce heat, cover and steam until done. Add cashews before serving.

SWEET FRIED CORN

QUICK & EASY

Yield: 4-6 servings
Assemble: 10 minutes
Cook: 5 minutes

Note: Serve with Mexican Cheese Torte (page 202) for a terrific vegetarian taste treat.

Vegetable oil for deep frying
8 ounces cooked sweet corn kernels, or frozen corn, thawed
½ celery stalk, chopped
1 shallot, finely chopped
1 clove garlic, finely chopped
1 tablespoon chopped fresh parsley
½ teaspoon salt
¼ teaspoon pepper
2 eggs, beaten
2 tablespoons flour
⅓ cup diced red or green pepper
Sour cream

Heat 2 inches of oil in a large electric frying pan or skillet. Combine the remaining ingredients in a large bowl. Drop one tablespoon of the mixture at a time into the hot oil. Fry until crisp and golden. Drain on paper towels and serve with dollop of sour cream.

PENNSYLVANIA DUTCH-STYLE CORN PUDDING

Yield: 6 servings
Assemble: 10 minutes
Bake: 90 minutes

Note: Easily assembled and baked while grilling Lamb Shish Kabobs (page 198).

2 16-ounce cans cream-style corn
4 eggs, beaten until frothy
4 tablespoons flour
½ cup melted butter
1 cup milk
½ cup sugar
½ teaspoon salt

Combine all ingredients in a large bowl and pour into a well-buttered 2-quart casserole. Bake at 350° for 1½ hours.

EGGPLANT ROLLUPS

QUICK & EASY

Yield: 4 servings
Assemble: 30 minutes
Bake: 30 minutes

1 large eggplant (1½ pounds), peeled, sliced lengthwise into eight ¼-inch slices
½ teaspoon salt
½ cup cottage or ricotta cheese
1 egg
¼ cup diced mozzarella cheese
3 tablespoons fresh parsley, chopped and divided
2 tablespoons grated Parmesan cheese, divided
1 15½-ounce jar meatless spaghetti sauce, divided

In a large covered saucepan or skillet cook the eggplant for 3 minutes in enough lightly salted boiling water to cover. Remove and drain on paper towels. In a small bowl mix the cottage or ricotta cheese, egg, mozzarella cheese, 2 tablespoons parsley and 1 tablespoon Parmesan until well blended; set aside. Pour ½ cup spaghetti sauce in a 1½-quart shallow baking dish.

Spoon equal amounts of the cheese mixture near the center of each eggplant slice. Roll up. Place seam side down in casserole and spoon on remaining sauce. Sprinkle with remaining parsley and Parmesan. Bake at 400° for 15-20 minutes or until heated thoroughly and sauce bubbles.

ORIENTAL ASPARAGUS

BAKED EGGPLANT IN SOUR CREAM

Yield: 8 servings
Assemble: 20 minutes
Bake: 25 minutes

3 pounds eggplant, peeled and diced
4 cups water
2 chicken bouillon cubes
1 cup sour cream
1 teaspoon Worcestershire sauce
¼ teaspoon Tabasco sauce
Pinch of salt
Pepper to taste
¼ cups grated Parmesan cheese
½ teaspoon paprika
⅓ pound Provolone cheese, sliced
¼ cup sliced almonds

Peel and dice eggplant. In a large saucepan cook eggplant, uncovered, in broth for 10 minutes or until tender; drain. Mix eggplant with sour cream, Worcestershire sauce, Tabasco sauce, salt and pepper. Pour into buttered 1½-quart casserole dish. Sprinkle with grated Parmesan cheese, dust with paprika, then top with sliced Provolone cheese and sliced almonds. Bake at 325° for 25 minutes.

OLIVE-STUFFED ONIONS

Yield: 6 servings
Assemble: 20 minutes
Bake: 20 minutes

Note: An onion lover's delight. Great when "Walla Walla Sweets" are available.

6 medium onions
Vegetable oil
Paprika
4 tablespoons butter
4 tablespoons light cream
4 tablespoons chopped ripe olives
2 tablespoons chopped pecans
½ teaspoon salt
Dry bread crumbs
Paprika

Peel onions. Cut a thick slice from the top of each; reserve. Cut out the center of each onion and reserve. In a large kettle cook the onion shells until tender in enough boiling water to cover (approximately 15-20 minutes). Remove from the water and drain onions upside down.

Brush the outside of the shells with oil and sprinkle with a little paprika. Coarsely chop reserved onion and saute' in butter until tender. Stir in cream, olives, pecans and salt. Spoon into the onion shells. Sprinkle each onion with bread crumbs, then drizzle with melted butter. Top with paprika and bake at 350° for 20 minutes.

BEER-BATTER ONION RINGS

QUICK & EASY

Yield: 6 servings
Assemble: 10-15
   minutes
Cook: 15 minutes

2 large white onions
2 eggs
1 cup flour
Beer, enough to make a thin batter (6 ounces)
Vegetable oil for frying

Slice onions. Mix the eggs, flour and beer in a medium-size bowl to make a thin batter. Dip onions in the batter to coat. Heat oil in a deep fryer, wok or heavy skillet to 400°. Fry coated onions, turning until golden on both sides. Drain on paper towels; salt to taste

POTATOES WITH ONIONS

Yield: 8 servings
Assemble: 30 minutes
Bake: 45 minutes

4 pounds potatoes cooked, peeled and mashed
½ cup heavy cream
¼ cup grated onions
1 teaspoon salt
½ cup butter, softened
2 egg yolks
Salt and white pepper to taste
2 egg whites
Pinch of salt
Pinch of cream of tartar
Onion slices
Melted butter

In a large bowl combine the mashed potatoes with heavy cream, grated onion and 1 teaspoon salt. Beat in softened butter, egg yolks, adjust seasoning with salt and white pepper to taste. In a separate bowl beat egg whites with a pinch of salt and a pinch of cream of tartar until they hold stiff peaks. Fold into potato mixture. Transfer the mixture to a buttered shallow 2-quart casserole. Top with onion slices and brush the top with melted butter. Bake at 325° for 45 minutes, or until golden and heated thoroughly.

CRISP WORCESTERSHIRE POTATOES

Yield: 6 servings
Assemble: 15 minutes
Bake: 1½ hours

¼ cup butter or margarine
¼ cup Worcestershire sauce
6 unpared potatoes, cut lengthwise into strips

Preheat oven to 350°. Melt butter in a 9 x 13-inch pan in oven. Put potatoes in pan and coat in Worcestershire and butter mixture. Bake for 1½ hours.

NEW POTATOES WITH LOW-CAL HERB SAUCE

QUICK & EASY

Yield: 6 servings
Assemble: 15 minutes
Cook: 20 minutes

6-8 uniformly sized new potatoes, cleaned and unpared
Fresh parsley for garnish

LOW-CAL HERB SAUCE:
1 cup milk
2 tablespoons flour
¼ teaspoon salt
⅛ teaspoon garlic powder
⅛ teaspoon pepper
⅛ teaspoon oregano
⅛ teaspoon thyme or tarragon
¼ cup chopped green onion

Cook potatoes in a medium-size saucepan with water to cover until tender (about 20 minutes). While potatoes are cooking, blend milk and flour in a small saucepan over medium heat until bubbly and thick. Cook stirring constantly for one minute more. Stir in seasonings and onion. Drain potatoes and serve sauce over top. Garnish with parsley.

COMPANY POTATOES

QUICK & EASY

Yield: 12 servings
Assemble: 5 minutes
Bake: 55 minutes

2 pounds frozen hash brown potatoes, thawed
¼ cup chopped onions
2 10¾-ounce cans cream of potato soup
1 pint sour cream
10 ounces medium-sharp Cheddar cheese, grated
½ cup Parmesan cheese

Mix potatoes, onions, soup, sour cream and grated cheese. Place in a greased 9 x 13-inch casserole and sprinkle Parmesan cheese over top. Bake at 350° uncovered for 55 minutes.

CROOKNECK CASSEROLE

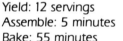

QUICK & EASY

Yield: 8 servings
Assemble: 20 minutes
Bake: 30 minutes

Note: Dresses up a ham or grilled knockwurst dinner.

3 pounds yellow crookneck squash, thickly sliced
1 small onion, chopped
1 2-ounce jar pimiento, chopped
1 10¾-ounce can cream of chicken soup
¼ cup butter or margarine
1 carrot, grated
1 cup sour cream
1½ cups Pepperidge Farm cornbread dressing mix, divided
1 teaspoon Beau Monde seasoning, divided
¼ cup butter, melted

In a large saucepan steam squash until crisp-tender. Drain and set aside. In a medium-size skillet saute' onion and carrot in butter. Add dressing mix and combine well. Place half of dressing mixture in bottom of greased 1½-quart casserole. Add squash and pimiento. Sprinkle with ½ teaspoon Beau Monde. Cover with other half of dressing mixture. Mix soup and sour cream and pour over all. Sprinkle with remaining Beau Monde and ½ cup dressing crumbs. Drizzle butter over all. Bake at 350°, uncovered, for 30 minutes until bubbly and light brown.

SAUTÉED SNOW PEAS

QUICK & EASY

Yield: 4 servings
Assemble: 5 minutes
Cook: 5 minutes

¾ pound fresh snow peas, cleaned, ends trimmed
1 tablespoon minced shallots
1 tablespoon vegetable oil
½ teaspoon basil
1 tablespoon beef broth

In a large skillet saute' snow peas and shallots in oil for about 3 minutes. Add basil and broth. Cook, stirring, for 1 minute. Serve immediately.

S.O.S. CASSEROLE

QUICK & EASY

Yield: 6 servings
Assemble: 20 minutes
Bake: 30 minutes

2 pounds fresh spinach, washed and stems removed (or
  4 10-ounce packages frozen chopped spinach)
1 cup sour cream
1 envelope dry onion soup mix
¼ cup finely crushed soda cracker crumbs
½ cup grated sharp Cheddar cheese
½ teaspoon grated fresh nutmeg

Cook spinach in boiling water and drain well. Preheat oven to 350°. Combine hot cooked spinach with remaining ingredients, blending well. Place spinach mixture into a well-greased 1½-quart casserole dish. Bake uncovered for 30 minutes at 350° until bubbly and top is slightly browned.

PECAN-TOPPED SWEET POTATOES

QUICK & EASY

Yield: 6 servings
Assemble: 30 minutes
Bake: 25-30 minutes

3 cups cooked, mashed sweet potatoes
1 cup sugar
¼ cup butter, melted
2 eggs, well beaten
1 teaspoon vanilla extract
⅓ cup evaporated milk
½ cup brown sugar
¼ cup flour
2½ tablespoons butter, melted
½ cup pecan pieces

Preheat oven to 350°. In a large bowl mix the first six ingredients and place into a 2-quart casserole. Combine last four ingredients and sprinkle on top of sweet potatoes. Bake uncovered at 350° for 25-30 minutes, or until crispy.

SPINACH LOAF À LA BERNOISE

Yield: 8-10 servings
Assemble: 40 minutes
Bake: 30 minutes

Note: Rich and elegant as a first course or accompaniment to grilled fish.

2 pounds fresh spinach, washed and stems removed
2 tablespoons unsalted butter
⅓ cup finely minced green onions
2 eggs
2 egg yolks
1 cup light cream
½ cup fresh bread crumbs
2-3 tablespoons freshly grated Parmesan cheese
Pinch of nutmeg
Pinch of salt
Freshly ground pepper to taste
2 tablespoons unsalted butter
½ pound mushroom caps, quartered
1 tablespoon butter
1 tablespoon flour
1 cup heavy cream
Salt
Pepper
2 tablespoons finely minced chives

In a large kettle cook spinach in rapidly boiling water for 2-3 minutes and drain thoroughly. When cool enough to handle, squeeze out all remaining moisture. Finely mince spinach and transfer to a large mixing bowl. Preheat oven to 350°.

Generously butter a 9 x 5-inch loaf pan and line with buttered waxed paper. Melt 2 tablespoons unsalted butter in a small heavy skillet over medium heat, add green onion and saute' 2-3 minutes, until softened but not browned. Add to spinach.

Combine eggs, egg yolks and light cream in a small mixing bowl and blend thoroughly with whisk. Combine egg mixture and spinach mixture. Add bread crumbs, Parmesan, nutmeg, salt and pepper. Spoon into the prepared loaf pan. Place in a larger baking dish and add boiling water to the outer dish to a depth of 1 inch. Cover the loaf pan loosely with foil and bake for 50 minutes or until a knife inserted into the center comes out clean. Remove from the oven and set aside.

Melt 2 tablespoons of unsalted butter in a large skillet over medium heat and saute' mushrooms for 3-4 minutes until nicely browned. Combine butter and flour and mix into a paste. Add cream to mushrooms and add flour mixture gradually, beating constantly until the sauce lightly coats a spoon. Remove from heat immediately and stir in chives.

Run a knife around the edges of spinach loaf and unmold onto a rectangular serving platter. Discard waxed paper and cut the loaf into ½-inch slices. Spoon the mushroom sauce over the loaf and serve immediately.

APRICOT SWEET POTATO BAKE

Yield: 6-8 servings
Assemble: 40 minutes
Bake: 20-30 minutes

4 or 5 sweet potatoes or yams, unpared
1 17-ounce can apricot halves
3 tablespoons brown sugar
1 tablespoon cornstarch
¼ teaspoon salt
⅛ teaspoon cinnamon
⅓ cup golden raisins
3 tablespoons dry sherry
½ teaspoon grated orange peel

Cook sweet potatoes or yams in a large kettle with boiling water to cover until tender (30 minutes). Drain, peel and slice sweet potatoes thickly on the diagonal. Place in a 9 x 13-inch serving dish; set aside. Drain apricots reserving syrup and set apricots aside. Add water to apricot juice, if necessary, to equal 1 cup liquid. Place liquid in a small saucepan. Add brown sugar, cornstarch, salt and cinnamon. Cook and stir over medium-high heat until thickened. Remove from heat and add raisins, sherry and orange peel. Arrange apricot halves over sweet potatoes and cover with sauce. Bake uncovered in 350° oven, basting occasionally for 20-30 minutes until well-glazed.

TOMATO AND ZUCCHINI RATATOUILLE

Yield: 6-8 servings
Assemble: 30 minutes
Bake: 60 minutes

3 medium zucchini, sliced
1 10-ounce package frozen corn, thawed (or equivalent
**   freshly cut from cob)**
1 large onion, cut into rings
½ pound fresh mushrooms, sliced
4 large fresh tomatoes, cut into wedges
1 medium green pepper, sliced into rings
2 cloves garlic, minced
1 teaspoon oregano, crushed
1 teaspoon sweet basil, crushed
¼ cup minced parsley
½ cup butter, softened
½ cup Parmesan cheese, ¼ cup reserved

Layer zucchini, corn, mushrooms, onion, green pepper and tomatoes in a 9 x 13-inch oven-proof dish. Combine butter and the remaining ingredients together. Dot the top with the herbed butter. Bake at 325° for 45-60 minutes until most of the moisture has evaporated. Stir occasionally while baking. Before serving, sprinkle top with the remaining Parmesan cheese and serve.

TOMATO AND ONION CASSEROLE

QUICK
& EASY

Yield: 6 servings
Assemble: 30 minutes
Bake: 30 minutes

4 medium onions, thinly sliced
3 tablespoons butter
5 large tomatoes, peeled and thickly sliced
1½ cups grated Cheddar and Monterey Jack cheese, combined
1 cup bread crumbs
1 teaspoon paprika
2 eggs, beaten
1 cup sour cream
Salt to taste

In a medium-size skillet saute' onions. Grease a 2-quart casserole dish and layer half of the tomatoes, cheese, onion, salt, paprika and bread crumbs. Make a second layer ending with the cheese. Preheat oven to 375°. Beat the eggs and add sour cream; pour over casserole. Cover and bake for 20 minutes; uncover and bake 10 minutes longer.

TOMATO CHIVE PIE

QUICK
& EASY

Yield: 8 servings
Assemble: 10 minutes
Bake: 30 minutes

1 unbaked 9" pie shell (page 223)
2 cups ripe tomatoes, peeled and sliced ½-inch thick
¼ cup fresh chives
1 cup mayonnaise (no substitutes)
1 cup grated mozzarella or Monterey Jack cheese
¼ teaspoon lemon pepper
⅛ teaspoon basil

Preheat oven to 375°. Bake pie shell for 7 minutes. Drain tomatoes well on paper towels then layer slices into the pie shell, overlapping. Sprinkle with chives, lemon pepper and basil. Combine the cheese and mayonnaise and spread on top of the tomatoes and seasonings. Bake for 25 minutes.

SAUTÉED YAMS WITH GINGER

QUICK
& EASY

Yield: 4 servings
Assemble: 10 minutes
Bake: 5 minutes

1½ tablespoons unsalted butter, divided
1 tablespoon vegetable oil
½ pound yams, peeled and cut into julienne strips
½ small onion, minced
½ teaspoon peeled and grated gingerroot
1 teaspoon fresh lemon juice
½ teaspoon soy sauce

In a large heavy skillet heat 1 tablespoon butter and oil over high heat until it is hot but not smoking. Saute' yams, undisturbed for 1-2 minutes or until they are golden brown. Continue to saute' yams over moderately high heat, stirring occasionally, for 2 minutes. Add onion, gingerroot and the remaining ½ tablespoon butter. Saute' mixture, stirring, for 1 minute or until yams are tender. Transfer mixture to a serving dish and toss with lemon juice and soy sauce.

ZUCCHINI FRITTATA

Yield: 6-8 servings
Assemble: 20 minutes
Bake: 30 minutes

1¼ pounds zucchini
4 eggs
¼ cup flour
½ cup grated Parmesan cheese
1¼ teaspoons salt
3 tablespoons chopped fresh parsley
3 tablespoons thinly sliced green onions
1 clove garlic, minced
¾ teaspoon oregano leaves
¼ teaspoon pepper
10 cherry tomatoes, halved

Remove stem and blossom ends from zucchini; rinse well. Grate or finely chop zucchini to yield 4 cups. Press out as much moisture from zucchini as possible with paper towels. Beat eggs in a medium-size mixing bowl, then beat in the flour, half of the cheese, salt, parsley, onion, garlic, oregano and pepper. Stir in zucchini. Place mixture into a buttered, shallow 2-quart baking dish. Arrange the halved tomatoes, cut side up, on top; press lightly into the zucchini mixture. Sprinkle the remaining Parmesan cheese evenly over top. Bake, uncovered, in a 350° oven for 30 minutes or until zucchini mixture is set in center when lightly touched.

PESTO ALLA GENOVESE

Yield: 1 cup
Assemble: 10 minutes

Note: Pesto alla Genovese is so versatile it can even be made successfully in the winter.

½ cup pignoli (imported pine nuts—found in Italian
  specialty shops or deli)
1 cup chopped fresh basil
1 cup chopped fresh spinach leaves
1 large garlic clove (or 2 medium cloves)
¼ cup freshly grated Romano cheese
¼ cup freshly grated Parmesan cheese
6 tablespoons butter, softened
½ cup olive oil
⅛ teaspoon freshly ground black pepper

In bowl of a food processor fitted with metal blade add the pine nuts, basil, spinach, garlic, Romano and Parmesan cheese. Process for 30 seconds. With motor running, add the butter and olive oil. Mix in the black pepper. (Entire process should take no more than 1 minute.) Use the sauce on 1 pound of cooked spaghetti, fettuccine or linguine. Also great on grilled pork chops, as a last minute flavor to steamed julienne-sliced vegetables or in minestrone soup (use it sparingly). The sauce can be frozen, used immediately or stored in refrigerator in tightly capped jar for up to 1 week. (In winter substitute ¼ cup dried basil and 2 cups fresh spinach for the fresh basil.)

MINTED PASTA SAUCE

QUICK
& EASY

Yield: 1 cup
Assemble: 10 minutes

Note: Fantastic side
dish for lamb.

¼ cup butter, softened
1 cup fresh mint leaves, tightly packed
½ cup fresh parsley
2 tablespoons dried basil leaves
½-¾ cup Parmesan cheese
1 teaspoon salt
½ teaspoon pepper

Place all ingredients in bowl of a food processor fitted with a metal blade or blender and blend until smooth. Serve over hot fresh pasta. Sprinkle with additional Parmesan cheese.

FETTUCCINE ALLA CARBONARA

QUICK
& EASY

Yield: 8 servings
Assemble: 20 minutes
Cook: 15 minutes

½ pound bacon
1 pound fettuccine pasta
¼ cup butter, room temperature
4 eggs, room temperature
¼ cup heavy cream, room temperature
1 cup Parmesan cheese
Ground pepper
¼ cup chopped fresh parsley

Fry bacon crisply; drain and break into pieces. Cook pasta in a large kettle of boiling salted water until al dente'; drain. Place pasta in a large serving dish and toss with butter. Beat eggs and cream until just blended and pour over pasta; toss until well coated. Add bacon, cheese, pepper and parsley. Toss again and serve.

FRIED CHEESE, ITALIAN-STYLE

Yield: 4 servings
Assemble: 1½ hours
Cook: 3-5 minutes

1 16-ounce block mozzarella cheese
3 eggs, beaten
¼ cup flour
⅔ cup bread crumbs
1 clove garlic, minced
1 tablespoon vegetable oil
1 28-ounce can tomatoes, chopped
¼ teaspoon salt
Pinch of pepper
1 teaspoon dried crushed oregano
½ teaspoon sugar
¼ teaspoon dried crushed basil
¼ cup vegetable oil for frying

Cut cheese into 2½ x 2½-inch squares. Dip in egg, then flour, then egg again and, finally, in crumbs. Place on waxed paper and refrigerate 1 hour. Meanwhile, in a large skillet saute' garlic slightly in 1 tablespoon oil. Add tomatoes, salt, pepper, oregano, sugar and basil; mix well. Simmer, uncovered, for 45 minutes until tender.

In medium skillet fry cheese in hot oil until browned and cheese is thoroughly warmed. Turn only once (entire cooking takes 3-5 minutes). Drain on paper towels. Serve smothered with sauce.

DELICIOUSLY SIMPLE BAKED BARLEY

Yield: 6 servings
Assemble: 20 minutes
Bake: 1¼ hours

½ cup butter
½ pound fresh mushrooms, sliced
1 cup instant barley
2 cups canned onion soup
⅔ cup water
½ cup grated Cheddar cheese

In a large skillet saute' mushrooms in butter; add barley and let it brown. Pour soup into a buttered 2-quart covered casserole. Add water, barley and mushroom. Bake at 350° for 60-75 minutes. Just before serving sprinkle grated cheese on top.

GREEN CHILI BAKED BEANS

Yield: 16 servings
Assemble: 30 minutes
Bake: 2¼ hours

4 ribs celery, chopped
1 green pepper, chopped
1 onion, chopped
½ cup catsup
1 4-ounce can chopped green chilies
1 10½-ounce can tomato soup
1 8-ounce can tomato sauce
2 tablespoons prepared mustard
2 teaspoons brown sugar
1 29-ounce can pork and beans
1 29-ounce can baked beans
1 15-ounce can red kidney beans, drained
½ pound bacon
½ cup Cheddar cheese, grated

In a large skillet saute' bacon; drain, crumble and set aside. Pour off grease but do not wash pan. Add celery, green pepper, onion and saute' slightly. Add catsup, chilies, soup, tomato sauce, mustard and sugar; allow to cook for 5 minutes. Add all beans, combine and pour into a 4-quart baking dish. Place bacon on top of bean mixture. Top with cheese. Bake at 350° for 15 minutes, then lower temperature to 225° and continue to bake for 2 hours more.

SAVORY BEAN BAKE

Yield: 12-16 servings
Assemble: 20 minutes
Bake: 3 hours

1 large onion, chopped
1 large green pepper, chopped
⅔ pound bacon
2 31-ounce cans pork and beans
1 14-ounce bottle catsup
1 cup brown sugar
1 teaspoon dry mustard
1 teaspoon chili powder
¼ cup molasses

In a medium-size skillet cook bacon; drain and break into pieces. Drain grease from skillet but do not wash. Saute' onion and green pepper in skillet. Combine all ingredients in a 2-quart covered casserole. Bake at 300° for 3 hours.

WORLDLY WILD RICE

Yield: 8 servings
Assemble: 20 minutes
Soak: 6 hours
Bake: 1 hour

1 cup uncooked wild rice
1 cup grated sharp Cheddar cheese
1 cup sliced fresh mushrooms
1 cup chopped black olives
½ cup chopped onions
1 cup hot water
¼ cup vegetable oil
1 cup Italian-style stewed tomatoes, drained
½ teaspoon garlic salt

Soak wild rice in water to cover overnight or at least 6 hours. Drain the rice, rinse and drain again. In large bowl combine all ingredients in order listed. Place rice mixture in buttered 2-quart casserole dish. Cover and bake at 350° for 1 hour.

WILD RICE MAGNIFIQUE

Yield: 8 servings
Assemble: 30 minutes
Soak: 6 hours
Bake: 30 minutes

1 cup uncooked wild rice (or ½ cup white and ½ cup wild)
½ pound ground sausage
1 onion, finely chopped
1 tablespoon vegetable oil
1 cup chopped fresh mushrooms
1 tablespoon flour
¼ cup chicken stock
½ cup heavy cream
Pinch of thyme
Pinch of oregano
Pinch of marjoram
1 teaspoon Accent (optional)

Soak wild rice in water to cover overnight or at least 6 hours; rinse and drain. Cook rice in a medium-size saucepan in 3 cups boiling water for 30 minutes. In a large skillet cook and drain sausage; crumble. Saute' onion in oil; add mushrooms and flour and mix until combined. Add chicken stock and cream; stir until smooth. Add sausage, seasonings and rice. Place mixture into a 2-quart casserole dish, cover and bake at 325° for 30 minutes.

EASY BAKED RICE

QUICK
& EASY

Yield: 6-8 servings
Assemble: 5 minutes
Bake: 55 minutes

1¼ cups uncooked converted rice
¼ cup butter, melted
1 10½-ounce can beef consomme
1 10½-ounce can French onion soup
½ cup hot salsa (optional)
½ cup grated Cheddar cheese (optional)

Combine first 4 ingredients in a 2-quart covered casserole. Bake at 350° for 55 minutes. Add optional ingredients after baking if a Mexican-style rice is desired.

RICE PILAF

Yield: 6 servings
Assemble: 15 minutes
Cook: 25-30 minutes

Note: Wonderful with shrimp scampi (page 144), lamb or grilled chicken.

1 10¾-ounce can chicken broth
1 cup water
1 cup uncooked converted rice
½ cup golden raisins
¼ cup sliced green onions (green tops only)
1 tablespoon chopped fresh parsley
¼ cup dry sherry
3 tablespoons butter
½ cup peanuts or slivered almonds (optional)

In a large saucepan bring chicken broth and water to a boil. Add rice and simmer over low heat for 25-30 minutes. Add raisins and onions after the rice has been cooking for 15 minutes. Add parsley, butter and sherry after rice has been cooking for 20 minutes. Serve when rice has absorbed all the liquid (25-30 minutes total). Fold in nuts, if desired.

HAM FRIED RICE

Yield: 4-6 servings
Assemble: 25 minutes
Bake: 10-20 minutes

3 tablespoons butter
½ cup chopped green onions (include green tops)
1 cup finely chopped celery
1 carrot, grated
1 cup diced ham
1 cup sliced fresh mushrooms
2 tablespoons soy sauce
2½ cups hot cooked white rice

In a large skillet saute' onions and celery in butter. Add carrots, ham, mushrooms and soy sauce. Continue to saute' 5 minutes more. Add rice and toss lightly together. Transfer to 2-quart baking dish and bake at 275° for 10-20 minutes.

RICE AND VERMICELLI

Yield: 6 servings
Assemble: 10 minutes
Cook: 30 minutes

½ cup butter
1½ cups uncooked converted rice
1½ cups broken vermicelli coils
2 14-ounce cans chicken broth
2 chicken bouillon cubes
1 onion, sliced (optional)
½ pound fresh mushrooms, sliced (optional)

Melt butter in a large skillet with a cover. Add rice and broken vermicelli and brown (vermicelli will turn golden brown). Add chicken broth and bouillon cubes. Add optional ingredients (if desired), bring to a boil, cover and simmer for 25 minutes over low heat. (Rice and Vermicelli may also be baked, covered, at 350° for 30 minutes.)

SPINACH RICE SOUFFLÉ

Yield: 8 servings
Assemble: 30 minutes
Cool: 1½ hours
Bake: 35 minutes

1 cup uncooked converted rice
6 tablespoons butter
2 10-ounce packages frozen chopped spinach, thawed and
  well-drained
2 medium onions, finely chopped
2 cups cottage cheese
1 cup Parmesan cheese
4 eggs, beaten
4 tablespoons sour cream

Cook rice according to package directions. While hot, add 6 table-spoons butter, cool. Spread rice in a 9 x 13-inch pan. Mix remaining ingredients and spread over rice. Let stand 1 hour before baking. Bake at 350° for 35 minutes or until edges are brown and soufflé cuts into squares like a cake.

SCALLOPED PINEAPPLE

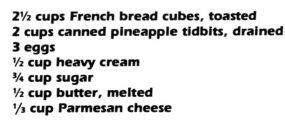

QUICK
& EASY

Yield: 4-6 servings
Assemble: 25 minutes
Bake: 45 minutes

Note: Really dresses
up a plain ham
dinner.

2½ cups French bread cubes, toasted
2 cups canned pineapple tidbits, drained
3 eggs
½ cup heavy cream
¾ cup sugar
½ cup butter, melted
⅓ cup Parmesan cheese

Toast bread cubes on cookie sheet under broiler. Combine drained pine-apple with bread cubes and place in a buttered 9 x 9-inch baking dish. In a small bowl beat eggs, cream and sugar together. Mix well and pour over pineapple and bread cubes. Drizzle melted butter over all. Bake at 325° for 40 minutes. Remove and sprinkle with cheese. Bake an additional 5 minutes or until the cheese melts.

ASPARAGUS AND EDAM SOUFFLÉ

Yield: 4-6 servings
Assemble: 30 minutes
Bake: 40-45 minutes

Note: Don't let the
convenience fool you.
Your guests will rave!

1 10¾-ounce can condensed cream of asparagus soup
7 ounces Edam cheese, grated
4 eggs, separated
Butter
Flour
Parmesan cheese

In a medium-size saucepan combine the soup and cheese. Heat just until cheese melts; remove from heat and set aside. Preheat oven to 375°. Beat yolks in a large bowl and gradually stir the cheese mixture into the yolks, beating constantly. Beat egg whites until stiff, but not dry. Fold into the cheese mixture. Turn into a 1½ quart soufflé dish or casserole which has been buttered and dusted with flour and/or Parmesan cheese. Place soufflé dish into a larger baking pan on center rack of oven. Pour 1 inch of water into the outer baking pan and bake 40-45 minutes or until done. Serve immediately.

SEAFOOD

Salt Lakers travel through time to an Elizabethan arena staged in Cedar City for the annual Shakespearean Festival. For decades, bearded bards, winsome wenches, and fatally-flawed heroes and heroines have drawn captivated audiences to the spectacle of seventeenth-century England. How better to awaken from **A Midsummer Night's Dream,** than to enjoy an evening dinner-on-the-knoll. Shrimp Croissants, fresh summer fruits and cheeses and Glazed Carrot Cake arouse contemporary taste buds.

HALIBUT WITH SPINACH FETTUCCINE

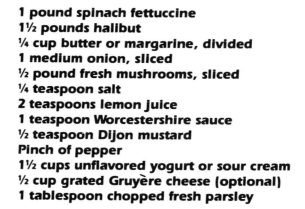

Yield: 4-6 servings
Assemble: 15 minutes
Cook: 15 minutes

Note: Low calorie,
low cholesterol when
using yogurt,
margarine and
omitting Gruyère
cheese.

1 pound spinach fettuccine
1½ pounds halibut
¼ cup butter or margarine, divided
1 medium onion, sliced
½ pound fresh mushrooms, sliced
¼ teaspoon salt
2 teaspoons lemon juice
1 teaspoon Worcestershire sauce
½ teaspoon Dijon mustard
Pinch of pepper
1½ cups unflavored yogurt or sour cream
½ cup grated Gruyère cheese (optional)
1 tablespoon chopped fresh parsley

Cook pasta al dente' while preparing halibut. Cut halibut into bite-size chunks, remove skin and bones. Melt 2 tablespoons butter in a large skillet. Saute' onions and mushrooms until tender. Remove from skillet; set aside. Add remaining butter and halibut to skillet and saute' until fish turns opaque and flakes.

In a small saucepan blend salt, lemon juice, Worcestershire sauce, mustard and pepper with yogurt or sour cream until smooth. Return onions and mushrooms to skillet. Pour yogurt mixture over all; stir and cook until heated thoroughly. (When using yogurt, heat carefully; it will curdle if overheated.) Drain pasta. Serve halibut over pasta. Sprinkle with Gruyère cheese and chopped parsley.

MARINATED HALIBUT WITH LEMON DILL SAUCE

Yield: 6 servings
Assemble: 15 minutes
Marinate: 40 minutes
Broil: 12 minutes

6 halibut fillets or steaks, 1-inch thick
½ cup Golden Caesar salad dressing

LEMON DILL SAUCE:
2 egg yolks
2½ tablespoons lemon juice
⅛ teaspoon white pepper
¼ teaspoon dill weed
½ cup butter, melted

Place halibut in shallow dish and pour salad dressing over. Allow fish to marinate for 20 minutes, then turn and marinate on other side for additional 20 minutes. Apply non-stick vegetable spray to broiler pan. Remove halibut from marinade and broil for 6-7 minutes on each side, approximately 4 inches from heat. Fish should be opaque when done. While fish cooks, place egg yolks, lemon juice, pepper and dill in a blender and blend for 10 seconds. Pour melted butter slowly into blender mixture while blender is operating at high speed. Pour sauce over halibut and serve at once.

HALIBUT WITH FRESH TOMATOES AND PARSLEY

QUICK & EASY

Yield: 6 servings
Assemble: 20 minutes
Cook: 20 minutes

1½ pounds halibut steaks
¼ cup chopped onion
1 clove garlic, minced
2 tablespoons butter
1 small tomato, chopped (approximately ½ cup)
⅓ cup dry white wine
1 tablespoon chopped fresh parsley
½ teaspoon salt
Pinch of pepper
⅓ cup milk
2 teaspoons cornstarch

Using a large skillet saute' onion and garlic in butter until onion is tender but not brown. Add halibut steaks, tomato, wine, parsley, salt and pepper. Cover and cook over low heat until fish flakes easily when tested with a fork (approximately 10-12 minutes). Remove fish to a heated platter; keep warm. Combine milk and cornstarch well and add to skillet. Cook and stir until thickened and bubbly. Cook 1-2 minutes longer. Pour over halibut and serve with parsleyed new potatoes and coleslaw.

ADRIATIC-STYLE RED SNAPPER

QUICK & EASY

Yield: 4 servings
Assemble: 10 minutes
Marinate: 30 minutes
Cook: 20 minutes

Note: a very low-sodium entre'e.

3 tablespoons unsalted butter, melted
3 tablespoons olive oil
Juice of 1 lemon
½ teaspoon dried thyme
2 tablespoons chopped fresh basil (or 2 teaspoons dried basil)
1 tablespoon finely chopped fresh parsley
1 clove garlic, finely minced
2 red snapper fillets about 1 pound each
Freshly ground pepper to taste

Combine the butter, oil, lemon juice, thyme, basil, parsley and garlic in a flat dish large enough to hold the fish pieces in one layer. Sprinkle the fish on all sides with pepper then place into the oil mixture and turn to coat on all sides. Let stand at least 30 minutes. Heat two non-stick skillets large enough to hold the fish pieces in one layer. Add fish to the skillet and cook over relatively high heat about 1 minute or until golden brown on one side. Turn and brown the other side. Cover tightly and simmer approximately 8-10 minutes or until cooked through; do not overcook. Pour remaining marinade over the fish and serve.

SWORDFISH WITH MUSTARD SHALLOT BUTTER

Yield: 4 servings
Assemble: 15 minutes
Broil: 6 minutes

4 tablespoons unsalted butter, softened
1 tablespoon coarse-grained mustard
1 large shallot, minced
¼ teaspoon salt
¼ teaspoon white pepper
4 swordfish steaks, approximately 6-ounces each, about
**   1-inch thick (salmon steaks also work well)**
2 tablespoons vegetable oil

Preheat the broiler and broiler pan. In a small bowl cream together the butter, mustard, shallot, salt and pepper until well-blended; set aside. Pat the fish dry and brush both sides lightly with half the oil. Brush the hot broiler pan with remaining oil. Broil fish about 4-inches from the heat, turning once, until just opaque throughout (approximately 3 minutes on each side). Place 1 heaping tablespoon of the mustard butter on each piece of fish. Place under the broiler for about 20 seconds to start the butter melting; serve hot.

"GABBY'S" MARINATED SWORDFISH STEAKS

Yield: 4 servings
Assemble: 10 minutes
Marinate: 1-3 hours
Grill: 10-12 minutes

Note: The "Gabby Gourmet" is a Salt Lake-based chef known for his radio and TV kitchen wizardry.

4 large swordfish steaks, cut 1½-inches thick

MARINADE:
⅓ cup light-style soy sauce
½ cup peanut oil
¼ cup fresh lemon juice
1 tablespoon Dijon mustard
2 green onions, finely chopped
2 tablespoons finely chopped fresh parsley
Zest from 1 fresh lemon
1 clove garlic, minced

Place the steaks in a shallow 9 x 13-inch glass baking dish. Combine marinade ingredients in a small bowl, mixing well. Pour marinade over the steaks. Marinate, covered, 1-3 hours in the refrigerator.

Broil steaks 5-6 minutes per side, 3-5 inches under the broiler or over gray-hot charcoal. Brush with marinade several times while cooking.

SEA BASS AND PINEAPPLE SHISH KABOBS

Yield: 4-6 servings
Assemble: 30 minutes
Marinate: 2 hours
Grill: 10-12 minutes

Note: Fabulous with Easy Baked Rice (Mexican-style) page 131.

½ cup fresh lemon juice
¼ cup olive oil
4 cloves garlic, minced
1 teaspoon ground cumin
½ teaspoon salt
½ teaspoon pepper, freshly ground
2-3 pounds sea bass fillets
Fresh pineapple chunks
2 Bermuda onions, quartered
Bamboo skewers

continued

continued

In a deep bowl combine the first 6 ingredients for the marinade. Cut sea bass into large chunks and marinate, uncovered, in refrigerator for 2 hours, turning occasionally. Remove from marinade and thread on skewers alternating with pineapple and onion. Barbecue or broil kabobs about 10-12 minutes turning until done.

GRILLED TROUT WITH HERBS

Yield: 6 servings
Assemble: 10 minutes
Grill: 10-30 minutes

Note: Herb Butter is not only delicious on grilled fish but great on other grilled meats or chicken, steamed vegetables or garlic bread.

6 fresh trout (or salmon or bass)

GARLIC HERB BUTTER:
2 medium cloves garlic, minced
¼ teaspoon dried oregano
¼ teaspoon dried basil
½ cup butter, softened
2 tablespoons chopped fresh parsley
1 tablespoon Parmesan cheese

In a medium-size bowl combine garlic, oregano, basil and butter. Mix in the chopped parsley and cheese. Cover the bowl and allow the mixture to mellow at room temperature for 2 hours.

For whole trout (salmon or bass), place cleaned fish on heavy-duty foil. Place Garlic Herb Butter inside fish (amount depends on size and number of fish, but be generous). Spread additional Garlic Herb Butter over skin. Place fish and foil on grill over gray coals but do not wrap foil over fish. Barbecue covered (indirect method) for 10-30 minutes, depending on size of fish, until fish flakes with fork.

SALMON WITH MUSTARD DILL SAUCE

QUICK & EASY

Yield: 6-8 servings
Assemble: 10 minutes
Marinate: 15 minutes
Broil: 10-15 minutes

Note: Mustard Dill Sauce is terrific over any fish; try with snapper or sea bass.

6-8 salmon fillets, skinned
1 cup dry white wine
½ cup butter, melted
1 cup sour cream
3 finely chopped green onions
1-2 tablespoons Pommery mustard (French-style)
1 teaspoon dill weed
1 tablespoon finely chopped fresh parsley
⅛ teaspoon ground white pepper

Place the salmon fillets in a 9 x 13-inch glass baking dish and pour wine over all. Allow the fish to marinate in wine for 15 minutes. Dry fish with paper towels. Brush both sides with melted butter and place on broiling rack. Broil 6-inches away from heat for 5-7 minutes (depending on thickness of salmon).

During the broiling period, prepare the sauce by combining the sour cream, mustard, dill weed, parsley and white pepper, stirring to blend well. The sauce should be spread on the salmon prior to removing from the oven; then broil for another 2 minutes.

DEER VALLEY SALMON WITH PESTO SAUCE

Yield: 4 servings
Assemble: 45 minutes
Cook: 30 minutes

Note: Deer Valley is one of Utah's newest mountain resorts. It offers excellent skiing and cool summer recreation and, of course, delicious cuisine.

4 6 to 8-ounce salmon fillets
Court Bouillon for poaching (ingredients below)
1 teaspoon fresh Pesto alla Genovese (page 128)
Veloute Sauce (ingredients below)
4 large cherry tomatoes, cut into a rose formation
Fresh basil leaves for garnish

COURT BOUILLON:
1 quart water
2 bay leaves
6 fresh basil leaves
1 clove garlic, halved
2 green onions, cut into 2-inch lengths
10 peppercorns
1 lemon, sliced

VELOUTE SAUCE:
1½ tablespoons butter
1½ tablespoons flour
1¼ cups fish stock
½ cup heavy cream
Salt and cayenne pepper to taste
1 tablespoon butter

Prepare Veloute Sauce first. Whisk butter and flour together in a medium-size saucepan over moderate heat until foamy; do not brown. Add fish stock, whisk briskly to avoid lumps. Boil slowly for 20 minutes to completely cook flour; whisk occasionally. If sauce is too thick, add more stock. Add cream and boil for 2-3 minutes. Adjust seasoning with salt and cayenne pepper. Strain and keep warm. Float butter on top to prevent skin from forming.

Poach salmon in boiling Court Bouillon in a large saucepan or skillet until salmon is almost firm (4-8 minutes, depending on thickness of fillets); do no overcook. Place on serving dish and keep warm while preparing Pesto Sauce. For Pesto Sauce bring Veloute Sauce back to a boil; add 1 teaspoon Pesto alla Genovese, whisk, pour over salmon and garnish with a tomato rose and fresh basil leaves.

GRILLED SALMON WITH TARRAGON MAYONNAISE

Yield: 6 servings
Assemble: 10 minutes
Chill: 2 hours
Grill: 8-10 minutes

2 cups mayonnaise
¼ cup chopped fresh tarragon
3 tablespoons finely minced green onion
2 tablespoons fresh lemon juice
2 tablespoons chopped capers
Salt and freshly ground pepper to taste
6 salmon steaks, approximately 1-inch thick
Lemon slices for garnish

Combine first 6 ingredients and blend well. Cover and chill 2-4 hours. Top each salmon steak with 2 tablespoons of tarragon mayonnaise and grill or broil for 4-6 minutes. Repeat for other side. Arrange on serving platter and garnish with lemon slices. Pass remaining tarragon mayonnaise.

CAMPFIRE SALMON

Yield: 8-10 servings
Assemble: 15 minutes
Bake: 45 minutes

Note: This recipe is
great for camping or
for a large crowd.

1 cup butter, melted (no substitutes)
1 cup lemon juice
1 teaspoon Worcestershire sauce
2 packages dry onion soup mix
1 large salmon, approximately 10 pounds
Pepper to taste
Garlic powder to taste

Combine first 4 ingredients together in a small saucepan. Heat slowly
until mixture boils and then thickens. Simmer while preparing fish.

Sprinkle pepper and garlic powder inside of the salmon and on skin.
Place the salmon in 2-3 layers of heavy-duty foil and pour sauce over,
covering thoroughly. Wrap the fish and sauce tightly in foil. Grill over the
flame for 30-45 minutes, or until fish flakes with a fork. Turn occasionally.

LEMON BREAD STUFFING FOR SALMON

Yield: 10-14 servings
Assemble: 20 minutes
Bake: 30-40 minutes

½ cup butter
4 tablespoons finely chopped onion
4 cups soft bread crumbs
4 tablespoon lemon juice
4 teaspoons grated lemon rind
½ teaspoon thyme
½ teaspoon salt
¼ teaspoon pepper
1 5-10 pound salmon
Melted butter, seasoned with garlic salt and pepper

Preheat oven to 350°. In a large skillet saute' onion in butter until
tender. Add next 6 ingredients; blend well. Stuff inside salmon, loosely
truss and baste with seasoned butter. Make a foil tent, cover fish loosely
and bake for 30-40 minutes (10 minutes per inch of thickness of fish).

SEAFOOD SAND DOLLARS

Yield: 12 open-faced
  sandwiches
Assemble: 30 minutes
Bake: 15 minutes

Note: Hearty and
nutritious served with
a vegetable soup.

1 pound cooked crab or shrimp (or a combination)
1 cup grated sharp Cheddar cheese
6 green onions, finely chopped
⅔ cup finely chopped celery
1 teaspoon chopped pimiento
1 tablespoon chopped green pepper
1 tablespoon minced fresh parsley
3 hard-boiled eggs, chopped
1½ cups mayonnaise
6 English muffins, split
Fresh parsley sprigs for garnish

In a medium-size bowl combine the first 8 ingredients. Fold in the
mayonnaise. Mound the filling on each muffin half; spread over edges so
they will not burn. Place on baking sheet and bake at 375° for 15
minutes. Place under broiler for 1 minute until lightly toasted. Remove
from oven and garnish each with a parsley sprig.

CREPES WITH CRAB AND SPINACH

Yield: 12 crepes
Assemble: 1 hour
Bake: 20 minutes

CREPES:
2 eggs
1 cup milk
3 tablespoons butter, melted
Pinch of salt
½ cup flour

CRAB AND SPINACH FILLING:
1 10-ounce package frozen chopped spinach
¼ cup chopped onion
½ pound fresh mushrooms, sliced
7 tablespoons butter, divided
1 cup crab meat (not imitation)
5 tablespoons flour
2 cups milk
1 cup heavy cream
¾ teaspoon salt
⅛ teaspoon pepper
1½ cups grated Swiss cheese
⅓ cup Parmesan cheese

Prepare crepe batter by placing ingredients in a blender and blend until smooth. Chill for 30 minutes. Brush a small amount of oil on the surface of a 6 x 7-inch crepe pan. Heat and cook 2 tablespoons batter for each crepe. (Spread batter evenly by tilting pan.) Cook until light brown, about 1 minute per side. Crepes may be prepared in advance, layered between waxed paper, refrigerated or frozen.

To make filling, prepare spinach according to package directions. Drain **very** well. Saute' onions and mushrooms in 2 tablespoons of butter. Add crab and spinach. In a saucepan melt the remaining 5 tablespoons of butter and blend in flour. Add milk and cream and simmer, stirring constantly, until mixture is thickened and smooth. Add seasonings. Add half of the cream sauce to crab and spinach mixture. Add Swiss cheese to remaining sauce. Spread crab mixture down the center of each crepe and roll. Spread a thin layer of cheese sauce in the bottom of a buttered 9 x 13-inch baking dish. Arrange rolled crepes over the sauce. Pour remaining sauce on top and sprinkle with Parmesan cheese. Bake for 20 minutes at 350°.

This recipe may be doubled and phyllo pastry may be used instead of crepes. Spread 8 buttered phyllo sheets in a buttered baking dish. Combine the crab mixture and cheese sauce. Pour onto the phyllo. Spread 6-8 more buttered phyllo sheets over the crab and cheese mixture. Bake for 20-30 minutes at 350°, or until phyllo is golden.

CRAB AND ARTICHOKE AU GRATIN

QUICK
& EASY

Yield: 4 servings
Assemble: 30 minutes
Bake: 30 minutes

½ pound fresh mushrooms, sliced
1 shallot, minced
½ cup finely chopped celery
2 tablespoons butter
1 cup light cream
1 cup mayonnaise
½ pound crab meat
6 hard-boiled eggs, chopped
2 tablespoons sherry
1 8½-ounce can artichoke hearts, drained and quartered
½ cup seasoned bread crumbs
¼ cup Parmesan cheese

In a large skillet saute' mushrooms, shallot and celery in butter. Preheat oven to 325°. Mix mayonnaise and cream with crab in a bowl. Stir in eggs, sherry and artichokes. Add mushrooms to crab mixture. Pour mixture into individual serving shells or au gratin dishes. Sprinkle with bread crumbs and Parmesan cheese. Bake for 30 minutes.

BAY SHRIMP STIR-FRY

Yield: 6 servings
Assemble: 30 minutes
Cook: 15 minutes

3 tablespoons peanut oil
1½ pounds uncooked tiny bay shrimp
½ cup sliced fresh mushrooms
2 cups coarsely diced celery
1 bunch fresh broccoli, separated into flowerettes
½ cup green onions, sliced into ½-inch pieces
2 cups fresh sugar pea pods, stems and strings removed
3 tablespoons soy sauce
3 tablespoons Aji Mirin (Japanese sweet cooking rice wine) or sherry
1 tablespoon light corn syrup
1 tablespoon cornstarch
2 cloves garlic, minced
3 cups hot cooked white rice
Chinese noodles as topping, if desired

Heat peanut oil in wok. Add shrimp and quickly stir-fry until shrimp turn pink and are soft, approximately 2-3 minutes. Remove shrimp and drain on paper towels. Add mushrooms, celery, broccoli and onions to wok and stir-fry until vegetables are almost tender, approximately 3-4 minutes. Add pea pods for an additional 1-2 minutes. Return shrimp to wok and stir-fry all together. Place soy sauce, rice wine or sherry, corn syrup, cornstarch and garlic into a half-pint jar; shake vigorously. Add this mixture to wok and stir-fry for 1-2 minutes until thoroughly heated and sauce is thickened. Serve over hot rice and garnish with Chinese noodles.

SHRIMP JAMBALAYA

Yield: 6 servings
Assemble: 45 minutes
Cook: 45 minutes

¼ pound sliced bacon, cut in 1-inch pieces
½ cup finely chopped onion
½ pound sausage (optional). Use a Spanish link or spiced breakfast sausage.
2 medium-size green peppers, seeded and cut in 1-inch strips
½ cup finely chopped celery
1 clove garlic, finely chopped
1 cup uncooked converted long-grain rice
1 16-ounce can whole tomatoes, drained and coarsely chopped
½ teaspoon thyme
1 teaspoon salt
½ teaspoon freshly ground pepper
1½-2 cups chicken stock
½ pound cooked smoked ham, cut in 2-inch by ½-inch strips
1 pound uncooked medium-size shrimp, shelled and deveined
1 tablespoon finely chopped fresh parsley

In a heavy 3-4 quart Dutch oven fry the bacon over moderate heat until it has rendered fat and browned, but not crisped. Drain on paper towels and set aside. Add onions to the bacon drippings in the skillet along with the sausage and cook for 8-10 minutes, stirring occasionally, until the onions are transparent but not brown, and the sausage is no longer pink. Mix in the green peppers, celery and garlic. Cook and stir until the peppers are limp, about 3 minutes. Preheat oven to 350°. Stir in the rice and fold with the vegetables over moderate heat until the grains become somewhat opaque and milky. Add the tomatoes, bacon, thyme, salt and pepper, stirring thoroughly. Pour in 1½ cups chicken stock and bring to a boil. Add the ham and stir again. Cover casserole tightly and place in the lower one-third of the oven. After 10 minutes add the shrimp, pushing them down beneath the rice, and continue cooking, tightly covered, for about 10 minutes longer or until all of the stock is absorbed and rice is tender. If at any point during the cooking rice appears dry, add a few more tablespoons stock. Serve directly from the casserole or mound on a large heated platter. Garnish with fresh chopped parsley.

SCAMPI

QUICK
& EASY

Yield: 4 servings
Assemble: 30 minutes
Cook: 10 minutes

¼ cup butter
3 cloves garlic, minced
¼ cup chopped fresh parsley
1 pound uncooked medium-size shrimp, shelled and deveined
½ teaspoon dried basil leaves
¼ cup dry white wine
¼ cup herbed bread crumbs
1 tablespoon grated Parmesan cheese
1 cup sliced fresh mushrooms
Juice of ½ lemon

Melt butter in a large skillet. Stir in garlic and saute' for one minute. Add parsley, shrimp and basil and continue to saute' until shrimp turn pink. Do not overcook. Add wine, bread crumbs, cheese and mushrooms. Stir until thickened and mushrooms are heated through. Add lemon juice, stir and then serve.

SHRIMP CREOLE

Yield: 4-6 servings
Assemble: 30 minutes
Cook: 90 minutes

3 tablespoons butter
1 green pepper, finely diced
1 large onion, finely diced
1½ cups finely diced celery
1 tablespoon flour
1 16-ounce can tomato sauce
1 teaspoon chili powder
Pinch of garlic salt
Pinch of cayenne pepper
Pinch of black pepper
1 pound uncooked medium-size shrimp, shelled and deveined
½ pound sliced fresh mushrooms
¼ cup sherry (optional)
2-3 cups hot cooked white or brown rice

GARNISHES:
Chopped green onions, grated sharp Cheddar cheese and sliced
  black olives

Melt butter in a large, heavy skillet. Add green pepper, onion and celery. Saute' until tender. Add flour, tomato sauce, chili powder, garlic salt, cayenne pepper and black pepper. Let simmer for 1 hour. Add shrimp and mushrooms and simmer 30 minutes more. Serve over rice. Serve small bowls of green onions chopped fine, grated sharp cheese and sliced ripe black olives on the side as condiments.

PICADILLY SHRIMP

QUICK
& EASY

Yield: 12 servings
Assemble: 20 minutes
Bake: 15-20 minutes

1½ cups butter
1½ cups margarine
3 lemons, sliced
5 ounces Worcestershire sauce
1 tablespoon tarragon vinegar
2 teaspoons salt
1 teaspoon Tabasco sauce
3 cloves garlic, minced
1 teaspoon rosemary
2 tablespoons finely ground pepper
1 bay leaf
5 pounds uncooked large shrimp, in shells

In a medium-size saucepan melt butter and margarine. Add lemon slices. Add Worcestershire sauce, vinegar, salt, Tabasco sauce, garlic, rosemary, pepper and bay leaf. Stir thoroughly and simmer for 10-15 minutes. Preheat oven to 400°. Divide shrimp between 2 large, shallow pans. Pour hot butter sauce over each pan of shrimp and stir to coat well. Cook for 15-20 minutes at 400°, turning once. Shells should be pink and shrimp should be white. Serve in cones made from newspaper just for fun.

COLORFUL SHRIMP FETTUCCINE

QUICK
& EASY

Yield: 6 servings
Assemble: 40 minutes
Cook: 20 minutes

Note: Compliment
this entree by serving
crusty French Bread
(page 68), Green
Salad with Almonds
and Orange Dressing
(page 90) and Fresh
Plum Cake (page
259) for dessert.

2 tablespoons olive oil
2 cloves garlic, minced
1 large onion, sliced into rings
½ cup thinly sliced celery
1 teaspoon crushed dried basil
1 teaspoon crushed dried oregano
1 tablespoon chopped fresh parsley
1 10¾-ounce can cream of shrimp soup (or shrimp bisque soup)
½ cup heavy cream
Juice of ½ lemon
¼ cup sherry
3 tablespoons butter
1 pound uncooked medium-size shrimp, shelled and deveined
1 pound fresh tomato fettuccine pasta (see recipe page 94)
1 teaspoon vegetable oil
Freshly ground pepper to taste
1 tablespoon chopped fresh parsley
1 cup grated fresh Parmesan cheese, divided

In a medium-size skillet sauté garlic, onion and celery in olive oil until onion is translucent. Add basil, oregano and parsley and sauté slightly to blend. Transfer to a medium-size saucepan (reserve skillet, unwashed, for later use), and add the soup, cream, lemon and sherry to mixture. Allow to simmer while preparing shrimp and fettuccine. In a large kettle bring 4-quarts of water to a boil. Add 1 teaspoon oil and fettuccine, cook until pasta is al dente (approximately 4 minutes). In the same skillet used to prepare herb mixture heat 3 tablespoons butter and sauté the shrimp until they turn pink (medium-high heat for 3-4 minutes). Drain fettuccine and place into a heated 2-quart serving dish. Pour sauce over pasta and grate fresh pepper over top. Sprinkle with half the Parmesan cheese, spoon shrimp on top and garnish with the remaining Parmesan and fresh parsley. Pass additional Parmesan at the table.

FUSILLI WITH SHRIMP AND ROASTED PEPPERS

Yield: 4 servings
Assemble: 30 minutes
Cook: 15 minutes
Marinate: 2 hours

1 large red bell pepper
1 large green bell pepper
¾ pound fusilli pasta
Salt and freshly ground pepper to taste
½ cup white wine vinegar
1 tablespoon Dijon mustard
½ cup olive oil
8 ounces cooked tiny bay shrimp
2-3 tablespoons chopped fresh basil, or 1 teaspoon dried, crumbled basil

Char peppers under broiler, turning until skins blacken. Wrap in plastic bag and let rest 10 minutes. Remove skin and seeds from peppers. Rinse and pat dry. Cut into strips the same size as fusilli pasta. Cook fusilli in large pot of rapidly boiling water until firm but still tender to bite. Drain, rinse under cool water and drain again. Sprinkle with salt and pepper. Bring to room temperature. Blend vinegar and mustard in bowl. Whisk in oil in a thin stream. Add peppers, fusilli, shrimp and basil and toss well. Adjust seasonings. Let stand at room temperature for 2 hours before serving, stirring often.

CAJUN SHRIMP (Pictured on Cover)

Yield: 4-6 servings
Assemble: 30 minutes
Cook: 5-7 minutes

Note: Pepper pods release just enough heat to enhance flavor, yet this unusual combination of ingredients will not overpower the delicate flavor of the shrimp.

1 bunch green onions
6 tablespoons butter, softened and divided in half
1 clove garlic, minced
2 teaspoons lime juice
2 teaspoons peanut butter
3 tablespoons dry sherry
1 teaspoon Old Bay seasoning (available at fish markets) or Beau Monde seasoning
1½ pounds uncooked large shrimp (20), shelled, deveined and butterflied
20 small dried Japanese pepper pods
⅓ cup minced fresh parsley, divided
½ cup dry-roasted peanuts, coarsely chopped
3-4 cups hot cooked white rice

Cut green onions into fine slivers 2-inches long. Place in a small bowl of ice water to develop curl; set aside. In another small bowl combine 3 tablespoons butter, garlic, lime juice and peanut butter. Add sherry and Old Bay; mix until smooth. Set sauce aside.

Melt 3 tablespoons butter in a large heavy skillet. Heat until almost ready to turn golden. Add shrimp and saute' for 2-3 minutes (they should begin to turn pink). Pour sauce over and add red peppers continuing to saute' for 2-3 minutes more. Add 2 tablespoons of the parsley, saute' for 1 minute more (or until shrimp are cooked thoroughly but not overly cooked) and turn off heat while preparing to serve. Drain onion curls. Place hot rice in a large, shallow heated serving dish. Add remaining parsley and toss. Place shrimp, peppers and any pan juices over rice; garnish with onion curls and chopped peanuts. Warn guests not to eat pepper pods unless they have cast-iron mouths!

BROILED SHRIMP INDIENNE

Yield: 2 servings
Assemble: 15 minutes
Marinate: 2 hours
Broil: 6 minutes

Note: Serve with chutney and a chilled tabbouleh salad.

1 pound uncooked large shrimp (12), shelled and deveined
¼ cup olive oil
1 teaspoon ground tumeric
½ teaspoon garlic powder
¼ teaspoon cracked black pepper
1 teaspoon Beau Monde seasoning
1 teaspoon chili powder
1 tablespoon red wine vinegar
1 teaspoon basil, crushed
2 teaspoons mint, crushed

Place shrimp in dish suitable for marinating. Combine remaining ingredients in a small dish; pour over shrimp. Marinate, turning often, for at least 2 hours at room temperature. Broil shrimp in the marinade under a preheated broiler for 2 to 3 minutes per side. Shrimp will turn pinkish, curl and begin to brown. Do not overcook.

SHRIMP AND ARTICHOKES IN PATTY SHELLS

QUICK
& EASY

Yield: 4 servings
Assemble: 30 minutes
Cook: 30 minutes

1 pound medium-size shrimp, shelled and deveined
5 tablespoons butter, divided
1 cup sliced fresh mushrooms
2 tablespoons flour
½ cup light cream
1 10¾-ounce can cream of mushroom soup
⅓ cup sherry
3 tablespoons Parmesan cheese
1 14-ounce can drained artichoke hearts, cut into fourths
4 patty shells, baked
½ cup slivered almonds, toasted
¼ cup chopped green onions

In a large skillet saute' shrimp in 3 tablespoons butter until pink. Remove shrimp and liquid and set aside. Saute' mushrooms in 2 tablespoons butter in the same skillet. Blend in flour. Gradually add the cream and bring mixture to a boil and cook for 1 minute. Blend in soup, sherry and cheese. Stir in the shrimp and artichoke hearts. Allow to heat thoroughly and serve over patty shells. Garnish with green onions and toasted slivered almonds.

SHRIMP CROISSANT

Yield: 8 servings
Assemble: 20 minutes
Marinate: 8 hours

Note: Marinade can be used with jumbo shrimp as an hors d'oeuvre or with medium-size shrimp in a main course salad.

2 pounds cooked tiny bay shrimp

MARINADE:
½ cup vinegar
20 bay leaves, divided
2 medium onions, thinly sliced
2 cups vegetable oil
Dash of Tabasco
¼ cup Worcestershire sauce
1 teaspoon paprika

2 thinly sliced avocados
4 ounces alfalfa sprouts
8 croissants, split

Rinse shrimp in cold water; drain. In a medium-size saucepan heat vinegar and half of the bay leaves; do not boil. Remove bay leaves and let vinegar cool. In a 1½-quart storage container layer shrimp, then onions, then remaining bay leaves until all the shrimp has been used. Prepare marinade of cooled vinegar, oil, Tabasco, Worcestershire sauce and paprika. Shake well or mix in a blender or food processor. Pour marinade over shrimp and refrigerate overnight. Drain shrimp and serve in a croissant with avocado slices and alfalfa sprouts.

LASAGNE DI MARE

Yield: 8 servings
Assemble: 45 minutes
Bake: 30 minutes

9 lasagne pasta strips
4 tablespoons butter
4 tablespoons flour
2 cups milk
Salt and pepper to taste
2 tablespoons sherry
1 tablespoon butter
1 tablespoon finely chopped shallots
¾ pound uncooked medium-size shrimp, shelled and deveined
1 pint sea scallops, cut into bite-size pieces, if necessary
Salt and freshly ground pepper to taste
½ cup dry white wine
2 cups thinly sliced fresh mushrooms
1 cup crushed canned tomatoes
½ cup heavy cream
¼ teaspoon crushed hot red pepper flakes
3 tablespoons finely chopped fresh parsley
4 small skinless, boneless flounder fillets (or any thin
**   white fish to equal approximately 1 pound)**
1 cup grated Gruyère or Swiss cheese
6 strips bacon, cooked and crumbled

Prepare lasagne pasta according to package directions. Place in cold water and set aside.

Prepare a Béchamel sauce by melting butter in a small saucepan; add flour and whisk together. Add milk and stir rapidly. Add salt, pepper and sherry. Increase heat and allow to thicken. When thick, simmer for 5 minutes while preparing seafood.

In a large skillet melt butter and add shallots; cook 30 seconds. Add shrimp and scallops and season with salt and pepper. When shrimp start to turn pink, add the wine and stir until mixture comes to a boil. Just as boil begins, turn off heat. With a slotted spoon, transfer seafood to a bowl; set aside. Bring cooking liquid to a simmer; add the mushrooms and cook for 5 minutes. Stir in Béchamel sauce. Add tomatoes and simmer 5 minutes. Add cream, pepper flakes, parsley, salt and pepper to taste. Add any liquid drained from shrimp and scallops to the sauce and stir in bacon. Preheat oven to 375°.

Butter bottom and sides of 9 x 13-inch baking dish. Spoon a layer of the sauce over the bottom of the dish. Add half of the shrimp and scallops. Spoon some sauce over the seafood. Cover with 3 strips of lasagne pasta. Add a layer of white fish fillets. Add salt and pepper to taste and a thin layer of sauce. Cover with 3 strips of lasagne pasta. Scatter remaining shrimp and scallops over pasta and add a light layer of sauce. Cover with the 3 remaining strips of lasagne pasta and top with remaining sauce. Garnish with cheese. (May be prepared in advance to this point and refrigerated or frozen.) Bake for 30 minutes or until bubbly.

TESTERS' CHOICE CLAM SAUCES

Yield: 6 servings
Assemble: 5 minutes
Cook: 10 minutes

Note: Serve linguine
with the sauce that
suits your tastes.

1 pound linguine pasta, fresh or dried
Grated fresh Parmesan cheese for topping

CREAMY CLAM SAUCE:
2 cups sliced fresh mushrooms
2 cloves garlic, minced
½ cup butter
6 tablespoons flour
3 6½-ounce cans chopped or minced clams (reserve juice)
2 cups light cream
½ cup Parmesan cheese
2 tablespoons chopped fresh parsley
½ teaspoon pepper

GARLIC OIL-BASED SAUCE:
½ cup butter
½ cup garlic oil (can substitute ½ cup olive oil with 2-3
** cloves minced garlic)**
1 large onion, chopped
1 cup chopped fresh parsley
1 teaspoon dried oregano
2 6½-ounce cans chopped or minced clams (reserve juice)
1 cup dry white wine
2 cups sliced fresh mushrooms
Salt and pepper to taste

Cook pasta according to package directions for either sauce. For Creamy Clam Sauce: saute' mushrooms and garlic in butter in a large skillet. Stir in flour. Gradually add clam juice and cream; stir until mixture thickens. Add clams, cheese, parsley and pepper. Drain pasta and serve topped with sauce. Sprinkle liberally with Parmesan cheese.

For Garlic Oil-Based Sauce: heat the butter and garlic oil in a large skillet. Add onion and saute' until golden. Stir in parsley, oregano, clam juice, white wine and mushrooms. Simmer for 5 minutes. Add clams and allow to heat thoroughly. Season to taste with salt and pepper. Drain pasta and serve topped with sauce. Sprinkle liberally with Parmesan cheese.

FRUITS DE MER EN CASSEROLE

Yield: 6-8 servings
Assemble: 30 minutes
Cook: 15 minutes

1 cup dry white wine
1 small onion, thinly sliced
1 tablespoon minced fresh parsley
1 teaspoon salt
1 pound sea scallops, halved if too large
½ pound fresh mushrooms, thinly sliced
¼ cup butter, divided
2 teaspoons lemon juice
4 tablespoons flour
1 cup heavy cream
⅓ cup grated Gruyère cheese
Pepper to taste
½ pound cooked bay shrimp
½ pound fresh or canned crab, flaked (do not use imitation)

continued

continued

1 cup buttered soft bread crumbs
4 cups hot cooked white rice

Combine first four ingredients in a medium-size saucepan and bring to a boil. Add scallops and poach for 4 minutes. Drain scallops saving liquid.

In a large skillet saute' mushrooms in 2 tablespoons butter for 3-4 minutes; sprinkle with lemon juice. Remove mushrooms with slotted spoon, saving liquid. Combine scallop liquid and mushroom liquid together, measure, and add enough water to equal 2 cups.

Melt remaining 2 tablespoons butter in skillet; blend in flour, 2 cups liquid and cream. Cook, stirring over low heat until thickened and smooth. Add cheese and pepper, stirring until cheese melts. Fold in scallops, mushrooms, shrimp and crabmeat. Heat to serving temperature. Turn into a shallow 2-quart casserole and sprinkle with buttered bread crumbs. Brown under broiler. Serve over rice.

SCALLOPS DENISE

QUICK
& EASY

Yield: 4-6 servings
Assemble: 30 minutes
Cook: 15 minutes

1 pound bay scallops, rinsed
2 cups water
Juice of 1 lemon
2 tablespoons butter
2 tablespoons flour
1 cup light cream
2 teaspoons finely chopped green onion tops
2 dashes of Tabasco sauce
¼ teapoon ground white pepper
¼ teaspoon grated nutmeg (fresh is best)
2 egg yolks, slightly beaten
½ cup grated Monterey Jack cheese
2 tablespoons dry white wine
¼ cup dry bread crumbs
2 tablespoons butter, melted with a pinch of garlic powder
**   or garlic puree**
Paprika for garnish

Preheat oven to 350°. Lightly butter 4 shallow 5-inch ramekins, shells or 1-quart au gratin dish. Bring water and lemon juice to a boil; add scallops. Reduce heat to simmer and cook scallops for 2 minutes **only** then drain.

In a small saucepan melt the butter and add flour to make a roux. Let roux cook for 1 minute. Stir the cream in slowly until sauce thickens. Add the onion, Tabasco, pepper and nutmeg. Stir some of the hot cream mixing into egg yolks and then slowly stir the egg yolk mixture back into hot cream mixture. Add the cheese and wine and stir until cheese melts. Stir in scallops until they are warm. Pour into prepared dish or dishes and top with bread crumbs drizzled with garlic butter. Sprinkle with a dash of paprika. Bake for 15 minutes at 350°, until bubbly and golden on top.

PASTA PRIMAVERA WITH CAMEMBERT AND SCALLOPS (Pictured)

Yield: 4-6 servings
Assemble: 45 minutes
Cook: 15 minutes

8 ounces fettuccine (white, green, red or a mixture)
1 pound sea scallops, rinsed
1 cup water
2 cups broccoli flowerettes
2 cups sliced celery
1 red pepper, sliced
2 cups sliced fresh mushrooms
1 clove garlic, minced
2 tablespoons butter
1½ cups heavy cream
4 ounces Camembert cheese, rind removed
4 ounces fresh Parmesan cheese, grated and divided in half
1 teaspoon salt
Pinch of nutmeg
½ cup toasted walnuts
Coarsely ground pepper to taste

Cook fettuccine according to package directions. While pasta cooks, poach scallops in 1 cup water in a large saucepan or skillet for approximately 3 minutes; do not overcook. Drain, return to pan and set aside. In another large saucepan blanch broccoli, celery and red pepper by covering with boiling water for 5 minutes. Drain well and allow to stand in colander. Saute' mushrooms and garlic in a large skillet in butter for 2 minutes then add to the scallops; set aside. In the pan used to saute' mushrooms add cream, Camembert cheese, half of the Parmesan cheese, salt and nutmeg. Simmer together until cheeses are melted, approximately 5 minutes. Drain fettuccine. Toss vegetables, mushrooms, scallops, pasta and walnuts with cheese sauce. Add remaining Parmesan cheese and pepper to taste.

CHEF DENNIS BIRD'S SCALLOPS SAUTE' WITH MUSHROOMS AND TOMATO

Yield: 4 servings
Assemble: 20 minutes
Cook: 15 minutes

Note: Dennis Bird is the chef/owner of Bird's Cafe in Salt Lake City, which specializes in seafood cuisine.

1½ pounds sea scallops, halved if too large
3 tablespoons butter
2 tablespoons chopped shallots
6 large fresh mushrooms, sliced
Juice from ½ medium lemon
1 large tomato, peeled, seeded and diced
1 cup dry white wine
Salt and freshly ground pepper to taste
2 tablespoons chopped fresh parsley
3 cups hot cooked white rice

Salt and pepper scallops. Saute' lightly in butter in a large skillet until firm but not quite done (3 minutes). Remove scallops from skillet and set aside. Reserve scallop liquid. Add more butter to skillet, if necessary, to saute' shallots and mushrooms with lemon juice. Add tomatoes and saute'. Add scallop liquid and white wine. Cook quickly until liquid is reduced by half. Add scallops and parsley. Cook until scallops are done (about 45 seconds). Serve over rice or in individual casserole dishes.

PASTA PRIMAVERA WITH CAMEMBERT AND SCALLOPS

COQUILLES A LA NAGE

Yield: 6 servings
Assemble: 45 minutes
Cook: 15 minutes

Note: An exceptional
seafood entre'e as
well as a first-course
appetizer or luncheon
entre'e.

¾ cup water
1 carrot, peeled and thinly sliced
1 tablespoon chopped shallot or onion
Pinch of salt
¾ cup white wine
1 pound sea scallops, sliced or 1¼ pounds bay scallops
4-5 fresh mushrooms, sliced
1 tablespoon butter
1 tablespooon flour
½ cup crème fraîche (page 218) or heavy cream
Salt and pepper to taste
½ cup grated Gruyère cheese
Chopped fresh parsley for garnish

Preheat oven to 350°. In a large skillet combine water, carrot, shallots
and a pinch of salt; cook, covered, about 10 minutes. Add wine and bring
to a simmer. Add scallops and poach for about 2 minutes. Add
mushrooms and simmer for 1 minute. Drain scallops and vegetables,
reserving liquid;. reduce liquid to half by boiling.
In a small saucepan make a roux of butter and flour. Add ½ cup of the
liquid and the cream and cheese. Stir until smooth and thickened; season
with salt and pepper to taste. Arrange scallops and vegetables in 6
individual dishes. Pour sauce over each and bake in oven for a few
minutes until bubbly. Scallops and sauce may be served in pastry shells
also. Serve garnished with chopped parsley.

COQUILLES SAINT-JACQUES SAUTÉ PROVENÇALE

Yield: 4 servings
Assemble: 10 minutes
Cook: 6 minutes

1 pound sea scallops
1 tablespoon lemon juice
Salt and pepper to taste
½ cup flour
2 tablespoons olive oil
2-3 tablespoons minced shallots
2 tablespoons minced garlic
2-3 tablespoons butter, sliced
2 tablespoons chopped fresh parsley

Poach scallops in 1-quart boiling water for 30-60 seconds until scallops
turn white. Remove from water, drain and dry thoroughly. (This process
seals scallops and will allow them to brown successfully.) Sprinkle with
drops of lemon juice and season with salt and pepper to taste. Just
before saute'ing, dredge with flour and shake in a sieve to release excess
flour. Pour a **thin** layer of olive oil in a large skillet. When the oil is
heated to almost smoking, add the scallops. Toss for 3 minutes over high
heat until they are lightly browned. Add the shallots and garlic. Stir for 1
minute; do not let garlic brown. Add the butter in slices that will melt
easily. Garnish with parsley and serve. (Entire saute'ing process takes only
4-5 minutes. Do not overcook or scallops will be tough.)

POULTRY

 The Alpine Loop, a canyon passage with pastoral meadows, verdant nature trails and gaping caves, is a favorite of the Salt Lake photographer, hiker and spelunker. To capture all three titles, board the early Heber Creeper, an authentic, steam-powered train, for some camera-worthy scenery; then drive the Loop to Timpanogos Cave for a memorable hike and a first-hand view of stalactites and stalagmites. Complete the outing with a sunset picnic of Cold Lemon Chicken, Chilled Rice and Artichokes, Best Hard Rolls and Orange Kiss-Me Cake.

CHRISTMAS GOOSE WITH APPLE SAUSAGE STUFFING

Yield: 8 servings
Assemble: 30 minutes
Roast: 1½ hours

Note: Traditionally, a goose served at Christmas-time brings good luck for the coming year to all who partake.

1 5-pound goose, wild or domestic
2 teaspoons salt, divided
1 tablespoon butter
¾ pound ground sausage
2 unpared apples, chopped
1½ cups finely chopped onions
½ teaspoon pepper
1 teaspoon sage
2 tablespoons chopped fresh parsley
1 teaspoon Beau Monde seasoning
4 cups toasted bread cubes
½ cup milk
1 egg, slightly beaten
½ cup chopped carrot
½ cup chopped celery
1 cup chicken stock
1½ cups currant jelly
1 teaspoon onion powder
¼ teaspoon pepper
2 cups water
2 tablespoons cornstarch
1 cup water

Wash goose well; pat dry inside and out. Sprinkle 1 teaspoon salt inside goose cavity and ½ teaspoon salt over skin. Saute' sausage in butter in a skillet until well-browned. Add onions, pushing sausage to side. Also add apples at this point; saute' until tender. Add ½ teaspoon pepper and next 6 ingredients, mixing well. Spoon into goose cavity. Truss and place in a Dutch oven. Surround goose with carrot, celery and chicken stock. Bake, covered, at 425° for a maximum of 1½ hours, or until tender. Remove goose to heated platter. Remove dressing and wrap in foil. Keep warm in oven until ready to serve. Skim off excess fat from pan juices, strain broth and mix in the jelly, onion powder, remaining ½ teaspoon salt and pepper with 2 cups of water. Cook until well blended, stirring constantly. Combine cornstarch with 1 cup cold water; stir into au jus. Cook until thick, stirring constantly. Carve goose and serve with currant gravy and apple stuffing.

SUCCULENT BAKED PHEASANT

Yield: 6-8 servings
Assemble: 30 minutes
Bake: 1½ hours

2 tablespoons butter
2 tablespoons flour
1 cup light cream
1 10¾ ounce can cream of mushroom soup
2 tablespoons chopped fresh parsley
¼ teaspoon paprika
½ cup sherry
¾ cup flour
1 tablespoon lemon pepper
6-8 pheasant breasts
3 tablespoons vegetable oil
4 tablespoons butter or margarine

In a medium-size saucepan melt butter. Add flour gradually and cook for 2 minutes without browning. Add the cream all at once and stir until thick. Add soup, parsley, paprika and sherry. Set aside and keep warm. Mix flour with lemon pepper. Roll breasts in seasoned flour. Pan brown in oil. Place a dot of butter or margarine under each breast as placed in a 9 x 13-inch casserole dish. Then pour warmed sauce over breasts covering each completely. Cover casserole and bake 1 to 1½ hours at 350°.

TURKEY SCALLOPINI WITH MARSALA

QUICK
& EASY

Yield: 4 servings
Assemble: 30 minutes
Cook: 20 minutes

1½ pounds turkey breast fillets, ½-inch thick
½ pound fresh mushrooms, thinly sliced
1½ tablespoons lemon juice
4 tablespoons butter or margarine, divided
¼ cup flour
½ teaspoon salt
¼ teaspoon pepper
¾ cup Marsala or dry sherry
1 teaspoon beef stock base or 1 bouillon cube
1 tablespoon minced fresh parsley

Place several pieces of turkey between sheets of waxed paper and pound each piece gently but firmly with a mallet to about ¼-inch thickness.

Melt 2 tablepoons of the butter in a large skillet. Add mushrooms, sprinkle with lemon juice and saute' over medium heat just until mushrooms are limp. Place mushrooms and juices in a dish and set aside.

Cut turkey into strips about 1-inch wide and dust in flour seasoned with salt and pepper; shake off excess. Melt remaining butter in the skillet and brown meat on high heat, turning to brown both sides. Set aside as browned. Pour in wine, add beef stock base and cook rapidly, stirring constantly, until all browned particles are incorporated into sauce. Return mushrooms and meat to the pan, heat thoroughly and serve at once. Garnish with minced parsley.

TURKEY LASAGNA TO GO

Yield: 8-10 servings
Assemble: 25 minutes
Bake: 35 minutes

Note: A lasagna that
assembles easily,
costs little, travels well
and, best of all, is a
delicious way to use
leftover turkey.

8 ounces lasagna pasta
1 10¾ ounce can cream of chicken soup
1 10¾ ounce can cream of mushroom soup
1 cup grated Parmesan cheese
1 cup sour cream
1 onion, finely chopped
1 cup sliced black olives
¼ cup chopped pimiento
½ teaspoon garlic salt
3 cups cooked turkey cut into matchstick-size slices
2 cups mild Cheddar cheese, grated

Cook and drain lasagna pasta according to package direction ; set aside. Combine next 8 ingredients and mix well. Stir in pieces of turkey. Place ¼ of the soup mixture in the bottom of a well-greased 9 x 13-inch baking dish. Use ⅓ of the pasta and ⅓ of the Cheddar cheese for the for the first layer. Repeat, layering with another ¼ of the soup mixture, ⅓ of the lasagna pasta and a ⅓ of the cheese. Use ¼ of the soup mixture and the final ⅓ of the lasagna pasta for the next layer. (Cheese not used for this layer.) Finally, cover with the remaining ¼ of the soup mixture.

Cover and bake for 20 minutes at 350°. Uncover and add the remaining ⅓ of the cheese mixture. Continue baking, uncovered, for 15 minutes.

POULET FLAMBÉ

Yield: 4-6 servings
Assemble: 10 minutes
Cook: 25 minutes

Note: As always, take
extreme precaution
when flaming chicken.
Flambe' startles the
novice but the results
are worth a few
skipped heart-beats!

8-10 chicken thighs
2 tablespoons unsalted butter
2 tablespoons vegetable oil
Salt and pepper to taste
½ cup bourbon, divided
4 shallots, minced
¾ teaspoon thyme
3 tablespoons minced fresh parsley
½ cup heavy cream

In a large skillet brown chicken thighs in butter and oil until golden. Salt and pepper to taste. Lower heat and cook chicken for 15 minutes, turning often. Remove chicken from skillet. Pour grease off and place chicken back in skillet. Add ¼ cup bourbon, keep skillet away from face (at arm's length) and ignite with a match. When flames die down, place chicken on a heated platter; set aside. Add shallots to pan, saute' for 1 minute. Add the rest of the bourbon, thyme, parsley and cream. Cook rapidly for 2 minutes, pour over chicken and serve.

CARIBBEAN CHICKEN

Yield: 4 servings
Assemble: 15 minutes
Marinate: 1 hour
Grill: 10 minutes

3 whole chicken breasts, skinned, boned and cut into skewer size-chunks
2 teaspoons crushed garlic
1 teaspoon salt
½ teaspoon dried oregano leaves
⅛ teaspoon coarsely ground black pepper
4 tablespoons olive oil
4 tablespoons red wine vinegar
½ teaspoon lemon juice
Pineapple chunks
Green pepper chunks
Cherry tomatoes

In a dish suitable for marinating place chunks of chicken in a mixture of the next 7 ingredients. Let stand at room temperature for at least 1 hour. Skewer the chicken alternating with pineapple chunks, green peppers and cherry tomatoes. Grill until tender but thoroughly cooked.

CHICKEN CACCIATORE

Yield: 6-8 servings
Assemble: 30 minutes
Cook: 1½ hours

Note: Although the aroma of the simmering cacciatore is heavenly, it is great for preparing ahead, refrigerating and heating just prior to serving.

½ cup olive oil
1 Bermuda onion, chopped
3 cloves garlic, minced
1 fryer chicken, cut into pieces and skinned
½ cup tomato paste
1 cup dry white wine or apple juice
Pinch of salt
½ teaspoon pepper
1½ cups chicken stock
1 bay leaf
¼ teaspoon thyme
¼ teaspoon marjoram
2 tablespoons brandy
1 cup sliced fresh mushrooms
1 pound spaghetti pasta, cooked

In a large skillet saute' the onion and garlic in olive oil until translucent and then let brown lightly. Remove from pan with slotted spoon and set aside. Dredge chicken in flour and saute' in the olive oil until golden brown. Place the chicken in a deep Dutch oven.

Place the garlic and onions from the pan into a blender and add tomato paste, wine or apple juice, salt, pepper, chicken stock, bay leaf, thyme, marjoram and brandy; blend thoroughly. Pour the mixture over chicken.

Simmer in Dutch oven for 1½ hours on top of stove, checking often to prevent sticking. During the final 30 minutes of cooking, add mushrooms. Cook pasta according to package directions; drain. Serve chicken and sauce over hot buttered spaghetti.

GAME HENS WITH MANDARIN GLAZE

Yield: 6 servings
Assemble: 30 minutes
Bake: 1¼ hours

6 Cornish game hens, thawed and rinsed
1 6¼-ounce package long grain and wild rice
½ cup chopped onions
½ cup chopped celery
4 tablespoons butter
1 cup pitted black olives, sliced
1 11-ounce can mandarin oranges

MANDARIN GLAZE:
¼ cup reserved mandarin orange juice
¼ cup teriyaki sauce
1 teaspoon cornstarch
1 tablespoon butter

Prepare rice according to package directions. Saute' onions and celery in butter until onions are translucent; combine with rice. Add olives to rice mixture. Drain mandarin oranges reserving ¼ cup juice for sauce and 12 orange segments for garnish. Add oranges to rice.

Preheat oven to 350°. Stuff each hen with rice mixture (approximately ¾ cup in each); truss. Place in a shallow baking dish and roast 1 to 1¼ hours.

As hens roast, combine glaze ingredients in a small saucepan. Heat, stirring constantly, until glaze is clear and slightly thickened. Brush over hens after they have roasted for 45 minutes. Baste every 10 minutes and continue to roast for approximately 30 minutes more or until hen drumsticks move freely. Garnish with reserved orange segments.

CHICKEN ROLLS WITH MUSHROOM SAUCE

Yield: 6-8 servings
Assemble: 1 hour
Cook: 20 minutes

Note: A nice entre'e for entertaining. Serve with a crisp salad and sourdough French bread.

4 whole chicken breasts, skinned, boned and halved
1 teaspoon salt
⅛ teaspoon pepper
½ cup cold butter
3 tablespoons each of chopped parsley and chives
¼ teaspoon each of marjoram and garlic powder
¼ cup flour
Dash of cayenne pepper
1 egg
2 tablespoons water
½ cup fine dry bread crumbs
Vegetable oil for frying
½ pound fresh mushrooms, sliced
3 tablespoons butter
½ cup dry white wine

Pound chicken between sheets of waxed paper until about ⅛-inch thick. Sprinkle the insides of the 8 chicken pieces with salt and pepper. Place 1 tablespoon of cold butter at one end of each chicken piece. Mix parsley, chives, marjoram and garlic powder together. Sprinkle ⅛ of herb mixture over each butter slice. Starting at butter end, roll chicken breasts

continued

continued

tightly, folding edges to enclose filling, and fastening ends with small skewers or wooden toothpicks.

Mix flour and cayenne pepper. Beat egg with water. Coat chicken rolls with flour, then egg mixture and roll in bread crumbs. Pour oil into a heavy skillet to depth of about ½-inch and heat to 350°. Saute' chicken rolls in hot oil until well-browned (about 4 minutes on each side); use tongs to turn. Drain on paper towels and keep warm.

In a medium-size skillet saute' mushrooms in butter. Stir in wine and cook quickly to reduce liquid by half. Pour over chicken rolls, remove toothpicks and serve.

ASPARAGUS CHICKEN WITH BLACK BEAN SAUCE

QUICK & EASY

Yield: 6 servings
Assemble: 30 minutes
Cook: 15 minutes

Note: A unique and classy treat using fresh asparagus. Wild asparagus grows prolifically along Utah's stream banks. Harvest some for a truly gourmet dining experience!

1 tablespoon salted Chinese black beans
2 cloves garlic, minced
2 whole chicken breasts, skinned, boned and cut into bite-size pieces
1 tablespoon soy sauce
1 tablespoon cornstarch
4 tablespoons peanut oil, divided
4 cups fresh asparagus, trimmed into 1½-inch diagonal slices
Pinch of salt
1 tablespoon water
1 teaspoon sugar
1 tablespoon cornstarch
1 tablespoon soy sauce
¾ cup (scant) chicken broth
4 cups hot cooked white rice

Rinse black beans in a strainer and drain. Mash with garlic in a small bowl. Place chicken in a large bowl, add black bean paste, soy sauce and constarch. Mix well and set aside.

Heat 2 tablespoons oil in a wok or large skillet until a drop of water sizzles. Add asparagus and stir-fry for 1 minute. Add water, cover, and steam for 30 seconds. Remove from pan and set aside.

Combine sugar, cornstarch, soy sauce and chicken broth in a shaker jar. Shake vigorously to combine; set aside. Add 2 tablespoons oil to the wok, heat to high and add coated chicken pieces. Sear until cooked (approximately 3 minutes). Add broth mixture in a shaker jar and stir until thickened. Return asparagus to chicken in wok. Toss until heated thoroughly and serve over rice.

SZECHUAN CHICKEN

Yield: 4 servings
Assemble: 30 minutes
Cook: 10 minutes

Note: This is a **spicy** Chinese dish. Use the crushed red pepper sparingly if not accustomed to this style of cooking. For those faint of heart, the dish still has a good flavor without the red pepper.

2 whole chicken breasts, skinned, boned and cut into bite-size pieces
3 tablespoons cornstarch
1 tablespoon peanut oil
3 cloves garlic, minced
5 tablespoons soy sauce
1½ tablespoons wine vinegar
1 teaspoon sugar
¼ cup water
1 bunch green onions, cut at 45° degree angles into 1-inch pieces
⅛ to ¼ teaspoon crushed red pepper
½ pound snow peas (optional)
½ pound mushrooms (optional)
4 cups hot cooked white rice

Place cornstarch in a paper bag. Add chicken pieces and toss to coat. Heat oil in wok or large, shallow skillet until hot enough for a drop of water to sizzle. Stir-fry chicken and garlic until lightly browned, taking care not to burn the garlic. Add soy sauce, vinegar, sugar and water. Cover and cook 3 minutes or until chicken is done. Uncover and add green onions and pepper. Add optional ingredients, if desired. Stir-fry an additional 2 minutes. Serve over rice.

CHICKEN WITH CASHEWS

Yield: 4-6 servings
Assemble: 30 minutes
Cook: 8 minutes

2 whole chicken breasts, skinned and boned
1 egg white, slightly beaten
¼ cup soy sauce
¾ teaspoon sugar
1 tablespoon cornstarch
¾ cup chicken broth
1 medium red pepper, cut into squares
½ pound fresh mushrooms, thinly sliced
½ pound fresh spinach, cleaned, stems removed
1 clove garlic, minced
½ inch fresh ginger, grated
4 scallions, sliced, include green tops
¾ cup unsalted cashews
5 tablespoons peanut oil, divided
4 cups hot cooked white rice

Cut chicken into 1-inch cubes; dip into egg white and set aside. In a pint jar shake together soy sauce, sugar and cornstarch. Add broth and shake until combined well.

Preheat wok containing 1 tablespoon oil and add cashews when hot. Cook over moderate heat until cashews are lightly toasted. Remove nuts and set aside. Add remaining oil and stir-fry chicken for about 3 minutes until it turns opaque. Remove chicken and set aside. Add red pepper, mushrooms, spinach, garlic and scallions and stir-fry about 2 minutes. Lower heat, stir in sauce and chicken, and cook until sauce thickens. Serve over rice and sprinkle with toasted cashews.

CHINESE STIR-FRY

Yield: 4-6 servings
Assemble: 60 minutes
Cook: 25 minutes

2 whole chicken breasts, skinned, boned and cut into bite-size pieces
½ cup catsup
2 tablespoons soy sauce
1 clove garlic, minced
1 onion, chopped
1 green pepper, cut into strips
½ pound broccoli flowerettes
2 ribs celery, sliced
¼ pound pea pods
1 8-ounce can water chestnuts, sliced
2 carrots, thinly sliced
1 zucchini, sliced
¼ cup water
4 cups hot cooked white rice

ORIENTAL SAUCE:
¼ cup cornstarch
2 cloves garlic, minced
1 teaspoon ground ginger
¼ cup white vinegar
½ cup soy sauce
½ cup dark corn syrup
1 14-ounce can beef broth
¼ teaspoon black pepper
Water

In a medium-size dish suitable for marinating combine catsup, soy sauce and garlic. Marinate the chicken pieces in this mixture for a few hours or overnight.

Prepare the sauce in a medium-size saucepan stirring together the cornstarch, garlic and ginger until well combined. Add vinegar and stir until dry ingredients are dissolved. Add the soy sauce, corn syrup, broth and pepper; mix well. Stir in enough water to make 4 cups total. Heat, stirring until mixture boils. Keep warm.

Saute' the marinated chicken in a large skillet using the necessary oil. Cook until tender, about 15-20 minutes; keep warm. Just before serving, begin to stir-fry the chopped onion and green peppers in a wok for approximately 1-2 minutes. Then add broccoli pieces, celery, pea pods, water chestnuts and cook approximately 2 minutes. Add carrot slices and cook 1 minute, then add zucchini and cook about 2 minutes. Add water and steam for 2 minutes.

Place the rice on a large platter and spoon a bit of Oriental Sauce over it. Top with cooked chicken, then all the vegetables. Spoon Oriental Sauce over all; pass remaining sauce. Garnish, if desired, with almonds, Spanish peanuts or quartered tomatoes.

POLLO CON CAPELLINI

Yield: 4-6 servings
Assemble: 30 minutes
Cook: 20 minutes

2-3 whole chicken breasts, skinned, boned and sliced
into ½-inch wide strips
1 large onion, sliced
1 tablespoon Hungarian paprika
¼ teaspoon freshly ground pepper
½ cup chicken broth or stock
1 pound capellini pasta
1 pint sour cream
2 tablespoons flour
½ cup butter
2 cloves garlic, minced
½ cup dry bread crumbs
Finely chopped fresh parsley for garnish

In a large skillet melt the butter over medium-high heat. Add the chicken slices and brown lightly. Add the onion, paprika and pepper. Allow this mixture to cook, stirring until onion is limp. Stir in broth or stock. Reduce heat, cover and let simmer until the chicken is tender.

Meanwhile, cook pasta according to package directions; drain well. Combine the sour cream and flour; stir into the chicken mixture and heat thoroughly but do not boil. In another large skillet melt ½ cup butter over medium-high heat until butter is almond color. Add the garlic, drained pasta and the bread crumbs. Allow the mixture to saute', stirring well, until lightly browned.

Place the pasta mixture into a large bowl. Pour the chicken mixture over the pasta and garnish with the chopped parsley. Serve immediately.

MICROWAVE CHICKEN DIJON

Yield: 6-8 servings
Assemble: 15 minutes
Cook: 20 minutes

4 whole chicken breasts, skinned, boned and halved
3 tablespoons butter
Chicken broth
2 tablespoons flour
½ cup light cream or milk
2 tablespoon Dijon mustard
4 cups cooked wild rice

In an oblong glass baking dish melt the butter in microwave on high setting for 30-40 seconds. Coat the chicken with the butter and arrange in dish. On high setting cook the chicken for about 12 minutes, turning and rearranging about every 4 minutes. Remove the chicken to a warm platter. Measure the pan juices and add chicken broth to equal 1 cup. Return this to the pan and cook on high for 1 minute. Add the flour and cream and stir until well blended. Cook this mixture for 5 minutes, stirring every 2 minutes until the sauce becomes thick and bubbly. Stir in the mustard. Spoon wild rice on platter, arrange chicken on top and spoon sauce over chicken.

POACHED CHICKEN BREASTS IN TARRAGON

QUICK
& EASY

Yield: 8-10 servings
Assemble: 20 minutes
Cook: 30 minutes

4-6 whole chicken breasts, skinned, boned and halved
Salt and freshly ground pepper
3 cups chicken broth
1 teaspoon dried tarragon leaves, divided
5 tablespoons butter
5 tablespoons flour
1½ cups heavy cream
Juice of 1½ lemons
5 cups hot cooked white rice
2 tablespoons finely chopped fresh parsley

Sprinkle both sides of chicken breasts lightly with salt and pepper. Arrange breasts in a large Dutch oven or covered skillet. Mix chicken broth with half of the tarragon and pour over chicken breasts. Bring broth to a simmer over moderate heat and poach about 10 minutes or until chicken is cooked through. Remove breasts from pan and keep warm. Reduce broth over high heat until 2 cups remain. Strain broth and set aside.

Rinse and dry pan and then melt butter over low heat. Add flour and cook for 1 minute, stirring constantly. Gradually add the 2 cups of reduced chicken broth and cream, stirring constantly with a wire whisk or wooden spoon. When sauce is thickened and smooth, stir in lemon juice and remaining tarragon. Return chicken breasts to pan. Simmer two minutes while spooning sauce over breasts.

Make a bed of rice on a shallow serving platter and arrange breasts over rice. Spoon a little sauce over chicken breasts and sprinkle with parsley. Serve remaining sauce separately.

RITZY CHICKEN WITH POPPY SEEDS

Yield: 8-10 servings
Assemble: 20 minutes
Cook: 1 hour

1 cup sour cream
2 tablespoons lemon juice
2 teaspoons Worcestershire sauce
2 teaspoons celery salt
1 teaspoon paprika
2 cloves garlic, minced
½ teaspoon salt
¼ teaspoon pepper
5 whole chicken breasts, skinned, boned and halved
1½ cups crushed Ritz crackers
½ cup butter
2 tablespoons poppy seeds

Combine first eight ingredients in a container suitable for marinating. Add chicken breasts and marinate refrigerated overnight. Remove the coated chicken from mixture and roll in cracker crumbs. Arrange in a single layer in a 9 x 13-inch pan. Melt butter and pour half over the chicken. Bake uncovered for 45 minutes at 350°. Spoon the remaining butter and the poppy seeds over the chicken and cook 15 minutes longer.

CHICKEN BREASTS WITH CHIVE SAUCE

Yield: 4-6 servings
Assemble: 20 minutes
Cook: 30 minutes

½ pound fresh mushrooms, cut into quarters
2 tablespoons sliced green onions with tops
1 tablespoon lemon juice
2 tablespoons butter
¼ cup flour
1 teaspoon salt
¼ teaspoon pepper
3 whole chicken breasts, skinned, boned and halved
3 tablespoons butter
¾ cup chicken broth
1 tablespoon flour
1 tablespoon butter, softened
1 cup heavy cream
2 tablespoons chopped fresh chives

In a medium-size skillet saute' mushrooms and onions in 2 tablespoons butter for 2 to 3 minutes. Add lemon juice and set aside.

Slightly flatten chicken breasts. Mix ¼ cup flour, salt and pepper; coat chicken. Saute' chicken in 3 tablespoons butter in a large skillet over medium heat, turning frequently, for 2 to 3 minutes (do not brown). Add chicken broth and heat to boiling. Reduce heat and simmer covered for 15 minutes. Remove chicken from skillet and keep warm. Mix 1 tablespoon flour and 1 tablespoon butter in a small bowl until smooth; stir in ¼ cup pan juices gradually. Stir flour mixture into remaining juices in skillet. Cook over low heat, stirring constantly, until thickened, 2 to 3 minutes. Add cream gradually. Cook, stirring constantly, until smooth. Stir in reserved mushrooms, onions and the snipped chives. Arrange chicken on a serving platter and spoon part of sauce over; pass remaining sauce.

CHICKEN SIMON AND GARFUNKEL

Yield: 4-6 servings
Assemble: 30 minutes
Bake: 50 minutes

3 whole chicken breasts, skinned, boned and halved
½ cup butter, softened and divided
Salt and pepper to taste
6 slices mozzarella cheese
Flour
1 egg, beaten
Fresh bread crumbs
2 tablespoons chopped fresh parsley
¼ teaspoon sage
¼ teaspoon rosemary
¼ teaspoon thyme
½ cup dry white wine

Flatten chicken breasts between sheets of waxed paper. Spread each breast with 1 teaspoon butter and sprinkle with salt and pepper. Place 1 slice of cheese on each piece of chicken, then roll and tuck ends, fastening with toothpicks if necessary. Coat lightly with flour. Dip in egg. Roll in bread crumbs and arrange in a baking dish. Melt remaining butter and add parsley, sage, rosemary and thyme. Pour butter mixture over chicken. Bake, uncovered, 30 minutes at 350°. Pour wine over chicken and baste with butter drippings; bake 20-30 minutes longer. Remove toothpicks and serve.

ITALIAN CREPES

Yield: 10 servings
Assemble: 60 minutes
Bake: 30 minutes

CREPES:
2 eggs, beaten until frothy
¾ teaspoon salt
2 tablespoons butter, melted
1 cup flour
1⅓ cups milk

CHICKEN FILLING:
2 cups diced cooked chicken breasts
5 ounces Italian sausage, cooked and drained
1 clove garlic, ground or crushed
**1½ packages (15-ounce) frozen chopped spinach, thawed
   and drained**
¾ cup grated Parmesan cheese
Pinch of onion salt
½ teaspoon Italian seasoning
Pinch of anise (optional)

CHEESE SAUCE:
6 tablespoons butter
6 tablespoons flour
3 cups milk
½ cup grated Parmesan cheese
1 cup grated sharp Cheddar cheese
1 scant teaspoon curry
Dash Tabasco sauce, or more to taste

Beat crepe ingredients together. Mixture will be the consistency of thick cream. Cook crepes in a crepe pan or skillet, and layer between waxed paper; set aside.

Mix all filling ingredients together in a mixing bowl; set aside.

Make sauce by melting the butter in a medium-size saucepan. Blend in flour and add milk a little at a time, stirring to a smooth consistency. Heat, stirring constantly, until thickened. Add remaining ingredients and stir until cheese is melted. Turn heat to low while assembling crepes.

Fill crepes with filling, arranging them seam-side down in a large baking dish. Pour sauce over crepes and bake at 350° for 30 minutes.

INDIAN CHICKEN CURRY (Pictured)

Yield: 4 servings
Assemble: 30 minutes
Cook: 2 hours

Note: One may cut chicken into bite-size chunks, however, the authentic preparation calls for chicken pieces with bones. The tortillas are traditionally used along side to scoop up the savory juices.

15 coriander seeds
10 allspice berries
10 opened cardamon seeds
3-4 tablespoons corn oil
½ teaspoon saffron
1 bay leaf
½ cinnamon stick
10 cloves
2 medium onions, minced
2 cloves garlic, minced
1 inch gingerroot, grated
1 8-ounce can tomato sauce
1 teaspoon tumeric
½ teaspoon chili powder
1 teaspoon curry powder
½ cup unflavored yogurt
Salt to taste
1 large frying chicken, skinned and cut into pieces
  (see note)
3-4 cups hot cooked white rice
Flour tortillas
Bengal hot chutney
Unsweetened shaved coconut

Using a mortar and pestle, crush coriander, allspice and inner cardamon seeds. Heat the oil in a large, deep skillet. When oil is very hot, drop in crushed seeds, saffron, bay leaf, cinnamon stick and cloves. Quickly add onions, garlic and ginger. Saute' until light brown in color, 5-7 minutes. Add the tomato sauce, tumeric, chili powder and curry powder. Continue to fry about 10 minutes more until the oil has separated and the color is red-brown.

Add the chicken pieces, continuing to cook over medium to high heat until meat changes color. Add salt and yogurt and continue to cook until these ingredients are well-blended. Cover and simmer about 1½ to 2 hours. Remove bay leaf and cinnamon stick. Serve over white rice, or with flour tortillas. Pass Bengal hot chutney and garnish with unsweetened, shaved coconut.

MARINATED GRILLED CHICKEN

Yield: 3-4 servings
Assemble: 10 minutes
Marinate: 12-24 hours
Bake: 1-1½ hours

¼ cup packed brown sugar
¼ cup bourbon
¼ cup soy sauce
¼ cup Dijon mustard
1 small onion, thinly sliced
1 teaspoon salt
Dash Worcestershire sauce
1 large roasting chicken

Combine first 7 ingredients and place in a container suitable for marinating. Add chicken, marinate 12-24 hours; baste occasionally. Remove from marinade and bake at 350° for 1 to 1½ hours, uncovered, or put on barbecue spit. Onions may be drained, baked for 15 minutes and served over sliced chicken.

INDIAN CHICKEN CURRY

CHICKEN SAUTÉ WITH PEPPERS, TOMATOES AND OLIVES

Yield: 6-8 servings
Assemble: 30 minutes
Cook: 20 minutes

**4 whole chicken breasts, skinned, boned and cut into
  bite-size pieces**
Salt and pepper to taste
¼ cup olive oil
**2 large onions, cut lengthwise in half and then into ¼-inch
  wide strips**
**2-3 small green peppers, seeded and cut lengthwise into
  ¼-inch wide strips**
6 medium ripe tomatoes, or 1 16-ounce can tomatoes, drained
2 tablespoons finely chopped garlic
Pitted black olives for garnish (about 16-20)
4 cups hot cooked saffron-flavored white rice

Season chicken with salt and pepper. In a heavy skillet or wok heat the
oil over high heat until a drop of water sizzles. Sauté chicken pieces,
tossing constantly, until cooked through (approximately 5-7 minutes).
When all chicken is lightly cooked, transfer to a serving platter.

Pour off most of the oil, leaving just enough to coat the bottom of the
skillet. Add the onions and peppers and immediately reduce heat to low.
Cook, stirring frequently, for 8-10 minutes until the onions are limp and
transparent, not browned, and the bell peppers retain some crispness.
This process is best achieved if the skillet is tightly covered with a lid. Add
the tomatoes, increase the heat to moderate-high, and cook briskly until
most of the liquid in the pan evaporates and the sauce coats the spoon
lightly. Stir in the garlic so it can release its flavor without being sautéed.
Return chicken to the skillet, mixing it well into the vegetables. Cover
tightly and simmer on low heat for 5-8 minutes or until the chicken is
warmed again. Stir in the black olives and taste for seasoning. Transfer
the entire contents of the skillet to a heated serving platter and serve
over saffron rice.

BENGAL TIGERS' CHICKEN DELIGHT

Yield: 6-8 servings
Assemble: 30 minutes
Bake: 60 minutes

Note: Delicious with
Rice Pilaf (page 132)
and cold Spiced
Peaches (page 45).

4 whole chicken breasts, skinned, boned and halved
1 10¾-ounce can cream of mushroom soup
1 cup mayonnaise
1 teaspoon curry
1 cup Parmesan cheese
½ cup herb seasoned bread crumbs
8 tablespoons melted butter

Make a roll or form a loose pocket of each chicken breast and place
into a low-sided casserole dish. In a small bowl combine soup,
mayonnaise and curry. Cover chicken with soup mixture and bake,
uncovered, for 40 minutes at 350°. Combine cheese and bread crumbs
and sprinkle over chicken. Then drizzle with melted butter. Bake 20
minutes longer.

RASPBERRY CHICKEN

QUICK
& EASY

Yield: 4 servings
Assemble: 15 minutes
Bake: 20 minutes

Note: May be
assembled and
prepared early to
baking step. Just
refrigerate and bake
until sauce bubbles
(approximately 40
minutes). Serve with
Rice and Vermicelli
(page 132).

3 whole chicken breasts, skinned, boned and halved
Salt and pepper to taste
3 tablespoons butter
1 tablespoon vegetable oil
4 tablespoons flour
1¼ cups chicken broth
1 cup heavy cream
½ cup raspberry vinegar
2 tablespoons raspberry liqueur
Salt and pepper to taste
Fresh raspberries, kiwi or avocado slices for garnish

Saute' chicken in butter and oil in a large skillet until golden but not brown, or chicken will be dry. Salt and pepper if desired. Place chicken in a casserole just large enough to hold all the pieces without overlapping; set aside.

Pour off all but 3 tablespoons of oil. Add flour and cook roux 3-5 minutes over medium-high heat. Remove from heat and add chicken broth; stir until smooth. Return to heat and add cream, stirring constantly. Add raspberry vinegar, salt and pepper to taste. Add raspberry liqueur. Pour sauce over chicken, completely covering. Cover and bake at 350° for 15-20 minutes. Do not overbake. Garnish with fresh raspberries and either sliced kiwi or avocado.

COLD LEMON CHICKEN

Yield: 4-6 servings
Assemble: 10 minutes
Cook: 15-20 minutes
Chill: 1 hour

½ cup dry white wine
1 cup water
1 bay leaf
1 clove garlic, peeled and cut in half
½ cup lemon juice
3 whole chicken breasts, skinned, boned and halved
¼ cup mayonnaise
4 teaspoons finely chopped cucumber, peeled and seeded
2 teaspoons grated lemon rind
2 teaspoons lemon juice
¼ teaspoon each salt and pepper
6 lemon slices for garnish
Parsley sprigs
Paprika

In a large saucepan combine the first 5 ingredients. Bring to a boil and add chicken. Cover and poach over medium-low heat for 15-20 minutes until done in center of breasts. Remove chicken from broth, cover and refrigerate to cool thoroughly.

Mix mayonnaise, cucumber, lemon rind, 2 teaspoons lemon juice, salt and pepper. Spread in a thin layer over chicken pieces. Top each with a lemon slice. Garnish with parsley sprigs and a sprinkle of paprika.

CHICKEN PICCATA

Yield: 6-8 servings
Assemble: 15 minutes
Cook: 15 minutes

4 whole chicken breasts, skinned, boned and halved
½ cup flour
¼ teaspoon pepper
Paprika
¼ cup butter
1 tablespoon olive oil
2-4 tablespoons Madeira wine
3 tablespoons lemon juice
2 tablespoons capers
¼ cup minced fresh parsley (optional)
8 thin slices of lemon

Flatten chicken breasts between 2 sheets of waxed paper and pound them to a ¼-inch thickness. Combine flour, pepper and paprika in a bag. Add chicken and coat well; gently shake off excess.

Heat butter and olive oil in a large skillet until bubbling. Saute' chicken breasts 2-3 minutes on each side; do not overcook. Drain on paper towels and keep warm. Drain off all but 2 tablespoons of butter. Stir in wine and scrape bottom of skillet to loosen any browned bits. Add lemon juice and capers; heat briefly. Add chicken to skillet and heat until sauce thickens; sprinkle with parsley. A thin lemon slice may be placed on each piece for garnish.

CURRIED CHICKEN WITH VEGETABLE RICE

Yield: 6-8 servings
Assemble: 45 minutes
Bake: 1 hour

1 cup honey
½ cup butter
½ cup prepared mustard
2 teaspoons curry powder
3-4 whole chicken breasts, skinned, boned and halved
¼ cup chopped onions
¼ cup chopped green peppers
½ cup chopped celery
4 tablespoons butter
1 8-ounce can sliced water chestnuts, drained
1 cup sliced fresh mushrooms
2½ cups water
5 teaspoons granulated chicken bouillon
1 cup uncooked converted rice

In a medium-size saucepan bring first 4 ingredients to a boil. Place chicken in a casserole dish and pour sauce over the chicken breasts. Bake, uncovered, for 45 minutes at 350°. Turn breasts and continue baking an additional 15-20 minutes.

Meanwhile, in a medium-size skillet saute' onions, green peppers and celery in butter, then add the water chestnuts and mushrooms. Bring 2½ cups water to a boil in a large oven-proof saucepan. Add the bouillon, rice and the saute'ed vegetables. Bake covered for 45 minutes at 350°. Serve chicken breasts over rice.

LEMON CHICKEN WITH SPINACH

QUICK
& EASY

Yield: 6 servings
Assemble: 20 minutes
Cook: 20 minutes

Note: Just like warm
spinach salad topped
with luscious chicken!

¼ cup sugar
2 tablespoons cornstarch
1 cup chicken broth
2 tablespoons soy sauce
⅓ cup lemon juice
3 whole chicken breasts, skinned, boned and halved
Vegetable oil
Butter
1 pound fresh spinach, cleaned and torn
2 lemons, thinly sliced
Cherry tomatoes
Paprika

In a small saucepan combine sugar, cornstarch and broth. Cook until opaque. Add soy sauce and lemon juice. Keep sauce warm.

Saute' chicken breasts in skillet in oil and butter until lightly browned. Place hot chicken on a bed of spinach on serving platter. Pour the warm sauce over all and serve immediately. Top with lemon slices and garnish entire edge of platter with cherry tomatoes. Sprinkle very lightly with paprika.

BLUE CHEESE CHICKEN ROLLS WITH DIJON

Yield: 6 servings
Assemble: 30 minutes
Cook: 45 minutes

2 ounces blue cheese
8 ounces cream cheese, softened
½ pound Gruyère cheese, grated
6 whole chicken breasts, skinned, boned and halved
Dijon mustard (for spreading)
4 eggs, beaten
1 cup flour
2 cups seasoned bread crumbs
4 tablespoons butter
4 tablespoons vegetable shortening

In a small bowl combine blue cheese with cream cheese and mix well. Form into 12 balls. Roll each ball into grated Gruyère cheese. Place balls in freezer for approximately 20 minutes, or until firm.

Flatten chicken breasts between sheets of waxed paper. Spread Dijon mustard on one side of a chicken breast. Place cheese ball in center and roll chicken. Secure with toothpicks. Dip chicken roll in flour, then in beaten egg and then roll in a generous amount of bread crumbs. Fry chicken rolls in mixture of half butter and half shortening until golden. Place rolls in a baking dish and bake for 30 minutes at 350°. Remove toothpicks and serve.

CHICKEN SHRIMP ROLLS

Yield: 6 servings
Assemble: 1 hour
Cook: 15 minutes

3 whole chicken breasts, skinned, boned and halved
¾ pound shrimp
Water
1 clove garlic, cut in half
1 bay leaf
10 peppercorns
½ cup butter or margarine
¼ cup chopped green onions, tops included
½ teaspoon salt
Vegetable oil
1 cup flour
1¼ teaspoons baking powder
¾ cup water
1 teaspoon salt
Fresh parsley sprigs for garnish
Remoulade Sauce (page 15) or cocktail sauce
4 cups hot cooked rice
1 tablespoon minced fresh parsley

Pound chicken to ¼-inch thickness between two sheets of waxed paper. Poach shrimp in boiling water, garlic, bay leaf and peppercorns for 2 minutes. Shell, devein and chop shrimp. Combine with butter, onion and salt. Divide the shrimp mixture into 6 equal parts and spoon into the center of the chicken breasts, leaving ½-inch on all sides. Roll and fasten with toothpicks to secure. Cover and refrigerate for 15 minutes.

Heat oil to 375° in a deep fryer or large electric frying pan. Mix together the flour, baking powder, water and salt. Dip the chicken rolls in this batter and fry for 10 minutes, turning often. Drain on paper towels. Remove toothpicks from chicken rolls. Toss rice with parsley and place in the center of a warmed platter. Arrange chicken breasts around the outside and garnish with parsley sprigs. Pass Remoulade Sauce or cocktail sauce.

PARMESAN CHICKEN

Yield: 4-6 servings
Assemble: 10 minutes
Marinate: 24 hours
Bake: 45 minutes

3 whole chicken breasts, skinned, boned and halved
1 16-ounce bottle Italian salad dressing
1 cup herb seasoned bread crumbs
½ cup grated fresh Parmesan cheese
⅛ teaspoon paprika
½ teaspoon Italian seasoning
¼ teaspoon salt
¼ teaspoon pepper
2 eggs, beaten

Marinate chicken in Italian dressing for 24 hours. Mix together the next 6 ingredients. Dip chicken pieces in beaten eggs and roll in crumb mixture. Place in a 9 x 13-inch baking dish and bake for 45 minutes at 350°.

CHICKEN BREASTS WELLINGTON

Yield: 6-8 servings
Assemble: 60 minutes
Cook: 60 minutes

4 whole chicken breasts, skinned, boned and halved
Salt and pepper to taste
½ cup dry white wine
2 tablespoons vegetable oil
½ pound fresh mushrooms, very finely chopped
4 green onions, sliced
¼ cup butter
1 teaspoon salt
2 17¼-ounce packages frozen puff pastry
1 egg, beaten
1 tablespoon cold water
Bearnaise Sauce (recipe below)

Lightly salt and pepper chicken. Turn breasts with hands into a contoured shape and arrange on a 15 x 10 x 1-inch jelly-roll pan. Add wine and oil to pan. Cover tightly with heavy-duty aluminum foil. Bake at 350° for 20 minutes. Remove chicken and reserve broth.

In a large skillet saute' chopped mushrooms and green onion in butter until soft. Season with salt and add enough of the chicken pan liquid to make a spreadable mixture (about 3 tablespoons). Cool mushroom mixture.

Thaw frozen puff pastry, one box at a time, following label directions. Separate each package into 2 strips. Cut each strip in half lengthwise and roll out to a 8 x 12-inch rectangle on a lightly floured pastry cloth. Coat the outside of each chicken breast with ⅛ of the cooled mushroom mixture and place on half of rolled-out pastry. Fold other half of pastry over. Trim and seal with a two-tined fork. Brush well with a mixture of beaten egg and 1 tablespoon cold water. When all chicken breasts are pastry-wrapped, take pastry trims and roll into thin ropes and shape a bow for each chicken bundle. Add additional strips to sides. Brush trims with egg mixture. Place on a large cookie sheet. Bake at 375° for 40 minutes, or until pastry is golden. Serve with Bearnaise Sauce.

BEARNAISE SAUCE

QUICK
& EASY

Yield: approximately
   1 cup
Assemble: 20 minutes

Note: Bearnaise
Sauce enhances grilled
fish fillets or steaks.

½ cup dry vermouth or white wine
2 green onions, sliced (white parts only)
1 teaspoon leaf tarragon
1 teaspoon leaf chervil (optional)
8 egg yolks
2 tablespoons cold water
1 cup butter, softened
½ teaspoon salt
¼ teaspoon white pepper

Combine vermouth or wine, onion, tarragon and chervil in a small saucepan; bring to a boil. Lower heat and allow to bubble until liquid is reduced by half. Strain with a fine strainer or through cheesecloth into a cup; cool.

Beat egg yolks until thick and lemon-colored with electric mixer on

continued

continued

high speed in top of double boiler. Beat in water and place over simmering, not boiling water. Heat, stirring constantly with a wooden spoon, 4 to 5 minutes, or until warm.

Cut each stick of butter into 4 pieces; add 1 piece at a time, stirring constantly. Continue to cook, stirring, until butter is all added and sauce is thick enough to coat a metal spoon. Remove pan from water and season sauce with salt and pepper. And wine mixture, a little at a time, and stir until smooth. Serve over Chicken Wellington.

LUNCHEON CHICKEN CRESCENTS

Yield: 8 servings
Assemble: 60 minutes
Bake: 20 minutes

Note: New twists to an old favorite. Each version is also tasty cold as picnic sandwiches.

¾ cup dry herb seasoned stuffing
½ cup finely chopped pecans, walnuts or almonds
6 ounces cream cheese, softened
4 tablespoons butter, softened
⅛ teaspoon pepper
2 cups diced cooked chicken
1 tablespoon chives or chopped green onions
1 tablespoon minced fresh parsley
⅔ cup chopped fresh mushrooms
2 8-ounce cans crescent rolls
3 tablespoons butter, melted

Crush seasoned stuffing and mix with nuts; set aside. In a large bowl cream together cream cheese, butter and pepper. Add chicken , chives, parsley and mushrooms; set aside. Separate crescent rolls to form 8 rectangles , press seams securely. Place ½ cup of chicken mixture in the center of each rectangle and fold up ends to cover filling. Seal edges securely. Dip each folded roll into melted butter and then roll carefully into stuffing mixture. Place on baking sheet and bake for 20 minutes at 400°.

CURRY CRESCENTS:

Follow the above directions but use the following substitutions:

Use dry roasted, unsalted peanuts for nuts in topping
Omit mushrooms
Add ½ cup finely chopped celery to chicken mixture
Add ¼ cup coarsely chopped peanuts to chicken mixture
Add 2 teaspoons of chutney to chicken mixture
Add ¼ teaspoon curry powder to chicken mixture

CHILI CRESCENTS:

Follow above directions but use the following substitutions:

Use roasted sunflower seeds for nuts in topping
Omit mushrooms
Add 1 4-ounce can diced green chilies to chicken mixture
Add ⅛ teaspoon chili powder to chicken mixture
Add ⅛ teaspoon cumin to chicken mixture
Top with dollops of Guacamole (page 19)

MEATS

For sheer exhilaration, Salt Lakers are beckoned by the white waters of the Colorado River. Rafting through Cataract Canyon rivals any amusement park giant thriller. Roaring rapids toss, jerk, plunge and catapult the white-knuckled rafters in every possible direction—even vertical! Their terror is heightened by the constant possibility of sudden ejection into the crested, churning water.

Pristine shorelines offer a quiet reprieve as the sun dims over the soggy but invigorated adventurers. A few campfire songs bouncing off of the canyon walls, and a pack-along dinner of Lamb Bandit in pita bread, Marinated Vegetable and Pasta Salad and Chocolate Caramel Delights soften the rigors of the day.

LOBSTER-STUFFED TENDERLOIN OF BEEF

Yield: 8 servings
Assemble: 45 minutes
Roast: 30 minutes

2 6-ounce lobster tails (about 12-ounces total weight)
3-4 pounds beef tenderloin
1 tablespoon butter, melted
2 teaspoons lemon juice
6 slices bacon, partially cooked
½ cup sliced green onion
½ cup butter
½ cup dry white wine
1 small clove garlic, minced

Place lobster tails in slightly salted boiling water to cover. Simmer for 5 minutes. Remove lobsters from shell. Cut in half.

Cut tenderloin lengthwise to within ½-inch of bottom. Place lobsters end-to-end inside beef. Combine melted butter with lemon juice; drizzle on lobster. Close meat around lobster and tie together with string. Place on rack in roasting pan. Roast for 30 minutes at 425°. Place bacon on top. Roast 5 minutes longer.

To make sauce, saute' green onions in ½ cup butter in a small saucepan. Add wine and garlic. Simmer while preparing meat. Slice roast, spoon on wine sauce and serve at once. (Note: Tenderloin may be stuffed ahead and refrigerated.)

BROWN-BAGGED SIRLOIN STEAK

QUICK & EASY

Yield: 4-6 servings
Assemble: 20 minutes
Roast: 30-60 minutes

2-3 pounds top sirloin steak, cut 2½-inches thick
¼ cup butter, softened
¼ cup vegetable oil
1 large clove garlic, minced
2 teaspoons seasoned salt
2 teaspoons seasoned pepper
1 cup grated sharp Cheddar cheese
1 cup bread crumbs

Trim excess fat from steak. In a small bowl blend butter, oil, garlic, seasoned salt and seasoned pepper. Spread on all sides of steak. Mix cheese and bread crumbs. Press into butter mixture, coating steak well. Place steak in a brown paper grocery bag. Fold end over and secure with staples or paper clips. (At this point steak may be refrigerated several hours.)

Before cooking, bring the steak to room temperature. Preheat oven to 375°. Place bag on a rimmed baking sheet and bake for 30 minutes. For medium-rare, increase oven temperature to 425° and bake 15 minutes longer. For medium-well, continue by reducing heat to 375° and baking 5 minutes longer before removing from oven. Remove steak from bag. Let stand for 5 minutes before carving into thin slices. Two steaks may be prepared in the same bag, double the recipe, but keep the baking time the same.

RICE-STUFFED FLANK STEAK

Yield: 6-8 servings
Assemble: 30 minutes
Roast: 45-60 minutes

1¾-2 pounds flank steak
1 medium clove garlic, minced
1 tablespoon soy sauce
¼ teaspoon coarsely ground pepper
1 tablespoon butter or margarine, softened
1½ cups cooked white rice
½ cup chopped onion
½ teaspoon salt
¼ teaspoon coarsely ground pepper
½ cup chopped fresh parsley
½ cup grated Parmesan cheese
2 tablespoons butter or margarine, softened
½ cup condensed beef broth
½ cup water
1 tablespoon chopped crystalized ginger or ¾ tablespoon ground ginger
Fresh parsley coarsely chopped for garnish

To prepare steak for stuffing, wipe with damp paper towel. With a sharp knife score both sides of steak lightly into diamonds; rub with crushed garlic. Brush both sides of steak with soy sauce and ¼ teaspoon pepper. Spread one side of steak with the butter or margarine.

In a medium-size bowl combine the rice, onion, ½ teaspoon salt, pepper, parsley and Parmesan cheese. Spread stuffing on steak, roll up and secure with wooden skewers. Rub steak rolls with 2 tablespoons butter and place on a roasting pan. Mix beef broth with water and pour over rolled steak. Sprinkle with ginger. Roast, uncovered, for 45-60 minutes at 350°. Baste as needed while cooking. Sprinkle with fresh parsley and serve pan juices as sauce with meat.

WESTERN BARBECUE SAUCE

Yield: 3 cups, approximately
Assemble: 15 minutes
Cook: 1 hour

2 cups catsup
½ cup lemon juice
½ cup brown sugar
¼ cup prepared mustard
½ cup finely chopped onion
2 tablespoons butter or margarine
¼ cup Worcestershire sauce
1 clove garlic, minced
½ teaspoon salt
⅛ teaspoon Tabasco
Liquid smoke to taste (optional)

Combine ingredients in a saucepan and bring to a boil. Simmer at least 1 hour. Use to baste any barbecued meats.

RIB EYES AND SHALLOT SAUCE

Yield: 4 servings
Assemble: 1 hour
Cook: 10-15 minutes

4 choice rib eye steaks, 1¼ inch thick
2 cloves garlic, pressed
2 tablespoons olive oil
2 tablespoons butter
Freshly ground pepper to taste
4 finely minced shallots
½ cup clear beef stock, or bouillon
½ cup brandy
½ cup heavy cream
¼ cup finely chopped fresh parsley

GARLIC TOAST:
4 large slices French bread
1 clove garlic, minced
2 tablespoons butter, softened

An hour before preparing this recipe, lay steaks on a platter and rub all sides with pressed garlic. Let sit at room temperature. Prepare garlic toast by combining garlic and butter. Spread over bread, toast and set aside. In a large skillet heat the oil and butter over medium-high heat. When this mixture is quite hot, add the beef and saute' 5-7 minutes per side, or until steaks are cooked to taste. Remove beef to a warmed serving platter.

In the same skillet add the fresh pepper and shallots and saute' in drippings for approximately 1 minute. Raise the heat and add the stock and brandy. Allow this mixture to simmer while scraping bottom of the pan with a spatula. When the sauce is reduced to half, lower heat and add the cream. Allow this mixture to cook until the sauce thickens. Place steaks over garlic toast points, pour the sauce over beef, and garnish each with fresh parsley.

BARBECUED LONDON BROIL

Yield: 6 servings
Assemble: 5 minutes
Marinate: 4-5 hours
Grill: 10 minutes

2 pounds London broil, cut into six serving pieces,
**   approximately 5-6 ounces each**
½ cup soy sauce
¼ cup white wine vinegar or rice vinegar
1 large clove garlic, minced
2 tablespoons sugar
2 tablespoons vegetable oil
½ teaspoon fresh grated ginger

Place pieces of London broil in a 9 x 13-inch size dish suitable for marinating. Combine the next 6 ingredients and pour over the meat. Marinate for 4-5 hours at room temperature, turning every 30 minutes. (Steak can also be marinated overnight in the refrigerator.) Broil over medium-hot coals until steaks are cooked to taste. They may be broiled in the oven, turning steaks after 5 minutes for medium-rare.

DILLED SHORT RIBS WITH CARROT GRAVY

Yield: 4-6 servings
Assemble: 30 minutes
Cook: 3 hours

2 tablespoons vegetable oil
4 pounds bone-in beef short ribs, trim excess fat
1 cup water
1 cup finely grated carrots
1 small onion, chopped
2 tablespoons cider vinegar
1 teaspoon salt
¼ teaspoon pepper
1½ teaspoons dill weed
8 ounces wide egg noodles
1 tablespoon butter
2 tablesoons flour
¼ cup water

In a Dutch oven heat oil over medium heat and brown the ribs well on all sides. Add 1 cup water, carrots, onions, vinegar, salt and pepper. Cover and simmer over low heat for 2½ hours until the meat is fork-tender. During the last hour of cooking, add the dill weed.

Cook noodles according to package directions. Drain and stir in the 1 tablespoon butter. Arrange noodles on a heated platter; place short ribs on top. Keep warm. Skim fat from the pan juices and add water to make 2 cups liquid. In a cup blend flour with ¼ cup water until mixture is smooth. Over medium heat, gradually add flour mixture to hot liquid. Cook, stirring constantly, until gravy is thickened and smooth; adjust seasoning. Spoon some gravy over the ribs and pass the remaining gravy.

ITALIAN POT ROAST

Yield: 6-8 servings
Assemble: 20 minutes
Cook: 3-4 hours

3-4 pounds chuck roast
1 large onion, chopped
3 tablespoons olive oil
3 8-ounce cans tomato sauce
1 6-ounce can tomato paste
1 cup water
½ teaspoon allspice
½ teaspoon poultry seasoning
½ teaspoon thyme
3 cloves garlic, minced
½ pound fresh mushrooms, sliced
8 ounces pasta shells, prepared according to package directions

In a Dutch oven brown meat and onions in the olive oil. Add the tomato sauce, tomato paste, water, seasonings and garlic. Cover and simmer **at least** 3 hours. Fifteen minutes before serving, add the mushrooms.

To serve, remove meat from pan and slice. Serve sauce over cooked pasta shells.

BEST-EVER BRISKET BARBECUE

Yield: 10-12 servings
Assemble: 15 minutes
Bake: 4 hours

1½ teaspoon salt
1½ teaspoons pepper
2 tablespoons chili powder
1 teaspoon crushed bay leaf
4 pounds fresh beef brisket, trimmed of excess fat

BARBECUE SAUCE:
1 cup catsup
⅛ teaspoon salt
1 cup water
½ cup cider vinegar
1 teaspoon sugar
1 teaspoon paprika
1 teaspoon chili powder
2 tablespoons chopped onion
3 stalks celery, chopped
4 tablespoons Worcestershire sauce
3 medium bay leaves
1 medium clove garlic, minced
Pinch of pepper

Mix first four ingredients. Place beef brisket, fat side up, in a Dutch oven. Sprinkle seasonings over top. Bake, covered, approximately 4 hours at 275°. Remove from oven and scrape off seasoning mixture. Cut into thin slices.

Before brisket is done, combine barbecue sauce ingredients in a large saucepan. Bring to a boil then simmer 15 minutes. Strain, pour over thinly sliced brisket. Serve brisket over or along side rye rolls, sourdough bread or pasta. Sauce is also wonderful for other types of grilled meats and chicken.

BULGOGI (MARINATED FLANK STEAK)

Yield: 6 servings
Assemble: 10 minutes
Marinate: 6 hours
Grill: 12 minutes

5 green onions, chopped
4 cloves garlic, minced
½ cup plus 2 tablespoons soy sauce
½ cup sugar
¼ cup sesame oil (dark)
¼ cup dry Sherry
1 teaspoon grated fresh ginger
½ teaspoon pepper
2 pounds flank steak

In a 9 x 13-inch dish suitable for marinating combine the first 8 ingredients for the marinade. Coat the steak thoroughly with the marinade. Cover and marinate for 6 hours or overnight in the refrigerator.

Grill steak over charcoals or broil for 6 minutes per side, turning once. Slice steak thinly against the grain.

PEPPER STEAK

QUICK
& EASY

Yield: 6-8 servings
Assemble: 30 minutes
Cook: 30 minutes

1½ pounds round steak or sirloin tip beef
⅛ teaspoon minced garlic
4 tablespoons butter or margarine
⅓ cup chopped onion
1½ green peppers, cut into strips
1 16-ounce can whole tomatoes
1 beef bouillon cube
1 tablespoon cornstarch
2 tablespoons soy sauce
1 teaspoon sugar
½ cup water
3-4 cups hot cooked white rice

Rub beef with garlic. Cut into 1-inch strips. In a large skillet melt butter and add beef. Saute', stirring occasionally, until beef is browned. Remove from heat. Add onion and green peppers to skillet and saute' 2 minutes. Return meat to skillet along with tomatoes and bouillon cube and simmer 10-15 minutes if using sirloin tip, or 20-25 minutes for round steak.

In a small bowl blend together the cornstarch, soy sauce, sugar and water. Add to meat mixture and cook, stirring constantly, until thickened. Reduce heat and cook 2 additional minutes. Serve over hot cooked rice.

POLPETTONE ALLA TOSCANA (ITALIAN MEATLOAF)

Yield: 6-8 servings
Assemble: 30 minutes
Bake: 1 hour

1 pound lean ground beef
1 slice white bread soaked in 1 tablespoon of milk
1 tablespoon finely chopped onion
½ teaspoon salt
1 teaspoon freshly ground pepper
¼ pound chopped Mortadella or Italian sausage
⅓ cup grated fresh Parmesan cheese
¼ teaspoon finely chopped garlic
1 egg yolk
Bread crumbs
1 tablespoon butter
2 tablespoons vegetable oil or olive oil
⅔ cup white wine
2 tablespoons tomato puree
5 large fresh mushrooms, thinly sliced

Mix together first 9 ingredients and form into a salami-shaped loaf. Preheat oven to 350°. Roll meat loaf in bread crumbs and saute' in butter and oil in a large skillet until browned on all sides. Transfer to baking dish and bake for 1 hour.

In the same skillet used to brown the meat, add wine and bring to a boil, scraping the bottom and sides of the dish. Add tomato puree and mushrooms. Cover skillet and simmer sauce for 30 minutes. Spoon sauce over loaf and allow to sit 10 minutes before serving. This also makes a delicious picnic sandwich; cold, sliced on French bread with mustard.

QUICK ITALIAN SAUTÉ

1 pound lean ground beef
½ cup chopped onion
¼ cup sliced fresh mushrooms
1 8-ounce can tomato sauce
2 tablespoons parsley flakes
½ teaspoon garlic powder
½ teaspoon dried basil leaves
½ teaspoon dried oregano leaves
⅛ teaspoon red pepper sauce
1 teaspoon seasoned salt
1 10-ounce package frozen chopped spinach, thawed
and well drained
1 cup low fat cottage cheese
1½ cups mozzarella cheese, grated

In a large skillet (with a lid) saute' beef, breaking it up as it cooks; drain off grease. Add onion and mushrooms and continue to cook until moisture is absorbed. Add tomato sauce, parsley flakes, garlic powder, basil leaves, oregano, red pepper sauce and seasoned salt. Cover and simmer for 5 minutes. Combine spinach and cottage cheese. Sprinkle ¾ cup mozzarella cheese over meat mixture. Spoon cottage cheese mixture evenly over meat. Spread remaining mozzarella cheese over top. Cover skillet and simmer 15 minutes. If too much moisture remains allow dish to cook uncovered for approximately 5 minutes longer.

SALSICCE CON PEPPERONI AND PASTA

8 links Italian sausage (available at Italian specialty stores)
½ cup water
2 tablespoons olive oil
2 large onions, sliced into rings
2 red bell peppers, sliced into strips
2 green bell peppers, sliced into strips
1 large clove garlic, minced
1 28-ounce can chopped Italian plum tomatoes
1 teaspoon dried oregano leaves
8 ounces pasta (linguine, fettuccine, etc.),cooked
and drained

Place sausage links in large skillet with the ½ cup water. Cover and cook over medium heat until lightly browned on all sides, approximately 20 minutes. In a separate skillet heat the olive oil. Add the onions, red peppers, green peppers and garlic. Cook and stir over medium heat until vegetables are slightly limp, approximately 5 minutes. Add the Italian tomatoes and oregano. Cook another 5 minutes. Remove from heat. When sausages are cooked, drain off excess grease and add links to the pepper mixture. Serve over the cooked pasta.

CALZONE WITH ITALIAN TOMATO SAUCE

Yield: 6 servings
Assemble: 2 hours
Bake: 30 minutes

ITALIAN TOMATO SAUCE:
4 tablespoons butter
2 medium onions, finely chopped
3 medium carrots, finely chopped
1 clove garlic, minced
12 ounces tomato paste
6-8 tomatoes (fresh or canned), cut into fourths, with some juice
¼ teaspoon oregano leaves
½ teaspoon basil leaves
1 tablespoon sugar
½ cup dry white wine

CALZONE:
1 pound loaf frozen white bread dough, thawed
3 tablespoons butter, softened
1 clove garlic, minced
8 slices Provolone cheese
8 slices hard salami
6 slices Mortadella (Italian bologna)
4 slices boiled or baked ham
2 green onions, sliced
Sesame seeds

At least two hours before serving, prepare Italian Tomato Sauce. Melt butter in a medium-size saucepan; saute' onion, carrot and garlic until onion is limp but not browned. Add tomato paste, tomatoes, oregano, basil, sugar and wine. Simmer uncovered, over low heat for two hours. Strain through sieve when ready to serve.

To prepare Calzone, grease a baking sheet. Roll dough out on lightly floured surface to 12 x 18-inch rectangle. Saute' garlic in butter for 2-3 minutes. Spread half of garlic butter mixture on top of dough. Arrange Provolone, salami, Mortadella and ham over dough; sprinkle with green onions. Fold top third of dough over middle, then fold bottom third up over top, as if folding business letter, enclosing filling. Transfer to baking sheet. Pinch ends to seal. Spread remaining garlic butter over top and sprinkle with sesame seeds. Bake for 30 minutes at 350° or until golden brown. Allow to cool 5 minutes. Slice and serve with Italian Tomato Sauce over slices.

FLANK STEAK MILANAISE

Yield: 4-6 servings
Assemble: 30 minutes
Cook: 2 hours

2 to 2½ pounds large flank steak, scored on one side
5 slices bacon
2 cups finely chopped fresh parsley
2-3 cloves garlic, minced
1 medium onion, minced
¼ cup grated Parmesan cheese
Salt and pepper to taste
½ teaspoon cinnamon
1 tablespoon dry basil leaves
1 clove garlic, minced
2 tablespoons vegetable oil
½ onion, sliced
1 teaspoon dry basil leaves
1 cup water
2 6-ounce cans tomato paste, or 2 8-ounce cans tomato sauce, or one of each
8 ounces spaghetti pasta
¼ cup grated Parmesan cheese

Score flank steak on one side. Fry bacon slightly, then cover steak lenthwise with bacon and spread with the following in the order given: finely chopped parsley, minced garlic, minced onion, ¼ cup grated Parmesan cheese, salt, pepper, cinnamon and basil. Roll steak and tie with string. In a large skillet, brown 1 clove garlic in oil. Add ½ sliced onion and 1 teaspoon basil. Brown meat on both sides. Add 1 cup water, cover tightly, and simmer for 30 minutes. Add tomato paste or sauce and continue to simmer 1 hour longer.

Cook spaghetti according to package directions. Drain and place back in pan; set aside. Remove steak from sauce and slice. Toss sauce and spaghetti together. Serve steak on a heated platter surrounded by spaghetti. Garnish with ¼ cup grated Parmesan cheese.

BEEF VEGETABLE STIR-FRY

QUICK
& EASY

Yield: 4 servings
Assemble: 30 minutes
Cook: 12-15 minutes

1 tablespoon cornstarch
1 teaspoon sugar
¼ teaspoon grated fresh ginger
2 tablespoons soy sauce
½ cup beef broth
1 pound boneless lean beef (flank or top round cut)
5 tablespoons vegetable oil, divided
1 clove garlic, minced
1 large onion, cut in half and then into ¼-inch slices
2 large carrots, peeled and cut into julienne slices
¼ pound fresh mushrooms, sliced ¼-inch thick
¾ pound snow peas, ends and strings removed
2-3 cups hot cooked rice

In a pint jar combine together the cornstarch, sugar, ginger, soy sauce and beef broth. Shake to blend and set aside. Cut beef with the grain into 1½-inch wide strips. Cut each strip across the grain in ⅛-inch thick slanting slices. Heat wok over high heat. When wok is hot, add 2 tablespoons of oil. Add the garlic and half of the beef. Stir-fry until the

continued

continued

meat is lightly browned (approximately 2 minutes); remove from wok and set aside. Repeat using an additional tablespoon of oil and the remaining meat. Heat the remaining 2 tablespoons of oil and add onion, carrots and mushrooms. Stir-fry for approximately 2 minutes. Add snow peas and stir-fry for 1 minute. Return meat to pan, add cornstarch mixture, and stir until sauce boils and thickens (approximately 1 minute). Serve over hot cooked rice.

Yield: 4-6 servings
Assemble: 40 minutes
Cook: 17 minutes

SUKIYAKI

¼ cup peanut oil
1 pound lean sirloin steak, cut into diagonal strips
    ¼-inch x 2 inches
1 clove garlic, minced
4 cups sliced fresh mushrooms
1 cup celery, sliced diagonally
1 cup julienne sliced carrots (matchstick size)
2 medium-size onions, sliced diagonally
1 8-ounce can drained bamboo shoots
2 8-ounce cans sliced water chestnuts, drained
1 chicken bouillon cube dissolved in ½ cup hot water
1 green pepper, sliced into thin strips
1 tablespoon brown sugar
½ cup soy sauce
3 cups fresh spinach leaves, cleaned and torn into
    large pieces
8 ounces vermicelli coils or mai fun rice sticks, prepared
    according to package directions

Pour oil into a wok. Preheat, uncovered, for 4 minutes until hot enough for a drop of water to sizzle. Place meat in hot oil and stir-fry for 2 minutes. Push meat up sides of wok. Add garlic and mushrooms and stir-fry for 2 minutes. Push garlic and mushrooms up sides of wok. Add celery and carrots and stir-fry for 2 minutes. Push vegetables up sides of wok. Add onions and stir-fry for 2 minutes. Push onions up sides of wok. Add bamboo shoots, water chestnuts and chicken broth. Stir once and cook for 2 minutes. Push shoots and chestnuts up sides of wok. Add green pepper, brown sugar and soy sauce. Stir once and cook for 30 seconds. Do not push up sides. Sprinkle spinach over top of all ingredients. Cover and simmer for 2 minutes. Reduce heat to warm for serving. Gently stir all ingredients together and serve immediately over hot vermicelli coils.

CANNELONI

Yield: 8 servings
Assemble: 3½ hours
Bake: 30 minutes

Note: Assembled
Canneloni can be
covered tightly with
plastic wrap and
refrigerated for up to
2 days.

PASTA:
1½ cups flour
1 egg
1 egg white
1 tablespoon olive oil
½ teaspoon salt
1 tablespoon water

FILLING:
2 tablespoons olive oil
¼ cup finely chopped onions
2 cloves garlic, minced
1 10-ounce package frozen spinach, thawed and squeezed dry
1 pound lean ground beef
¼ cup grated Parmesan cheese
2 tablespoons heavy cream
2 eggs, slightly beaten
¾ teaspoon crumbled oregano leaves
1 teaspoon salt
¼ teaspoon coarsely ground pepper

BÉCHAMEL SAUCE:
4 tablespoons butter
4 tablespoons flour
1 cup milk
1 cup heavy cream
½ teaspon salt
⅛ teaspoon white pepper

TOMATO SAUCE:
¼ cup olive oil
1 large onion, finely chopped
1 32-ounce can whole tomatoes, chopped but not drained
1 6-ounce can tomato paste
1 teaspoon dried sweet basil
¼ cup finely chopped fresh parsley
1 teaspoon sugar
½ teaspoon salt
¼ teaspoon coarsely ground pepper

TOPPING:
¼ cup Parmesan cheese
3 tablespoons butter

Mix pasta ingredients in the bowl of a food processor fitted with a metal blade. Process until dough forms a ball. Cover and let rest 30 minutes. On a floured board roll pasta into a thin 12 x 16-inch rectangle. Cut in 32 rectangles, each measuring 2 x 3-inches. (Dough may be rolled in a pasta machine as long as rectangle size and count remains the same.) In a stockpot bring 6 quarts of water to a boil. Add pasta, stir gently and

continued

continued

cook for 6-7 minutes. Drain, cool slightly and lay on paper towels to dry.

To prepare filling, saute' onion in oil in a large skillet until translucent. Add spinach and cook until moisture has evaporated. Transfer to a large mixing bowl and set aside. Brown ground beef in the same skillet, drain any grease and add to spinach mixture. Add Parmesan, cream, eggs, oregano, salt and pepper; set aside.

Make a roux of the butter and flour in a medium-size saucepan; do not brown. Add milk and cream all at once, whisk briskly until thickened. Season with salt and white pepper, remove from heat and set aside.

In a large saucepan make Tomato Sauce. Saute' onion in olive oil until tanslucent. Add the remaining 7 ingredients and simmer for 45 minutes; stir occasionally. Before assembling Canneloni, whirl sauce in a blender or strain through a sieve. Preheat oven to 375°.

To assemble Canneloni, place a heaping tablespoonful of filling on to each pasta rectangle and roll up. Pour 1 cup of Tomato Sauce on the bottom of a large baking dish. Lay the Canneloni side-by-side in one layer over the sauce. Pour Be'chamel Sauce over Canneloni and spoon the remaining Tomato Sauce over all. Sprinkle with Parmesan and dot with butter. Bake uncovered for 25-30 minutes or until cheese melts and sauce bubbles. Place under broiler for 30 seconds to brown on top.

FETTUCCINE VEGETARIAN

QUICK & EASY

Yield: 6 servings
Assemble: 30 minutes
Cook: 15 minutes

1 pound fettuccine pasta, fresh or dried
3 tablespoons butter
2-3 cloves garlic, minced
½ pound fresh mushrooms, sliced
2-3 fresh firm zucchini, sliced julienne (total weight about 1½ pounds)
1 tablespoon sliced pimiento, drained
½ cup butter, cut into small cubes
1 cup heavy cream
¾ cup grated fresh Parmesan cheese
¼-½ cup finely chopped fresh parsley
Freshly grated nutmeg to taste
Freshly ground black pepper to taste

Prepare pasta to al dente'. While pasta is cooking melt 3 tablespoons of butter in a large skillet; add garlic. Add mushrooms and saute' over a medium-high heat for 2 minutes. Add zucchini, pimiento, butter and heavy cream. Bring mixture to a simmer and let cook 3 full minutes.

Drain the pasta well, then add to the vegetables and sauce along with Parmesan, parsley, nutmeg and pepper. Toss pasta well over a medium heat. Pour the entire mixture onto a heated serving platter and garnish with more chopped fresh parsley and Parmesan cheese, if desired.

NEAPOLITAN PASTA EN CASSEROLE

Yield: 8-10 servings
Assemble: 45 minutes
Cook: 30 minutes

1½ pounds lean ground beef
1 cup finely chopped onions
1 cup chopped green peppers
2 cloves garlic, crushed
2 teaspoons dried basil leaves
1 teaspoon fennel seed
⅛ teaspoon crushed red pepper
2 tablespoons sugar
1½ teaspoons salt
2 16-ounce cans tomatoes (preferably Italian plum), undrained
1 pound fresh spinach, cleaned and stems removed
1 pound rigatoni pasta
1 cup grated sharp Cheddar cheese

In a large 5-quart saucepan saute' beef, onions, green peppers, garlic, basil, fennel seed and red pepper over medium heat until meat is browned and vegetables are tender (approximately 20 minutes). Add sugar, salt and tomatoes, mashing the tomatoes as added. Bring mixture to a boil. Reduce heat and simmer, uncovered, stirring occasionally until most of the liquid is absorbed (approximately 20 minutes).

Cook spinach in a large kettle, covered, 4-6 minutes or until spinach is just wilted. Drain well and set aside. (This step may be done in a microwave.) Cook pasta until al dente' and drain well. Add spinach and pasta to beef mixture and toss until well mixed. Place into a 3-quart casserole and sprinkle with cheese. Bake, uncovered, for 30 minutes at 350°, or until casserole is bubbly and lightly browned.

PAVÉ NORMAND ("THE STONE OF NORMANDY")

Yield: 8 servings
Assemble: 30 minutes
Bake: 30 minutes

2 sheets Pepperidge Farm Puff Pastry
8 ounces sour cream, or crème fraîche, divided
1 pound Swiss cheese, grated and divided
¼ pound boiled ham, thinly sliced
Salt and pepper to taste
1 egg yolk
1 drop water

Place 1 sheet of pastry on baking sheet. Spread half of sour cream over pastry; salt and pepper to taste. Sprinkle half of grated cheese over sour cream; salt and pepper to taste. Place ham over cheese leaving approximatley ½-inch around all edges. Place remaining cheese over ham. Dollop the remaining sour cream over the ham. Sour cream does not need to be spread. Place remaining pastry on top, pressing firmly and smoothing to spread layer of sour cream beneath. Use a small amount of the sour cream to adhere pastry edges together on all sides. Press firmly to seal. Preheat oven to 375°. Add 1 drop of water to egg yolk to thin and mix well. Salt and pepper to taste. Brush egg yolk over top of pastry. Use a knife tip to score pastry top for decoration and to let steam escape. Bake for approximately 30 minutes (check after 20 minutes).

MARINATED PORK CHOPS WITH DIJON

Yield: 6-8 servings
Assemble: 20 minutes
Marinate: 1 hours
Cook: 20 minutes

1½ cups white wine
½ teaspoon salt
¼ teaspoon pepper
½ teaspoon Bouquet Garni (basil, thyme, oregano)
8 loin pork chops, cut 1 to 1½-inches thick
¼ cup flour
3 tablespoons butter
¼ cup shallots
½ lemon
1 teaspoon Dijon mustard
¼ cup heavy cream

In a dish suitable for marinating combine the wine, salt, pepper and Bouquet Garni; add pork chops. Marinate ½ hour per side. Reserve marinade. Remove chops from marinade and dust each chop with flour. Clarify 3 tablespoons butter in a large skillet. Saute' chops on one side until lightly browned. Turn chops and add ¼ cup chopped shallots. Saute' 5-7 minutes longer. Pour marinade over chops. Squeeze juice of ½ lemon over chops. Simmer chops 5 minutes, turn, and simmer 5 minutes longer. Transfer chops to serving platter and keep warm. Add Dijon mustard to skillet and deglaze pan by boiling until liquid is reduced by half. Add cream, stirring until mixture is thickened. Pour sauce over chops.

SPICY STIR-FRY PORK WITH TOFU

QUICK
& EASY

Yield: 4 servings
Assemble: 20 minutes
cook: 20 minutes

1 pound tofu (fresh bean curd)
¾-1 pound ground unseasoned pork, or ½-inch pork cubes
1 heaping teaspoon grated fresh gingerroot
1 clove garlic, minced
½ cup chicken broth
1 tablespoon cornstarch
2-3 tablespoons soy sauce
1 tablespoon rice-wine vinegar or cider vinegar
¼-½ teaspoon ground cayenne pepper (adjust to taste)
1 tablespoon vegetable oil
1 onion, sliced
1 green pepper, sliced
2-3 cups hot cooked rice

Cut bean curd into ½-inch cubes. Drain well on several layers of paper towels. In a small bowl combine the pork, ginger and garlic. In a small jar with a lid shake together broth, cornstarch, soy sauce, vinegar and cayenne pepper; set aside. Heat wok or large skillet over medium heat. Add pork mixture. Cook, stirring to separate pork, about 3 minutes or until lightly browned; remove from skillet. Heat oil in same pan. Add onion and green pepper. Stir-fry for 4 minutes. Add pork and soy sauce mixture. Cook and stir until mixture boils and thickens. Gently fold in bean curd and heat thoroughly. Serve over rice.

GRETCHEN'S SUPER STUFFED SHELLS

Yield: 8-10 servings
Assemble: 1 hour
Bake: 50 minutes

1 pound Jumbo shell pasta, or any large shell-shaped pasta
1 pound extra-lean ground beef
1 pound mild sweet Italian sausage
½ cup finely chopped onions
½ teaspoon fennel seed
1-2 cloves garlic, minced
2 28-ounce cans Italian-style plum tomatoes, with juice
12 ounces tomato paste
½ teaspoon basil leaves
½ teaspoon oregano leaves
2 tablespoons dried parsley
2 tablespoons sugar
2 pounds fresh whole-milk ricotta cheese
2 eggs
1 tablespoon sugar
2 tablespoons dried parsley
2 pounds grated whole milk mozzarella cheese, divided
1 cup grated Parmesan cheese, divided

Cook pasta shells in 8 quarts of water according to package directions Drain and place in cold water.

In a large saucepan combine the beef, sausage (remove and discard casings), onions, fennel and garlic. Brown meat over medium-high heat. Drain off excess grease. Add tomatoes, breaking them up slightly. Add tomato paste, basil, oregano, dried parsley and 2 tablespoons sugar. Let mixture simmer over a low heat for 30 minutes, stirring occasionally.

Meanwhile, combine ricotta cheese, eggs, 1 tablespoon sugar and parsley in a large mixing bowl and beat until smooth. Add 1½ pounds mozzarella cheese and ½ cup grated Parmesan cheese and mix thoroughly. Set filling mixture aside. Preheat oven to 350°.

Spread a small amount of sauce over bottom of an 11 x 14-inch shallow baking dish. Fill the pasta shells generously with the filling mixture, place in pan and layer sauce over, reserving approximately 1½ cups of the sauce to add later.

Bake shells for 30-40 minutes. Remove from the oven and top with reserved sauce and remaining cheeses. Return to the oven and continue baking approximately 5-10 minutes until cheese topping has melted.

FETTUCCINE WITH PEAS AND HAM

QUICK
& EASY

Yield: 8 servings
Assemble: 20 minutes
Cook: 10 minutes

5 tablespoons unsalted butter
6 shallots, minced
½ pound fresh mushrooms, sliced
1¼ cups heavy cream
1 10-ounce package frozen tiny peas, thawed
4 ounces boiled ham, sliced into julienne slices
1 cup grated fresh Parmesan cheese
1 pound fettuccine, fresh or dried
Salt and freshly ground pepper to taste

continued

continued

Prepare fettuccine to al dente'; drain and set aside. Heat butter in a large heavy non-aluminum skillet. Add shallots and saute' until soft. Add mushrooms and increase heat to high. Cook until mushrooms are very lightly browned. Add cream and boil for 2 minutes. Stir in peas and cook approximately 30 seconds. Reduce heat to low and blend in ham, cheese and fettuccine. Toss mixture until heated through and combined well. Sauce should cling to pasta. Season with salt and pepper to taste.

SWEET AND SOUR BARBECUED SPARERIBS

QUICK & EASY

Yield: 4 servings
Assemble: 20 minutes
Grill: 30 minutes

Note: Sweet and Sour Sauce is also terrific on grilled chicken or fish.

4 pounds baby-back pork ribs
1 carrot, diced
1 sprig fresh parsley
1 sprig fresh basil
1 onion, diced
2 stalks celery, diced
1 bay leaf
1 sprig fresh thyme
½ teaspoon salt

SWEET AND SOUR SAUCE:
1 tablespoon vegetable oil
1 clove garlic, minced
¼ cup minced carrots
½ cup minced onions
¼ cup minced green peppers
2 tablespoons cornstarch
1 6-ounce can pineapple juice
1 8-ounce can sliced pineapple, drained and juice reserved
1 6-ounce can apricot nectar
¾ cup brown sugar, firmly packed
3 teaspoons soy sauce
¾ cup wine vinegar
½ teaspoon salt

Cut ribs into portions containing 3-4 ribs each. Place ribs in a large stockpot and cover with cold water. Add vegetables, herbs and salt. Bring to a boil and simmer for 15 minutes.

To prepare sauce, heat oil and minced garlic over medium-high heat. Add carrots and onions and saute' until cooked but still crisp. Add green peppers. In a small jar with lid mix cornstarch with pineapple juice and reserved juice from sliced pineapple; shake to blend and add to vegetable mixture. Add apricot nectar, brown sugar, soy sauce, vinegar and salt to vegetables. Cook, stirring constantly, until thick,(about 5 minutes). Dice 2 slices of pineapple and add to the sauce. (Reserve remaining pineapple.) Sauce may be prepared in advance.

Drain and pat the ribs dry. Place on a grill and cook over medium heat, turning frequently, until done (approximately 20-30 minutes). During the last 15 minutes of cooking, baste ribs often with Sweet and Sour Sauce. Garnish with pineapple slices and serve with individual servings of sauce.

ROAST PORK WITH CRABAPPLE JELLY SAUCE

Yield: 6-8 servings
Assemble: 10 minutes
Roast: 2-2½ hours

3-4 pounds boneless pork loin roast
2 cloves garlic, minced
1 tablespoon chili powder
½ cup crabapple jelly or plum jelly
½ cup catsup
1 tablespoon vinegar
½ teaspoon chili powder

Preheat oven to 325°. Place the pork roast in a roasting pan. Rub with the minced garlic and 1 tablespoon chili powder. Roast in oven or grill over medium-hot coals, baste often with sauce, for 2-2½ hours or until thermometer registers 180°.

For the sauce, place crabapple jelly, catsup, vinegar and chili powder in a small saucepan. Bring to a boil over medium heat, then simmer for 2 minutes. Slice and serve the roast with any remaining sauce, or double sauce recipe to have extra to pass at the table.

LAMB SHISH KABOB

Yield: 6 servings (2 shish kabobs per serving)
Assemble: 30 minutes
Marinate: 3 hours
Grill: 8 minutes

1 large clove garlic, minced
2 teaspoons salt
½ cup dry sherry
½ cup orange juice
1 teaspoon white vinegar
1 teaspoon dried basil leaves
½ teaspoon crumbled rosemary
1 tablespoon chopped fresh parsley
2 tablespoons Worcestershire sauce
2 tablespoons brown sugar
1 pound boneless lamb, cut into 1-inch cubes
12 bamboo skewers, 10 inches long
12 small whole peeled onions
12 1-inch pieces green pepper
12 cherry tomatoes
12 1-inch slices zucchini
12 large mushrooms

In a dish suitable for marinating combine the first 10 ingredients for the marinade; stir well. Add lamb cubes and marinate in the refrigerator for 2-3 hours. Place lamb on skewers alternately with the onions, peppers, tomatoes, zucchini and mushrooms, allowing one of each vegetable per skewer. Grill over medium coals; turn and baste with marinade every 2 minutes. Cook for about 8 minutes total.

LEMON GRILLED PORK CHOPS

Yield: 4 servings
Assemble: 10 minutes
Marinate: 8 hours
Grill: 30-40 minutes

¼ cup lemon juice
2 tablespoons vegetable oil
2 tablespoons water
2 tablespoons chopped fresh parsley
2 teaspoons chopped fresh chives
1 teaspoon salt
1 teaspoon crushed dried tarragon
1 teaspoon grated lemon peel
½ teaspoon crushed savory
4 pork loin chops, 1 to 1¼ inches thick

In a medium-size saucepan combine lemon juice, oil, water, parsley, chives, salt, tarragon, lemon peel and savory. Simmer 3-4 minutes; cool. Pour marinade over chops and marinate in refrigerator for 6-8 hours, or overnight, turning occasionally. Grill chops over medium coals for approximately 15-20 minutes per side.

DIJON LEG OF LAMB

Yield: 6-8 servings
Assemble: 20 minutes
Marinate: 8 hours
Roast: 35-50 minutes

6-7 pound leg of lamb, boned, trimmed and butterflied
1 large clove garlic, minced
¾ cup vegetable oil
¼ cup red wine vinegar
⅓ cup lemon juice
½ cup chopped onion
2 teaspoons Dijon mustard
2 teaspoons salt
½ teaspoon dried oregano leaves
½ teaspoon basil or thyme
3 drops Tabasco sauce
1 crushed bay leaf
Freshly ground pepper

Have butcher "butterfly" leg of lamb. Make a series of small slits in the meat so that it will lay flat. Place meat fat-side down in a pan suitable for marinating. In a small bowl blend remaining ingredients for the marinade. Pour marinade over the lamb, cover tightly and refrigerate 8 hours or overnight, turning occasionally. Remove from the refrigerator 1 hour prior to cooking.

Preheat broiler. Place lamb, with marinade, in broiler pan, fat-side up. Broil 4-inches from the heat source for 10 minutes. Turn lamb, baste and broil 10 minutes longer. Reduce oven temperature to 425° and roast meat for 15-30 minutes, depending on how well-done meat is desired. (It is recommended to use a meat thermometer at this point.) Remove lamb from marinade and transfer to a warm platter. Carve meat into thin slices. Smother with pan juices.

LAMB BANDIT-STYLE

Yield: 4 servings
Assemble: 30 minutes
Marinate: 60 minutes
Bake: 60 minutes

2 pounds lean lamb, cut into 1½-inch cubes
¼ cup olive oil
1 large clove garlic, minced
Juice of 1 lemon
1 large onion, sliced ¼-inch thick
½ cup dry sherry
1 teaspoon dried oregano leaves
Salt and pepper to taste
4 tomatoes slices, cut ¼ to ½-inch thick
1 cup crumbled feta cheese
Oregano to taste
4 tablespoons butter
2-3 cups hot cooked rice or 4 pita bread pockets
4 sheets (12 x 12-inch) heavy-duty aluminum foil

In a medium-size bowl mix lamb with olive oil, garlic, lemon juice, onion, sherry, oregano, salt and pepper. Marinate for 1 hour.

Brush 4 sheets of aluminum foil with olive oil and arrange portions of the meat mixture in the center of each sheet. Place 1 tomato slice on each portion of meat, crumble feta cheese over tomato slices, season with a sprinkling of oregano and place 1 tablespoon of butter on top. Fold the foil to enclose meat mixture and crimp edges tightly. Bake for 60 minutes at 375° on a flat baking sheet. (May also be grilled over medium-hot coals for 1 hour.) Serve with rice by spooning rice on individual plates, making a well in the center. Open the foil packet and slide the lamb into the well, keeping tomato slice and cheese on top. (May also be slightly drained and served in pita bread.) This is a great outdoor feast. Meat can marinate in the cooler and be grilled over a campfire.

CARBONADE OF LAMB WITH ORANGE MUSTARD

QUICK
& EASY

Yield: 6-8 servings
Assemble: 15 minutes
Grill: 40 minutes

5-6 pound leg of lamb, boned, trimmed and butterflied
4 tablespoons olive oil
1 teaspoon crumbled rosemary
Salt and pepper to taste
Juice and zest from 1 large orange
½ cup butter
3 tablespoons Dijon mustard

Have butcher "butterfly" leg of lamb. Rub both sides of lamb with olive oil and sprinkle on the rosemary, salt and pepper. Place lamb meat-side up in a 9 x 11-inch roasting pan. Broil 6-inches from the heat source for 20 minutes. Turn lamb and broil for another 15 minutes. While lamb is cooking, prepare sauce by heating the orange juice, zest and butter. Simmer mixture for 2 minutes. Remove from heat and whisk the mustard into the sauce. Spread mixture over lamb just before serving.

VEAL MARSALA

Yield: 8 servings
Assemble: 20 minutes
Cook: 15 minutes

2 pounds thin veal scallops or cutlets
⅔ cup flour
⅔ cup butter (no substitutes)
Salt and pepper to taste
½ cup dry Marsala wine
½ pound fresh mushrooms, sliced
3 tablespoons butter
2 tablespoons chopped fresh parsley

Pound veal until very thin, being careful not to tear meat. Dip into flour and saute' in butter 2-3 minutes on each side in a large, heavy skillet. (Do not overcook.) Sprinkle with salt and pepper. Remove veal cutlets to serving dish; keep warm.

Add Marsala to deglaze pan and simmer until thickened, about 2-3 minutes. In a separate skillet saute' mushrooms in butter for 2 minutes; pour over veal. Top with parsley and serve.

WIENERSCHNITZEL (VIENNESE CUTLETS)

Yield: 6 servings
Assemble: 15 minutes
Cook: 15 minutes

12 veal cutlets or pork cutlets (approximately
** 4 ounces each)**
Salt
1 cup flour
2 cups fresh bread crumbs
2 eggs
1 tablespoon milk
1 cup vegetable oil (for frying)
12 lemon wedges
Fresh parsley sprigs for garnish

Pound cutlets until thin and salt to taste. Place flour on a plate. Place bread crumbs on another plate. In a small, shallow bowl beat the eggs and milk. Dredge cutlets in the flour, shaking off excess. Dip floured cutlets into egg mixture, then into bread crumbs, patting well, shaking off excess.

In a large skillet heat ½-inch of oil over medium heat until a bit of bread crumbs placed in the oil bubbles. Cook a few cutlets at a time (about 2-3 minutes per side), until golden brown. Drain on paper towels. Keep cutlets warm while continuing to cook remaining meat. Serve two cutlets per person garnished with lemon wedges and sprigs of parsley.

SWEET AND PUNGENT GLAZE

Yield: 1 cup
Assemble: 10 minutes
Cook: 5 minutes

3 tablespoons brown sugar
¼ cup catsup
3 tablespoons wine vinegar
3 tablespoons olive oil
2 teaspoons soy sauce
1 clove garlic, crushed
3 tablespoons port wine
Salt and pepper to taste

Heat all ingredients thoroughly in a small saucepan. Glaze pork chops, spareribs or any grilled meat or chicken.

VENISON ROAST WITH ORANGE SAUCE

Yield: 8-10 servings
Assemble: 30 minutes
Roast: 1 hour

1 5-pound venison roast (tender cut preferred)
4 cloves garlic, slivered
Zest from 2 large oranges
1 pound sliced bacon
1 teaspoon anise seed

ORANGE SAUCE:
1¼ cups orange juice
½ cup brown sugar
Zest of 1 large orange
½ teaspoon anise seed
⅛ teaspoon thyme
⅛ teaspoon crushed bay leaf
¼ teaspoon salt
⅛ teaspoon pepper
1 tablespoon cornstarch
¼ cup water

14-16 small boiled new potatoes, unpared
Orange segments for garnish

Place roast in a large roasting pan. Preheat oven to 375°. Make small slits in roast approximately 1-inch apart. Insert garlic slivers into roast. Sprinkle with orange zest, salt, pepper and anise seed. Wrap bacon around roast and bake for approximately 1 hour, or until meat juices are clear.

For orange sauce, in a saucepan combine orange juice, brown sugar, zest of 1 large orange, anise seed, thyme, bay leaf, salt and pepper and bring to a boil. Continue to cook approximately 5 minutes. Add cornstarch and water mixture, cooking approximately 5 minutes or until sauce has thickened slightly.

Remove roast from oven and drain off juices. Add juices to sauce. Slice roast and serve on a platter with potatoes arranged around the edge. Top with orange sauce and garnish with orange segments.

MEXICAN CHEESE TORTE

QUICK
& EASY

Yield: 2 servings
Assemble: 20 minutes
Bake: 10 minutes

½ cup refried beans
3 flour tortillas, lightly crisped
2 tablespoons minced green pepper
2 tablespoons minced onion
4 ounces Monterey Jack cheese, grated
4 ounces Cheddar cheese, grated
½ cup mild green chili salsa
¼ cup shredded lettuce
2 tablespoons chopped tomato
2 tablespoons chopped ripe avocados
¼ cup sour cream

continued

continued

Preheat oven to 350°. Spread beans on one tortilla and place on oven-proof plate. Cover with second tortilla. Distribute green pepper, onion and Monterey Jack cheese evenly over the top. Cover with remaining tortilla and sprinkle with Cheddar cheese (can be frozen at this point). Bake in oven until cheese melts and starts to turn brown. Pour salsa evenly over and cover with lettuce, tomato and avocados. Top with a dollop of sour cream and serve immediately.

LASAGNA SWIRLS

Yield: 6 servings
Assemble: 45 minutes
Bake: 30 minutes

LASAGNA SWIRLS:
8 ounces lasagna pasta, spinach or regular (not extra-wide)
2 10-ounce packages frozen chopped spinach, thawed and well-drained
1 pound ricotta cheese
1 cup grated Parmesan cheese, divided
8 ounces cream cheese, softened
8 ounces mozzarella cheese, grated
½ teaspoon dried basil leaves
¼ teaspoon dried oregano leaves
Salt and pepper to taste

LIGHT TOMATO SAUCE:
1 large onion, chopped
2 cloves garlic, minced
3 tablespoons butter
2 1-pound 12-ounce cans crushed tomatoes in tomato puree
16 ounces tomato sauce
2 tablespoons sugar
2 tablespoons olive oil
2 teaspoons sweet basil leaves
1 teaspoon Italian herb seasoning
Pinch of red pepper flakes
Salt and pepper to taste
½ cup grated Parmesan cheese for topping

Prepare lasagna pasta according to package directions; set aside. Beat together the next 8 ingredients until blended; set aside.

To prepare sauce, saute' onion and garlic in butter in a large skillet. Combine next 8 ingredients and simmer 10 minutes. Lay out each lasagna noodle and spoon approximately ½ cup filling on the top of the noodle. Roll up jelly-roll fashion. Place rolls into an 11 x 14-inch pan, coiled side up. Preheat oven to 350°. Pour lighty sauce over the rolls and sprinkle top with Parmesan cheese. Bake, loosely covered, for approximately 30-40 minutes or until heated through and mozzarella in filling is melted.

DESSERTS & PIES

 The soul of the classic art lover triumphs in Salt Lake City. Whether thrilling to the piccolo trill of the world-class Utah Symphony, soaring with a pas de deux from Ballet West, sighing with the arias of the Utah Opera Company, or empathizing with one of live theatre's enticing characters, the aesthetic spirit thrives. An elegant evening celebrating the arts is highlighted by a late-night excursion through the historic streets of Salt Lake in a horse-drawn carriage. Savoring the evening over a sumptuous champagne and dessert buffet of Raspberry Walnut Torte, Stuffed Strawberries, Chocolate-on-Chocolate Mousse Cake, Raisin Cream Pie, Cashew Butter Toffee, Chilled Amaretto Mousse and assorted exotic coffees is the artistic finale.

FRUIT PIZZA

Yield: 2 fruit pizzas
Assemble: 1 hour
Bake: 12-15 minutes

SUGAR COOKIE CRUST:
1 cup butter, softened
1 cup powdered sugar
⅓ cup sugar
1 egg
2½ cups flour
2½ teaspoons baking soda
2½ teaspoons cream of tartar
½ teaspoon vanilla extract
¼ teaspoon almond extract

FILLING:
16 ounces cream cheese, softened
1 cup powdered sugar
1 teaspoon vanilla extract
Fresh fruits of choice: peaches, strawberries, kiwi, bananas, grapes, apples, mandarin oranges or any berry

ORANGE SAUCE:
½ cup sugar
1 cup orange juice
¼ cup lemon juice
¼ teaspoon grated orange peel
¼ teaspoon grated lemon peel
4 teaspoons cornstarch

Preheat oven to 325°. Prepare crust by creaming butter and sugars until light and fluffy in a large bowl. Add egg, vanilla and almond extracts, beating well. Combine dry ingredients and add to the creamed mixture, blending thoroughly. Divide dough in half. With lightly floured hands pat dough onto two lightly greased pizza-type pans. Bake for 12-15 minutes; cool.

To prepare filling, whip cream cheese, powdered sugar and vanilla. Spread mixture over cooled crust. Decorate with slices of fruit, completely covering the crust.

Combine orange sauce ingredients in a small saucepan. Cook over medium heat until the mixture is thick. Stir in the orange and lemon peel; cool. Glaze fruit pizzas with sauce.

POACHED PEARS

Yield: 6 servings
Assemble: 15 minutes
Bake: 30 minutes
Chill: 2 hours

Note: A refreshing make-ahead dessert.

6 fresh pears
18 whole cloves
½ cup sugar
1 cup heavy red wine
1 cup heavy cream, slightly whipped

Peel pears and insert 3 whole cloves at either end. Place in a Dutch oven with enough water to cover pears; add sugar. Cover and bake for 30 minutes at 350° until pears are tender. Remove pears with a slotted spoon (reserve juice) and rinse under cold water until pears are cool. Place pears in a covered container, add reserved juice and wine. Refrigerate until ready to serve, up to 2 days. Remove pears from liquid and serve with cream on top on dessert plates.

CHILLED AMARETTO MOUSSE

Yield: 6-8 servings
Assemble: 45 minutes
Chill: 6 hours

1 large orange
5 large egg yolks
½ cup sugar
2 envelopes unflavored gelatin
¼ cup cold water
½ cup Amaretto liqueur
5 large egg whites
1 cup heavy cream
1 orange, thinly sliced
Fresh mint leaves

Grate rind and extract juice from orange; set juice aside. Place the grated orange rind and egg yolks into large bowl. Beat at high speed until yolks are thickened slightly (approximately 1 minute). Gradually add the sugar. Beat until mixture forms a ribbon when beaters are lifted (approximately 3-5 minutes).

While egg yolks are beating, soften gelatin in the cold water in a small saucepan. Heat over low heat and stir until gelatin becomes clear. Remove from heat to cool to room temperature. Add cooled gelatin and Amaretto to egg yolks. Beat at medium speed for 1 minute.

Beat egg whites until stiff. Fold the whites, along with the reserved orange juice, into egg yolk mixture. Whip cream until stiff; fold into mousse. Pour the mousse into a greased 2-quart souffle' dish or into a decorative deep-sided bowl. Chill at least 6 hours. Garnish with thin orange slices and mint leaves.

FRENCH MOCHA POTS DE CREME

QUICK
& EASY

Yield: 6-8 servings
Assemble: 10 minutes
Chill: 10 minutes

1½ envelopes unflavored gelatin
¼ cup cold water
1 6-ounce package semi-sweet chocolate chips
½ cup hot milk
2 teaspoons instant coffee
1 tablespoon sugar
Pinch of salt
½ teaspoon vanilla extract
2 egg yolks
1¼ cups finely crushed ice, drained
1 cup heavy cream
1 chocolate bar, shaved for garnish

In a small dish soften gelatin in cold water. Place chocolate chips in blender and pour hot milk over; blend for 20 seconds. Add gelatin and coffee. Blend on high speed for 40 seconds. Add sugar, salt and vanilla; blend for 10 seconds. Keep motor running, remove cover and add egg yolks, ice and cream. Blend 20 seconds or until mixture begins to thicken. Pour into 6-8 ramekins or small sherbets. Chill approximately 10 minutes (for consistency of soft ice cream) or until ready to serve. Garnish with chocolate shavings.

SNOW PUDDING WITH CUSTARD SAUCE

Yield: 6 servings
Assemble: 45 minutes
Chill: 3 hours

PUDDING:
1½ tablespoons unflavored gelatin
¼ cup cold water
1 cup boiling water
¾ cup sugar
¼ teaspoon salt
¼ cup fresh lemon juice
3 egg whites, room temperature

CUSTARD SAUCE:
1½ cups milk
3 egg yolks
¼ cup sugar
⅛ teaspoon salt
1 teaspoon vanilla extract
½ teaspoon nutmeg
Fresh strawberries or raspberries for garnish (optional)

In a medium-size bowl sprinkle gelatin over cold water and allow to soften for 5 minutes. Add sugar, boiling water and salt to gelatin; stir until dissolved. Add lemon juice and grated lemon rind. Chill until thick and syrupy but do not let mixture begin to gel.

In a large bowl beat egg whites until stiff peaks form. Beat gelatin mixture until **very** foamy. Very carefully fold the beaten egg whites into the gelatin mixture. Turn mixture into 4-cup mold and refrigerate 2-3 hours or until set.

To make custard sauce, heat milk in a double boiler until bubbles appear around the edge of the pan. Beat egg yolks and sugar together. Very slowly pour the hot milk into the egg mixture, beating constantly. Place the mixture in double boiler again. Cook until the sauce thickens (it should form a thin coating of sauce on a metal spoon). Remove from heat, slightly cool, then add vanilla, salt and nutmeg; chill.

To serve, unmold pudding on a serving platter, garnish with fresh berries and spoon sauce over top. (Note: do not double this recipe).

PEACH MELBA

QUICK
& EASY

Yield: 6 servings
Assemble: 15 minutes
Chill: 30 minutes

Note: Best when fresh peaches are used. Serve with Angel Puffs (page 238) or Giant Sugar Cookies (page 237).

1 10-ounce package frozen red raspberries, thawed
⅔ cup sugar
⅛ teaspoon cream of tartar
Vanilla ice cream
Fresh peaches, peeled and halved

Press thawed raspberries through a sieve into a small saucepan. Add sugar and cream of tartar and boil for 3 minutes, stirring constantly. Cover and chill thoroughly. (Can freeze at this point.)

Serve over a scoop of vanilla ice cream topped with a fresh peach half. Garnish with a mint leaf.

PEPPERMINT SURPRISE

Yield: 10-12 servings
Assemble: 30 minutes
Freeze: 2 hours

Note: What a way to complete a Mexican dinner!

CRUST:
2 cups crushed vanilla wafers
5 tablespoons butter, softened

FIRST LAYER:
1 quart peppermint ice cream, softened slightly

SECOND LAYER:
2 1-ounce squares unsweetened chocolate
½ cup butter or margarine
3 egg yolks, beaten
1½ cups powdered sugar
1 tablespoon vanilla extract
½ cup chopped pecans
3 egg whites

Combine wafer crumbs and butter in a medium-size mixing bowl; reserve ¼ cup for topping. Press into the bottom of a 9 x 13-inch pan. Spread ice cream over and freeze.

In a medium-size saucepan melt chocolate and butter over low heat. Remove from heat and gradually add beaten egg yolks, stirring continuously. Add the powdered sugar, vanilla and nuts. Mix together and cool thoroughly. Beat egg whites until stiff and fold into cooled chocolate mixture. Spread over ice cream layer, sprinkle with reserved crumbs and freeze. Allow to soften slightly before cutting into squares and serving.

DOLCE (CHOCOLATE MOUSSE)

Yield: 12 servings
Assemble: 35 minutes
Chill: 8 hours

8 ounces semi-sweet chocolate
⅓ cup rum
3 eggs, separated
¼ cup sugar
½ cup butter, softened
¾ cup heavy cream
½ cup almonds, coarsely chopped
Whipped cream for garnish
Chopped almonds for garnish

Lightly oil a 1½-quart loaf pan and invert over paper towels to drain. Melt chocolate in a double boiler, stir in rum and cool to room temperature. Beat egg yolks and sugar until light (approximately 4-5 minutes). Add butter, a tablespoon at a time, beating until fluffy. Add to chocolate mixture; set aside.

In a large bowl beat egg whites until stiff. Beat cream to soft-peak stage in a separate bowl. Fold whites into chocolate mixture and then fold in cream; add almonds. Pour into loaf pan, spreading evenly, and chill over night until firm.

Run a knife around sides of pan and then dip pan into hot water a few seconds to unmold mousse. Garnish with whipped cream and almonds.

RHUBARB CRISP

Yield: 6-8 servings
Assemble: 10 minutes
Bake: 40 minutes

¾ cup sugar
1 egg, well beaten
2 tablespoons flour
3 cups fresh rhubarb, cut into ½-inch pieces
¼ cup butter, softened
⅓ cup firmly packed brown sugar
⅔ cup flour
1 cup heavy cream
2 teaspoons powdered sugar
½ teaspoon vanilla extract

Mix together the sugar, egg and 2 tablespoons flour in a large bowl. Add rhubarb and pour into a 9-inch glass pie plate. Preheat oven to 350°. Cream together the butter and brown sugar. Add ⅔ cup flour to butter mixture and combine until crumbly. Sprinkle mixture over rhubarb. Bake for 40 minutes or until rhubarb is tender.

Whip cream with sugar and vanilla. Serve over warm Rhubarb Crisp.

RASPBERRY WALNUT TORTE

Yield: 15 servings
Assemble: 1 hour
Bake: 30-35 minutes

½ cup butter or margarine, softened
1 cup flour
⅓ cup powdered sugar
1 10-ounce package frozen raspberries, drained and juice reserved
¾ cup walnuts, coarsely chopped
2 eggs
1 cup sugar
½ teaspoon salt
¼ cup flour
½ teaspoon baking powder
1 teaspoon vanilla extract
½ cup water
½ cup sugar
Liquid from raspberries
2 tablespoons cornstarch
1 tablespoon lemon juice
2 cups heavy cream, whipped

Preheat oven to 350°. Cut butter into flour and sugar and press into a 13 x 9-inch pan. Bake for 15 minutes; cool. Sprinkle walnuts and raspberries over crust.

In a medium-size bowl beat the eggs with 1 cup sugar until light and fluffy. Add salt, flour, baking powder and vanilla. Pour over walnuts and berries. Bake for 30-35 minutes; cool.

To prepare the sauce, combine water, sugar, reserved raspberry juice and cornstarch in a small saucepan. Cook over medium heat until thickened and clear. Stir in the lemon juice; cool. Serve torte garnished with whipped cream and sauce.

PEAR KUCHEN

1½ cups flour
2 tablespoons sugar
¼ teaspoon salt
¼ teaspoon baking powder
½ cup butter, softened
**4-5 pears, peeled and thinly sliced (peaches or apples may
  be used)**
¼ cup sugar
1 teaspoon cinnamon
½ teaspoon freshly grated nutmeg
½ cup heavy cream
1 egg yolk, beaten
½ cup coarsely chopped hazelnuts (sliced almonds may be used)
Powdered sugar

Preheat oven to 400°. Combine first 4 ingredients in a medium-size bowl. Cut in butter until mixture resembles coarse meal. Press over bottom and up sides of a 9-inch tart pan with removable bottom (mixture will be dry and crumbly). Arrange pears over crust. Combine ¼ cup sugar, cinnamon and nutmeg and sprinkle over pears. Bake 15 minutes.

Blend cream and egg yolk together. After kuchen has baked for 15 minutes, pour cream mixture over pears, sprinkle with nuts and bake until custard is set (approximately 30 minutes). Dust with powdered sugar and serve hot.

CASHEW BUTTER TOFFEE

2 cups butter
2½ cups sugar
¼ cup white corn syrup
½ cup water
2-3 cups cashews, broken
½ pound chocolate bar, melted
½ cup cashews, coarsely ground

Cut butter into chunks and combine with sugar, corn syrup and water in a large, heavy saucepan. Cook on high heat until mixture starts to boil. Reduce heat to low. DO NOT STIR once mixture boils. Cook to 280°. (This mixture must cook slowly and for quite a long time to reach this temperature.)

Lightly butter a 16 x 11-inch jelly roll pan and scatter with broken nuts. Pour hot toffee over nuts. Pour melted chocolate over toffee and sprinkle with ground nuts. Break into pieces when cool.

FRESH PEACH AND BLUEBERRY COBBLER

QUICK
& EASY

Yield: 6-8 servings
Assemble: 30 minutes
Bake: 25-30 minutes

1½ tablespoons cornstarch
¼ teaspoon ground mace
½ cup firmly packed brown sugar
¼ cup sherry
¼ cup water
1 tablespoon lemon juice
1 tablespoon butter
½ cup chopped pecans
5 cups sliced peaches
1 cup fresh or frozen blueberries
1 cup flour
1½ teaspoons baking powder
2 tablespoons sugar
⅛ teaspoon salt
¼ cup butter, softened
1 egg, slightly beaten
¼ cup milk
1 cup heavy cream for topping

Combine cornstarch, mace, brown sugar, sherry and water in a medium-size saucepan and cook, stirring, until thickened. Remove from heat. Add lemon juice, butter, pecans, peaches and blueberries. Coat fruit with sauce and set aside.

Sift flour, baking powder, sugar and salt into a small mixing bowl. Cut in butter until mixture is like coarse meal. Combine egg and milk, then add to dry ingredients. Stir just to moisten. Preheat oven to 400°. Pour fruit filling into a large round 1½ to 2-quart baking dish. Spoon topping over filling. Bake for 20-25 minutes. Serve warm with cream.

HONEYDEW LIME REFRESHER

QUICK
& EASY

Yield: 10-12 servings
Assemble: 10 minutes

1 large honeydew melon, chilled
1 pint lime sherbet
Juice of 1 large lime
Crushed ice (optional)
Fresh mint sprigs for garnish
Fresh strawberries or raspberries for garnish

Peel and seed melon. Dice into bowl of a food processor fitted with a metal blade. Add sherbet and lime juice; process until smooth. Divide among serving dishes (set in ice to keep longer), garnish with mint sprigs and berries. Serve immediately.

ORANGE PINEAPPLE OLD-FASHIONED FREEZER ICE CREAM

Yield: 1 gallon
Assemble: 30 minutes
Freeze: 20 minutes

2²/₃ cups sugar
1 quart whole milk
1 5-ounce can evaporated milk
3 cups heavy cream
12 ounces fresh orange juice (3-4 oranges)
6 ounces fresh lemon juice (3-4 lemons)
18 ounces pineapple juice
Ice
Rock salt

Dissolve 2²/₃ cups sugar in milk in the container of a 6-quart ice cream freezer; stir to mix. Add evaporated milk and heavy cream. Using a long handled wooden spoon, stir mixture several times to completely dissolve sugar. Refrigerate mixture* while preparing fruit juices.

Mix together orange juice, lemon juice and pineapple juice. Add all at once to the milk and cream mixture; blend well. Insert freezer dasher and process immediately according to freezer directions.

*For fresh fruit variation complete process up to this step. Puree fruit of choice below, add the indicated fruit juice(s), then add fruit mixture to cream mixture. Stir well to blend and freeze according to freezer instructions.

PEACH ICE CREAM:
3 cups pureed fresh, firm, ripe, peeled peaches
½ cup pineapple juice
Juice of 2 oranges
Lemon juice to taste

APRICOT ICE CREAM:
2½ cups pureed, firm, ripe apricots
½ cup pineapple juice
Juice of 2 oranges
Lemon juice to taste

CREAMY BERRY ICE CREAM

Yield: 1 gallon
Assemble: 10 minutes
Freeze: 20 minutes

3 ripe bananas
Juice of 3 lemons
Juice of 3 oranges
6 cups fresh strawberries or raspberries cleaned and hulled
3 cups sugar
4 cups heavy cream
2 cups whole milk
Ice
Rock salt

Place first 5 ingredients in bowl of food processor fitted with metal blade (or use blender and blend bananas and orange juice, then sugar, strawberries and lemon juice, then combine). If using raspberries, leave whole; do not process. Add cream slowly, then add milk. Pour entire mixture into 6-quart ice cream freezer and freeze according to freezer instructions.

APPLE ALMOND PUDDING WITH NUTMEG SAUCE

Yield: 12 servings
Assemble: 30 minutes
Bake: 1 hour

PUDDING:
½ cup butter
2 cups firmly packed brown sugar
2 eggs, beaten
½ teaspoon cinnamon
½ teaspoon nutmeg
2 teaspoons baking soda
½ teaspoon salt
2 cups flour
½ cup chopped, roasted, unsalted almonds
4 cups finely chopped or grated unpared apples
½ cup raisins

NUTMEG SAUCE:
2 cups sugar
1 cup butter
1 cup heavy cream
1 tablespoon vanilla extract
½ teaspoon nutmeg

Preheat oven to 325°. To make pudding, cream butter and sugar in a large bowl. Add eggs and combine well; set aside. Combine cinnamon, nutmeg, soda, salt and flour; add to butter mixture. Fold in fruit. Bake in 9 x 13-inch pan for 1 hour. To serve, crumble pudding into serving dishes and top with Nutmeg Sauce.

Prepare sauce by stirring sugar, butter and cream over low heat until butter melts and sauce is hot. Add vanilla and nutmeg. Serve over hot pudding.

IDLE ISLES CANDY

Yield: 2 pounds
Assemble: 2½ hours
Freeze: 8 hours

Note: Idle Isles Candy is impressive and irresistable; a most appreciated gift for friends.

1 cup butter, softened
1 14-ounce can sweetened condensed milk
¼ teaspoon vanilla extract
4 cups sifted powdered sugar
1½ pounds high quality dipping chocolate
1 pound roasted, salted, finely chopped almonds

Combine butter, vanilla, milk and powdered sugar. Mix well and refrigerate until firm enough to handle. Roll into balls using about ½ teaspoon per ball. Freeze creme balls overnight.

Melt dipping chocolate over hot water. Take extreme care not to let any water spill over into chocolate. Pour small amount of chocolate onto marble slab. Roll frozen creme ball in chocolate, coating completely. Roll in almonds and refrigerate until ready to serve.

SNOWBALL

Yield: 8-12 servings
Assemble: 30 minutes
Bake: 55 minutes
Chill: 8 hours

8 ounces semi-sweet chocolate
½ cup boiling water
1 cup sugar
1 cup butter, softened
4 large eggs
1 cup heavy cream
2 teaspoons powdered sugar
1 teaspoon vanilla extract

Use a round dome-shaped ovenproof bowl with a 6-8 cup capacity. Line the bowl with aluminum foil; set aside. Preheat oven to 350°. In a small saucepan melt the chocolate and sugar in boiling water. Transfer to a large mixing bowl. Gradually mix in butter and beat on low speed until mixture is smooth. Add eggs one at a time, beating well after each addition. Pour mixture into lined bowl and bake for 55 minutes. When done the top will be puffy with a thick, cracked crust. Allow the bowl to cool at room temperature. As it cools, shrinkage will occur, especially in the middle. Use a piece of waxed paper and press around the edges as it cools in order to keep it as flat as possible. When cool, cover and refrigerate overnight, several days or freeze.

To serve, whip cream, sugar and vanilla until stiff. Unmold dessert by inverting a flat dessert plate over bowl, turn over plate and bowl, remove the bowl and carefully peel off the foil. Frost with whipped cream.

MOLDED FRENCH CREME

Yield: 8 servings
Assemble: 30 minutes
Chill: 4 hours

Note: Try this in a
heart-shaped mold
for Valentine's Day.

1 cup sour cream
1 cup heavy cream
¾ cup superfine sugar
1 envelope unflavored gelatin
¼ cup cold water or scant ¼ cup Amaretto liqueur
8 ounces cream cheese, softened
½ teaspoon vanilla extract
Fresh strawberries or raspberries for garnish
Frosted grapes for garnish

Brush one 4-cup or eight 4-ounce molds lightly with vegetable oil; set aside. Combine sour cream and heavy cream in a medium-size saucepan. Beat in the sugar. Place pan over very low heat and warm. Sprinkle gelatin over water or liqueur in a cup to soften. Place cup in a saucepan with hot water to dissolve and liquify. Stir into the warm cream mixture and remove from heat. Beat cream cheese until soft in a medium-size bowl; stir in the cream mixture. Gradually add vanilla, blending thoroughly. Pour into prepared mold(s). Refrigerate 4 hours or until firm.

To unmold, dip mold into hot water for about 10 seconds, invert and shake gently onto a serving plate. Garnish with fresh berries and frosted grapes. (To frost grapes, dip in egg white then roll in granulated sugar; allow to dry for about 20 minutes.)

STRAWBERRY CHEESECAKE TRIFLE

QUICK
& EASY

Yield: 12 servings
Assemble: 20 minutes
Chill: 40 minutes

Note: Casual and
easy; a great summer
time treat.

16 ounces cream cheese, softened
2 cups powdered sugar
1 cup sour cream
2 teaspoons vanilla extract
¼ teaspoon almond extract
1 cup heavy cream
1 teaspoon vanilla extract
1 tablespoon sugar
1 angel food cake, cut into 1 to 1½-inch cubes
2 quarts fresh strawberries or peaches, thickly sliced,
**   or raspberries**
3-4 tablespoons sugar
2-3 tablespoons Amaretto liqueur (optional)
Whole berries for garnish
Mint leaves for garnish

In a large mixing bowl blend cream cheese and powdered sugar
together. Add the sour cream, vanilla and almond extract. In a small
bowl whip the heavy cream, vanilla and sugar until stiff. Fold the
whipped cream into the cream cheese mixture. Add the cake cubes and
coat well.

Thickly slice the strawberries, then add the sugar and Amaretto; mix well.
Layer into a trifle bowl, starting with a layer of strawberries, then a layer of
cake/cream cheese mixture. Continue layering, ending with strawberries.
Cover with plastic wrap and chill well before serving. Garnish with mint
leaves or whole berries.

CANTALOUPE MOUSSE

Yield: 8 servings
Assemble: 30 minutes
Chill: 4 hours

1 medium cantaloupe, seeded and peeled
2 envelopes gelatin
½ cup cold water
2 cups heavy cream
1½ to 2 cups sugar (depending on sweetness of cantaloupe),
**   divided**
4 egg whites
Strawberries for garnish
Fresh mint for garnish

Cut cantaloupe into small pieces. Puree pieces in a food processor
fitted with metal blade for 10-20 seconds to yield 2 cups puree. Sprinkle
gelatin in cold water. Place over boiling water to dissolve. Cool and add
to cantaloupe puree; set aside.

Whip cream to soft peaks; gradually add ½ to 1 cup sugar. Whip egg
whites until fluffy; add 1 cup sugar and whip to stiff peaks. Fold
cantaloupe mixture into whipped cream. Then fold in egg whites. Pour
into individual serving dishes or into a mold; refrigerate to set. Serve
within 8 hours or mousse will become drippy on bottom. Garnish with
fresh strawberries and mint sprigs.

APRICOT CHEESE PILLOWS

Yield: 8 crepes
Assemble: 60 minutes
Bake: 10 minutes

CREPES:
1½ cups milk
2 tablespoons vegetable oil
3 eggs
1½ cups flour
⅛ teaspoon salt

FILLING:
8 ounces cream cheese, softened
¼ cup butter, softened
¼ cup sugar
1½ teaspoons vanilla extract
1 teaspoon grated lemon rind
6 tablespoons sliced almonds
⅔ cup apricot jam
⅓ cup orange juice
Butter for topping

APRICOT SAUCE:
⅔ cup apricot jam
⅓ cup orange juice
2 tablespoons butter
1 tablespoon lemon juice
1½ teaspoons grated lemon
Sliced almonds for garnish

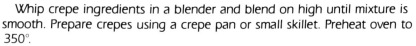

Whip crepe ingredients in a blender and blend on high until mixture is smooth. Prepare crepes using a crepe pan or small skillet. Preheat oven to 350°.

Combine filling ingredients, except almonds, and beat until fluffy. Spread each crepe almost to edge with approximately 3 tablespoons of filling. Fold as diagramed.

Arrange crepes in a buttered 9 x 13-inch baking dish. Dot with a small amount of butter. Bake crepes for 10 minutes at 350° until cheese filling bubbles. As crepes bake, mix and heat sauce ingredients in a small saucepan until warmed. Pour sauce over hot crepes. Garnish with sliced almonds.

RASPBERRY SORBET

QUICK
& EASY

Yield: 6 servings
Assemble: 10 minutes

24 ounces frozen raspberries
¼ to ½ cup sugar (adjust according to sweetness of berries)
1 cup plain yogurt
1-2 teaspoons fresh lemon juice
2-3 tablespoons Grand Marnier, Cointreau or Kirsch (to taste)
Fresh mint leaves for garnish
Fresh raspberries for garnish

Place all ingredients into bowl of food processor fitted with metal blade. (A blender may be used but berries must be slightly thawed in order to blend to sorbet consistency.) Process until desired texture is obtained. Serve at once, garnished with mint or berries or freeze in individual molds.

APPLE GALETTE WITH CRÈME FRAÎCHE

Yield: 6-10 servings
Assemble: 45 minutes
Bake: 45-60 minutes
Assemble: Crème
    Fraîche—32 hours
    in advance

Note: Apple Galette
with Crème Fraîche
not only makes a
terrific dessert but a
delightful addition to
a brunch menu.

PASTRY:
1½ cups flour
8 tablespoons butter, cold
¼ teaspoon salt
7-8 tablespoons ice water

FILLING:
5-8 peeled, cored and sliced apples; divided
¼ cup sugar
1 teaspoon cinnamon
3 tablespoons butter, cut into very small pieces

GLAZE:
4 tablespoons preserves
1 tablespoon rum or brandy

CRÈME FRAÎCHE:
1 cup heavy cream
1 tablespoon sour cream

In a medium-size bowl work flour, butter and salt together with fingers until well blended. Butter should be chunky. Add water and work into dough. Gather into a ball, cover and chill for at least 30 minutes. Chop enough sliced apples to yield 1 to 1½ cups. Reserve remaining sliced apples. Preheat oven to 400°.

On floured surface or pastry cloth roll out pastry into a large circle. Pastry should be approximately ¼-inch thick. Transfer dough to a baking sheet. Cover the center of the pastry with chopped apples, leaving a border of 1 to 1½-inches to be folded up. Arrange sliced apples over chopped apples. Fold pastry over the edges of the apples. Pastry will form a border edge. Sprinkle with sugar and cinnamon and dot with butter. Bake for 45-60 minutes until golden. After galette is baked, warm preserves and liqueur together in a small saucepan and brush over the warm apples and edges of the pastry. Make Crème Fraîche 32 hours ahead of serving. In a small bowl mix cream and sour cream together; let sit at room temperature 8 hours, cover and refrigerate 24 hours before using. Serve galette warm with Crème Fraîche, ice cream or whipped cream.

BITTERSWEET CHOCOLATE SOUFFLÉ

Yield: 8 servings
Assemble: 1 hour
Bake: 30-40 minutes

3 tablespoons butter
3 tablespoons flour
1 cup milk
½ cup sugar
3 1-ounce squares unsweetened chocolate
⅛ teaspoon salt
5 egg yolks, room temperature
5 egg whites, room temperature
½ teaspoon vanilla extract
Heavy cream, whipped and sweetened for garnish
1 tablespoon brandy (optional)

continued

continued

In a medium-size saucepan melt butter over low heat. Add flour and stir until smooth. Add milk a little at a time and continue to stir over low heat until mixture is slightly thickened. Add sugar and stir until dissolved. Next add chocolate and continue to stir until melted. Remove from heat, add salt and beat; cool.

Beat egg yolks in a separate bowl until lemon-colored. Add to cooled chocolate mixture. Beat until smooth. Allow sauce to come to room temperature (approximately 20 minutes). Meanwhile, beat egg whites until stiff. Add vanilla to cooled sauce, then fold in beaten egg whites, thoroughly and carefully. Preheat oven to 350°.

Butter 8 individual souffle' dishes and sprinkle with sugar. Tap gently and turn upside down to remove extra sugar. (A 2-quart souffle' dish treated with sugar may be used if preferred.) Fill dishes and bake for 30 minutes. (If using a 2-quart souffle' dish, bake for 40 minutes.) Remove from oven and serve immediately with whipped cream. Brandy may be added to whipped cream if desired.

ALMOND TART

Yield: 6-8 servings
Assemble: 15 minutes
Bake: 55-60 minutes

CRUST:
1 cup flour
½ cup unsalted butter, softened
1 tablespoon sugar
Pinch of salt
1 tablespoon vanilla extract
1½ teaspoons water

FILLING:
¾ cup sugar
¾ cup heavy cream
1 teaspoon orange juice
Almond extract to taste
1 cup sliced almonds

Position oven rack in lower third of oven and preheat to 400°. Combine flour, butter, sugar and salt in a small bowl. Beat with an electric mixer on low speed until mixture is consistency of coarse meal. Mix vanilla with water. With mixer running, gradually add to flour, blending lightly. Do not overmix. Gather dough into a ball. Press into a 9-inch tart pan with removable bottom. Bake until set, approximately 10-15 minutes; remove from oven. Reduce oven temperature to 350°.

Combine sugar, cream, orange juice, almond extract and salt in a small bowl and beat with a fork until slightly thickened. Stir in almonds, mixing well. Turn filling into crust. Return to oven and bake until golden brown (approximately 40-45 minutes). Allow to cool completely. Remove from pan and cut into wedges.

COLD LEMON SOUFFLÉ WITH LADYFINGERS (Pictured)

Yield: 10-12 servings
Assemble: 20 minutes
Chill: 4 hours

2 envelopes unflavored gelatin
½ cup cold water
6 egg yolks
½ cup sugar
½ cup lemon juice
6 egg whites
Pinch of salt
½ cup sugar
½ teaspoon cream of tartar
1 cup heavy cream
2 dozen ladyfingers
½ to ¾ cup heavy cream, sweetened and whipped (optional)
Thin lemon slice (optional)

Dissolve gelatin in cold water. Beat egg yolks in a medium-size bowl until light. Add sugar and gelatin mixture and lemon juice. Put bowl in hot water (as in preparing hollandaise) and cook, whisking steadily, until mixture is smooth and slightly thickened. Remove from heat and cool.

Beat egg whites until stiff and glossy, having added the ½ cup sugar. Add salt and cream of tartar. Fold egg whites into egg yolk mixture. Whip cream until thickened but not completely stiff. Fold into egg mixture. Butter bottom of a 9-inch springform pan and line with ladyfingers. Stand ladyfingers up around the sides. Spoon souffle mixture into pan and refrigerate a minimum of 4 hours. Optional but beautiful: pipe rosettes of whipped cream sweetened with powdered sugar. Take a thin slice of lemon cut through the middle and twisted into an "S" shape and place in the middle. Remove from springform pan.

CRÈME BRÛLÉE

Yield: 8 servings
Assemble: 30 minutes
Bake: 1 hour
Chill: 4 hours

4 cups heavy cream
¼ cup sugar
8 egg yolks
¼ teaspoon salt
2 teaspoons vanilla extract
1 cup sifted brown sugar
Chopped ice

Preheat oven to 275°. Place cream in a double boiler. Heat but do not boil. Add sugar and stir until dissolved. Beat eggs with salt and vanilla. **Stir** hot cream into eggs. Do not beat or the custard will have air bubbles. Pour the custard into custard cups. Place filled cups into a water bath about half the depth of the cups. Bake for approximately 1 hour or until set. Remove from oven and cool. Chill until very cold.

Before serving, sprinkle custard with brown sugar. Make a bed or chopped ice in a baking pan. Place custard cups in the ice and broil until the sugar is melted and brown. Serve immediately, or custard may be chilled again.

COLD LEMON SOUFFLÉ WITH LADYFINGERS

SUMMER'S BEST FRESH FRUIT PIE

Yield: 6-8 servings
Assemble: 1 hour
Bake: 10-12 minutes
Chill: 2 hours

CRUST:
1 cup flour
¼ teaspoon salt
¼ cup butter, chilled
2 tablespoons vegetable shortening
3-4 tablespoons ice water

FILLING:
5 cups sliced fresh, peeled peaches or strawberries
1 tablespoon lemon juice
¼ cup sugar
Orange juice
Lemon juice
3 tablespoons cornstarch
2 tablespoons butter
Pinch of salt
3 tablespoons orange liqueur (Triple Sec)
8 ounces cream cheese, softened
1 tablespoon heavy cream
2 tablespoons powdered sugar
3 tablespoons butter
¾ cup chopped pecans or almonds
1 cup flaked coconut
1 cup heavy cream, whipped and sweetened

To make crust, stir flour and salt together in a medium-size bowl or in the bowl of a food processor fitted with a metal blade. Cut or process butter and shortening into flour until mixture resembles coarse meal. Add ice water until dough begins to form a ball. Wrap in plastic wrap and thoroughly chill. Preheat oven to 450°. Roll out dough on a lightly floured surface into a 12-inch circle. Place into a 9-inch pie plate, flute edges, prick bottom well and bake for 10-12 minutes or until golden; cool.

In a large bowl sprinkle sliced peaches or strawberries with lemon juice and sugar. Allow to stand for 1 hour; drain, reserving juice. To the fruit juice add enough orange juice and lemon juice to make 1 cup. Place juice in a small saucepan, add cornstarch; stir to blend. Cook over low heat until thick, stirring constantly. Remove from heat and add butter, salt and orange liqueur. Fold sliced peaches or strawberries into sauce; cool.

In a small bowl blend cream cheese, 1 tablespoon heavy cream and powdered sugar. Spread on bottom of baked pie shell. Pour cooled fruit mixture into pie shell; chill.

Before serving, preheat oven to 350°. Melt 3 tablespoons of butter and toss with nuts and coconut. Spread mixture on a baking sheet. Bake for 5-6 minutes, or until lightly browned, stirring often to prevent uneven browning; allow to cool. Top pie with whipped cream and sprinkle coconut mixture over top.

SUGAR TART SHELLS

Yield: 25 shells
Assemble: 20 minutes
Bake: 10 minutes

1 cup sugar
½ cup vegetable shortening
½ cup butter, softened
1 egg
1 teaspoon almond extract
2½ cups flour
Vegetable spray (such as PAM)

Cream sugar with shortening and butter until fluffy. Add egg and almond extract; mix in flour. Work mixture with hands until a dough forms. Preheat oven at 375°. Spray tart pans with vegetable spray; press dough into pans. Bake for approximately 10 minutes. Cool before filling. Fill shells with chocolate pudding, cherry pie filling or fresh fruit. Top with sweetened whipped cream.

APPLE PIE EN PAPILLOTTE

Yield: 6-8 servings
Assemble: 30 minutes
Bake: 90 minutes

Note: Fun to make and mysterious bake. Resist the urge to peek!

CRUST:
1½ cups flour
1½ teaspoons sugar
1 teaspoon salt
½ cup vegetable oil
2 tablespoons cold milk

FILLING:
4 cups peeled, thinly sliced apples
½ cup sugar
2 tablespoons flour
1 teaspoon cinnamon
1½ teaspoons nutmeg

TOPPING:
½ cup flour
½ cup sugar
½ cup cold butter

Vanilla ice cream

Mix flour, sugar, salt, oil and cold milk together with a pastry blender, or food processor, until crumbly. Press into a 9-inch pie plate; set aside.

To make filling, combine apples, sugar, flour, cinnamon and nutmeg together and pour into the pie shell.

Mix topping of flour, sugar and cold butter together with a pastry blender, or in food processor, and sprinkle mixture on top of pie. Place pie in a large paper bag, seal with staples or pins and bake 90 minutes at 350°. Serve warm with vanilla ice cream.

MEXICADO LIME PIE

Yield: 6-8 servings
Assemble: 30 minutes
Chill: 3 hours

Note: This will become a favorite dessert after a Mexican dinner. Try it after Mexican Cheese Torte (page 202).

1 9-inch pie shell, baked and cooled (see page 223)
1 large avocado, peeled
½ cup fresh lime juice (about 5 limes)
1 cup sugar, divided
1 envelope unflavored gelatin
¼ teaspoon salt
3 eggs, separated, room temperature
½ cup whole milk
1 tablespoon grated lime peel
1 cup heavy cream
1 tablespoon powdered sugar
1 teaspoon vanilla extract
Sliced toasted almonds for garnish

Puree the peeled avocado with the lime juice in a food processor or blender. In the top of a double boiler, mix together ½ cup sugar, unflavored gelatin and salt. In a medium-size bowl, beat the egg yolks with the milk and grated lime peel. Add egg yolk mixture to the sugar mixture in top of double boiler and stir over boiling water for about 5 minutes or until gelatin dissolves. Remove from heat, cool slightly and stir in the avocado puree. Chill until the mixture mounds slightly, about 1 hour. Add the remaining sugar to the egg whites and beat until stiff. Fold into chilled avocado mixture and turn into baked pie shell. Chill until firm. Whip cream with sugar and vanilla. Garnish pie with whipped cream and toasted almonds.

PEACH PARFAIT PIE

Yield: 6-8 servings
Assemble: 40 minutes
Chill: 3 hours

CRUST:
1 cup quick-cooking oatmeal
½ cup slivered almonds
½ cup brown sugar
6 tablespoons butter, melted

FILLING:
1 3-ounce package lemon gelatin
1¼ cups boiling water
1 pint vanilla ice cream
½ teaspoon almond extract
2 cups fresh peaches
1 cup heavy cream whipped for topping

Spread oats on cookie sheet and bake for 5 minutes at 350°. Add almonds and cook 5 minutes longer. Add butter and brown sugar and mix. Press into 9-inch pie plate; chill.

In a large bowl combine lemon gelatin and boiling water; stir to dissolve gelatin. Add vanilla ice cream, cut into pieces; stir until melted. Blend in almond extract. Chill until thickened but not set (approximately 20 minutes). Fold in peaches and turn into cooled pie shell. Chill until firm. Top with whipped cream.

DERBY PIE

Yield: 6-8 servings
Assemble: 20 minutes
Bake: 40-50 minutes

1 9-inch pie shell, unbaked (see page 223)
¼ cup butter, softened
1 cup sugar
3 eggs
¾ cup light corn syrup
¼ teaspoon salt
1 teaspoon vanilla extract
½ cup semi-sweet chocolate chips
1½-2 cups coarsely chopped black walnuts or pecans
2 tablespoons bourbon
Whipped cream flavored with bourbon (optional)
Ice cream (optional)

Prepare crust but do not prick bottom. Preheat oven to 375°. In a large bowl cream butter and sugar until very light. Add eggs and beat. Add corn syrup, salt and vanilla. Add chocolate chips, nuts and bourbon and mix well. Pour filling into a 9-inch unbaked pie shell. Bake for 40-50 minutes. Serve with whipped cream or à la mode.

LEMON ANGEL PIE

Yield: 6-8 servings
Assemble: 30 minutes
Bake: 1 hour
Chill: 2 hours

Note: Splendid pie to serve after a spicy Italian meal.

MERINGUE CRUST:
4 egg whites
¼ teaspoon cream of tartar
1 cup sugar

FILLING:
4 egg yolks
½ cup sugar
⅛ teaspoon salt
Juice of 1½ lemons
1 tablespoon grated lemon rind
1 cup heavy cream
Lemon zest for garnish

In a medium-size bowl beat egg whites until foamy then add cream of tartar. Continue beating until mixture stands in peaks. Gradually add sugar, beating constantly. Continue beating until mixture is stiff and glossy. Preheat oven to 250°. Turn mixture into a **well greased** 9-inch glass pie plate, pulling meringue to edge and denting in center for filling. Bake for 60 minutes. Turn oven off, leave door ajar and cool shell slowly.

In a small bowl beat egg yolks slightly and add sugar, salt, lemon juice and grated rind. Cook in double boiler for 8-10 minutes or until mixture thickens; cool. Beat cream until stiff and fold into lemon mixture. Turn into cooled shell and refrigerate. Garnish with lemon zest before serving.

QUICK CRANBERRY MINCE PIE

Yield: 6-8 servings
Assemble: 25 minutes
Bake: 35 minutes

Pastry for 2-crust 9-inch pie (double 9-inch
   pie crust recipe, page 223)
1½ cups mincemeat
1 16-ounce can whole cranberry sauce
½ cup chopped walnuts
¼ teaspoon salt
2 teaspoons grated lemon rind
2 teaspoons flour
1 teaspoon cinnamon
2 tablespoons brown sugar
Ice cream

Prepare crust for two 9-inch pies. Sprinkle a bit of flour on 9-inch pie plate. Place 1 crust into the pie plate; do not prick bottom. Reserve 1 crust for lattice top. Mix next 8 ingredients in a large bowl. Preheat oven to 400°. Pour filling into pie shell and smooth the top. Cover with lattice top, flute edges and trim. Bake for 35 minutes. Cool before serving. Pie can be frozen. Serve à la mode.

KEY LIME PIE

Yield: 8 servings
Assemble: 30 minutes
Bake: 20 minutes
Chill: 2 hours

CRUST:
8 ounces chocolate wafers, crushed
½ cup butter, melted

FILLING:
1 14-ounce can sweetened condensed milk
⅓ cup fresh lime juice
1 tablespoon grated lime rind, divided
3 eggs, separated
¼ teaspoon salt
3-4 drops green food coloring (optional)
1 cup heavy cream, whipped
2 tablespoons sugar
1 tablespoon rum
Lime twists (optional)
Chocolate shavings (optional)

Preheat oven to 350°. Place wafers in a food processor or strong plastic bag and crush finely. Add melted butter and blend well. Press firmly onto the sides and bottom of a 10-inch pie plate. Bake for 10 minutes. Cool on rack for 30 minutes.

In a large bowl mix sweetened condensed milk with the lime juice, 1½ teaspoons of lime rind and beaten egg yolks. Add coloring, if desired, and mix. Beat egg whites and salt until stiff, but not dry. Fold into the milk and lime juice mixture. Pour into cooled pie shell. Bake for 10 minutes at 250°. Cool for 30 minutes. Refrigerate for 1 hour or until well chilled. Top with whipped cream to which sugar and rum have been added. Garnish with reserved 1½ teaspoons lime rind, lime twists or chocolate shavings.

RAISIN CREAM PIE

Yield: 6-8 servings
Assemble: 30 minutes
Chill: 2 hours

1 cup raisins
1 cup water
4 tablespoons flour
¾ cup sugar
1 cup heavy cream
2 egg yolks
1 tablespoon butter
1 teaspoon vanilla extract
1 9-inch pie shell, baked (see page 223)
1 cup heavy cream
2 teaspoons powdered sugar
½ teaspoon vanilla extract

In a large saucepan boil raisins in 1 cup water until liquid is absorbed. Mix flour and sugar in a small bowl. Add cream to raisins, then add flour mixture before cream is completely heated. Add egg yolks. Let mixture come to a boil, stirring constantly. Remove pan from heat and add butter and vanilla. Pour filling into baked pie shell and let cool. Before serving, whip cream with sugar and vanilla; spread on chilled pie.

CHERRY RASPBERRY PIE

Yield: 6-8 servings
Assemble: 45 minutes
Bake: 30 minutes

Pastry for 2-crust 9-inch pie (double 9-inch pie crust recipe, page 223)
1 10-ounce package frozen raspberries, thawed
3 tablespoons cornstarch
¼ teaspoon salt
¾ cup sugar
2 cups pitted fresh red tart cherries, or equal amount of canned or frozen cherries, drained, juice reserved
Ice cream

Using half the pastry, line a 9-inch pie plate. Drain raspberries, reserving syrup. Add enough water to syrup to make 1 cup. (If frozen or canned cherries are used, add ½ cup of cherry juice to ½ cup raspberry syrup to make 1 cup liquid.) Preheat oven to 425°. In a medium-size saucepan combine the 1 cup liquid with cornstarch, salt, sugar. When cornstarch is dissolved, add cherries. Cook over low heat, stirring constantly, until mixture is thick and clear (5-7 minutes). Stir in raspberries. Pour filling into pastry shell. Top with pastry top, crimping edge. Bake for 30 minutes; cool. Serve à la mode.

MACAROON ALMOND CRUST PEACH PIE

Yield: 6-8 servings
Assemble: 1 hour
Chill: 2 hours

CRUST:
1½ cups blanched almonds, toasted
1½ cups flaked coconut
½ cup sugar
6 tablespoons butter

FILLING:
6 tablespoons powdered sugar
1½ cups sour cream
4 teaspoons fresh orange juice
2 teaspoons orange zest
2 teaspoons vanilla extract
4 cups sliced fresh peaches
1 cup water
1 teaspoon lemon juice
1 cup heavy cream
¼ cup powdered sugar
½ teaspoon vanilla extract
1 teaspoon fresh orange juice

Preheat oven to 350°. Grind almonds to medium-fine. Mix with coconut. With fingers, blend coconut/almond mixture with sugar and butter. Reserve 4 tablespoons for topping; set aside. Press mixture into a 9-inch glass pie plate. Bake for 5 minutes, check to make sure that mixture has not puffed or slid down sides of plate. (Use a fork to return mixture to original position if this happens.) Lightly brown reserved portion in another pan. Remove both pans and place on rack to cool.

Combine powdered sugar, sour cream, orange juice and orange zest and beat until smooth. Spread mixture over bottom and up sides of cooled crust; refrigerate.

Dip sliced peaches in mixture of the water and lemon juice. Dry completely. Place peaches in pie shell, covering completely. In a small bowl add powdered sugar to cream and whip until soft peaks form. Add vanilla and orange juice. Spread over peaches and garnish with reserved crust mixture. Chill until ready to serve.

PRALINE PUMPKIN PIE

Yield: 6-8 servings
Assemble: 1 hour
Chill: 4 hours

1 envelope unflavored gelatin
½ cup cold water
1 teaspoon cinnamon
¾ cup brown sugar
1 16-ounce can pumpkin
1 cup heavy cream
¼ cup milk
¾ teaspoon nutmeg
½ teaspoon salt
1 9-inch pie shell, baked (see page 223)
¼ cup butter
½ cup sugar
1 cup finely chopped pecans
1 cup heavy cream, sweetened and whipped

In a small saucepan sprinkle gelatin over water and heat on low until gelatin is dissolved. Remove from heat and cool. Add brown sugar to gelatin and mix until dissolved. In a large bowl combine pumpkin, milk, salt, cinnamon and nutmeg. Add gelatin mixture and blend together until smooth. Whip cream in a small bowl until stiff. Fold into pumpkin mixture; set aside.

To make praline mixture, melt ¼ cup butter. Add ½ cup sugar and stir well. Add chopped pecans and cook over medium heat, stirring constantly, until golden brown. Remove from heat and turn onto foil to cool. Crumble mixture. Sprinkle 1 cup praline mixture on bottom of baked pie shell. Pour pumpkin mixture over praline, filling pie shell high as pumpkin mixture will settle. Chill until firm. Garnish with whipped cream and remaining crumbled praline mixture.

LAYERED MOCHA MUD PIE

QUICK
& EASY

Yield: 12 servings
Assemble: 15 minutes
Freeze: 45 minutes

1 13-ounce package Mother's Macaroon Cookies, crumbled
1 quart chocolate-fudge ice cream, softened slightly
1 quart coffee ice cream, softened slightly
1 to 1½ cups Hot Fudge Sauce, (page 231)
¼ pound Victorian toffee or Heath toffee bars, crumbled

Lightly oil bottom of 9-inch springform pan. Pat half of the crumbled cookies into the pan. Spread chocolate ice cream over cookies. Heat hot fudge slightly (just to spreadable consistency). Drizzle half of the fudge sauce over ice cream. To complete second layer, pat remaining cookies onto fudge sauce. Spread coffee ice cream over cookies. Drizzle remaining fudge sauce over the ice cream. Top with crushed toffee. Freeze until ready to serve.

WINNING PEANUT BUTTER PIE

Yield: 10-12 servings
Assemble: 35 minutes
Chill: 8 hours

Note: A prize winner
in a local dessert
contest!

CRUST:
25 vanilla wafers, crushed
½ cup finely chopped unsalted peanuts (without skins)
¼ cup butter, melted

FILLING:
1 cup smooth peanut butter
8 ounces cream cheese, softened
1 cup sugar
2 tablespoons butter, melted
1 cup heavy cream
1 teaspoon vanilla extract
½-1 cup Hot Fudge Sauce (recipe below)

Preheat oven to 350°. Combine vanilla wafers, peanuts and butter and press into a 10-inch pie plate. Bake for 15 minutes; cool.

In a large bowl cream peanut butter, cream cheese, sugar and butter together with an electric mixer on medium speed. Blend well. Whip cream until stiff and add the vanilla. Carefully fold the whipped cream into peanut butter mixture and blend well until texture is consistent and smooth. Place mixture into cooled pie shell and refrigerate for at least 2 hours.

Thin hot fudge topping by heating slightly. Allow to cool to just warm to touch. (It should not be so hot that it melts filling.) Spread a thin layer of fudge onto set pie. The fudge may be left smooth or incorporated into the peanut butter mixture by using a spatula creating a "flower-type" design (see diagram). Chill pie for at least 6 hours.

HOT FUDGE SAUCE

QUICK
& EASY

Yield: 2 cups
Assemble: 10 minutes

1 14-ounce can sweetened condensed milk
2 1-ounce squares unsweetened or semi-sweet chocolate
1 tablespoon vanilla extract
2 tablespoons butter

Combine milk and chocolate and cook over low heat until chocolate melts and mixture thickens. Microwave may be used, but process does not take long. Add vanilla and butter. Store, covered, in refrigerator. Use for Winning Peanut Butter Pie and Layered Mocha Mud Pie, or hot, over ice cream.

COOKIES & CAKES

A dramatic contrast to the progressive civilization of Salt Lake City is the primitive challenge of the high Uinta Mountains. Eager explorers with horses and packs, climb endlessly through a lush terrain of unforaged timber, tranquil ponds and meadows of unbounded natural color and texture. A saddlebag treat of Granola Bars and Wasatch Mountain Ranger Cookies provides that extra energy to establish camp.

At day's end, the embers of a tended campfire glow while the shouts of a screech owl and the wild ensemble of coyote calls echo through the hills. Accompanied by an exaggerated tale of the local "Big Foot," the trail blazers savor nature and the last bite of grilled fresh native trout.

DATE COOKIES WITH PENUCHE ICING

Yield: 4 dozen
Assemble: 45 minutes
Bake: 10 minutes

2 cups chopped dates
½ cup boiling water
1 teaspoon baking soda
¾ cup shortening
1½ cups firmly packed brown sugar
2 eggs
1 teaspoon vanilla extract
3 cups flour
½ teaspoon salt
1 cup chopped pecans or walnuts

PENUCHE ICING:
⅓ cup butter
1 cup firmly packed brown sugar
¼ cup milk
1¾-2 cups powdered sugar
4 dozen pecan halves

Preheat oven to 350°. In a small bowl mix together dates, water and soda. Set aside and allow to cool. Mix together shortening, sugar, eggs and vanilla in a large bowl. Add flour and salt and blend well. Stir date mixture and nuts into dough. Drop by teaspoonsful on greased baking sheet and bake for 10 minutes.

Melt butter in a medium-size saucepan. Add brown sugar and milk; boil over low heat for 2 minutes, stirring constantly. Cool to lukewarm. Gradually add powdered sugar and beat until thick enough to spread. (If too thick add a little water.) Frost cookies and top each with a pecan half.

BANANA JUMBOS

QUICK
& EASY

Yield: 4 dozen
Assemble: 20 minutes
Bake: 10 minutes

Note: Banana Jumbos are also delicious unfrosted or one can use a favorite cream cheese frosting.

½ cup butter or margarine
½ cup shortening
1 cup sugar
2 eggs
1 cup mashed ripe bananas (2)
½ cup buttermilk
1 teaspoon vanilla extract
3 cups flour
1½ teaspoons baking soda
½ teaspoon salt
1 cup coarsely chopped walnuts

In a large bowl combine first four ingredients; mix well. Add bananas, buttermilk and vanilla. Sift flour, soda and salt; stir into batter. Add walnuts. Chill 1 hour. Drop by tablespoonsful on greased cookie sheet and bake at 375° for 10 minutes. Cool and frost with Penuche Icing (recipe above), if desired.

PECAN PIE COOKIES

Yield: 4 dozen
Assemble: 30 minutes
Chill: 2 hours
Bake: 10 minutes

1 cup butter, softened
½ cup sugar
½ cup dark corn syrup
2 eggs, separated
2½ cups flour

PECAN FILLING:
½ cup powdered sugar
¼ cup butter
3 tablespoons dark corn syrup
½ cup chopped pecans

In a large bowl combine butter and sugar. Add corn syrup and egg yolks and beat until thoroughly blended. Mix in flour gradually. Chill dough for 1-2 hours.

Beat egg whites slightly in small bowl and set aside. Combine sugar, butter and corn syrup in small saucepan for filling; stir to blend. Cook over medium heat stirring occasionally until mixture reaches a full boil. Remove from heat and stir in pecans; chill.

When all ingredients are chilled, preheat oven to 375°. Using 1 table-spoonful of dough for each cookie, roll into balls. Make a thumb-size indentation in center of each ball. Brush cookie very lightly with egg whites. Place on a lightly greased cookie sheet, leaving 2 inches between each cookie and bake for 5 minutes. Remove from oven. Roll ½ teaspoon of the chilled pecan filling into a ball and press firmly into the center of each cookie. Return to oven and bake 5 minutes longer or until lightly browned. Cool 5 minutes on cookie sheet, remove and cool completely on rack.

COTTAGE CRESCENTS

Yield: 2 dozen
Assemble: 30 minutes
Chill: 1 hour
Bake: 20 minutes

Note: Excellent with fresh fruit ice creams (page 213).

1 cup butter or margarine, softened
1 cup cottage cheese, room temperature
2 cups flour
¼ cup butter or margarine, melted
¾ cup firmly packed brown sugar
¾ cup ground walnuts or pecans
Cinnamon to taste

In a large bowl cream cottage cheese and softened butter; combine well. Add flour, mixing well (should be a workable dough texture). Chill 1 hour.

Preheat oven to 350°. Roll out ⅛-inch thick into a 15 x 20-inch rectangle. Spread dough with melted butter. Sprinkle with brown sugar, nuts and cinnamon. Cut into 2½-inch squares. Roll each square starting at one corner and rolling to opposite corner to form crescent. Bake on a lightly greased cookie sheet for 20 minutes or until browned.

HAWAIIAN PINEAPPLE COOKIES

Yield: 3½ dozen
Assemble: 40 minutes
Bake: 8 minutes

½ cup vegetable shortening
½ cup firmly packed brown sugar
½ cup sugar
1 egg, beaten
½ cup drained crushed pineapple, reserve liquid
1 teaspoon vanilla extract
2 cups flour
¼ teaspoon salt
¼ teaspoon baking soda
1 teaspoon baking powder
½ cups nuts (walnuts, almonds or macadamia nuts)

PINEAPPLE ICING:
2 cups powdered sugar
2 tablespoons butter, softened
½ teaspoon vanilla extract
1-2 tablespoons reserved pineapple liquid

TOPPING:
½ cup flaked coconut, toasted (optional)

Cream shortening with sugars in a large bowl. Add egg, pineapple and vanilla; mix well. Sift together flour, salt, baking soda and baking powder; combine with creamed mixture. Add nuts. Drop by teaspoonsful on greased cookie sheet. Bake at 375° for 8 to 10 minutes. Frost, if desired.

To make icing combine powdered sugar, butter and vanilla in a medium-size bowl. Add pineapple liquid to make a good frosting consistency. Beat with mixer until light and fluffy. Ice cookies and dip the frosted side into coconut.

SLICED SPICED NUT COOKIES

Yield: 3-5 dozen
Assemble: 30 minutes
Freeze: 8 hours
Bake: 12-15 minutes

1 cup firmly packed brown sugar
1 cup sugar
2 cups butter
3 eggs
½ teaspoon cream of tartar
1 teaspoon baking soda
1 teaspoon nutmeg
1 teaspoon cinnamon
1 teaspoon allspice
5 cups flour
1 cup chopped nuts
4-5 teaspoons cocoa (optional)

In a large bowl cream sugars and butter; add eggs. Add all dry ingredients. Add nuts and mix well. Shape into a roll or rectangle and freeze overnight. Slice thinly and bake on a greased cookie sheet in a preheated 375° oven for 12 to 15 minutes. The rolls may be kept frozen for several months.

GIANT SUGAR COOKIES

Yield: 5 dozen
Assemble: 30 minutes
Bake: 12-15 minutes

Note: The dough doesn't need refrigeration before rolling.

2 cups butter, softened
2 cups powdered sugar
¾ cup (scant) granulated sugar
½ tablespoon vanilla extract
½ tablespoon almond extract
2 eggs
5 cups flour
¾ tablespoon baking soda
¾ tablespoon cream of tartar

Preheat oven to 325°. Cream butter, sugars, extracts and eggs until fluffy and mixed well. Add dry ingredients blending thoroughly. Roll out ¼ to ½-inch thickness. Cut with a cookie cutter the size of a salad plate. Sprinkle with sugar if desired. Bake on a greased cookie sheet for 12 to 15 minutes. Frost if desired.

PEANUT BUTTER AND CHOCOLATE BONBONS

Yield: 4 dozen
Assemble: 1½ hours
Chill: 2 hours

Note: If you have always wanted to know what it would be like to sit around and eat bonbons, here's your chance!

2 cups sifted powdered sugar
1 cup graham cracker crumbs
¾ cup chopped pecans
½ cup flaked coconut
½ cup butter
½ cup peanut butter, creamy or chunky
1½ cups semi-sweet chocolate pieces or chips
3 tablespoons shortening

In a large bowl combine powdered sugar, graham cracker crumbs, pecans and coconut. In a small saucepan melt butter and peanut butter; pour over the coconut mixture. Blend until moistened, then shape into 1-inch balls.

Melt chocolate and shortening together in a saucepan. Spear balls on toothpicks; dip or roll in chocolate mixture to coat and place on waxed paper. Chill to set. Store in a tightly covered container between layers of waxed paper in a cool place.

SCOTCH SHORTBREAD

Yield: 3-4 dozen
Assemble: 20 minutes
Bake: 8-10 minutes

4 cups flour
1½ cups powdered sugar, divided
2 cups butter, softened

Mix flour and 1 cup powdered sugar in a large bowl. Cut butter into mixture with pastry cutter. Divide dough into thirds; pat each third out to ¼-inch thickness onto a lightly floured surface. DO NOT ROLL WITH A ROLLING PIN!

Preheat oven to 350°. Cut dough into rectangular pieces 1 x 2 - inches and prick each with a fork. Sprinkle with a little reserved powdered sugar. Place on an ungreased cookie sheet and bake for 8 to 10 minutes (until very lightly browned). Watch closely, they burn easily. Sprinkle with more powdered sugar while still hot.

PARFAIT COOKIES (Pictured)

Yield: 3 dozen
Assemble: 20 minutes
Bake: 8-9 minutes

Note: These fantastic
Parfait Cookies
should be prepared
and served on the
same day as they do
not store well.

¾ cup sugar
¾ cup firmly packed brown sugar
¾ cup butter or margarine
2 eggs
2 teaspoons almond extract
3 cups flour, divided
½ teaspoon salt
½ teaspoon baking soda
8 ounces milk chocolate slab (with or without nuts),
cut into ½-inch chunks

Preheat oven to 350°. In a large bowl cream together sugars and
butter. Beat in eggs and almond extract. Blend in 2 cups of the flour
mixed with salt and soda. With a wooden spoon add additional flour so
that dough just barely ceases to be sticky, about 1 more cup. Stir in
chocolate chunks. Drop by heaping teaspoonsful onto greased baking
sheet. Bake for 8-9 minutes or until done; do not overbake. Cookies
should have just a tinge of brown but mostly remain white, soft and high.

ANGEL PUFFS (Pictured)

QUICK
& EASY

Yield: 2 dozen
Assemble: 15 minutes
Bake: 15 minutes

Note: These are
wonderful plain or
glazed with
chocolate. Serve
with ice cream or
fresh fruit—light and
mysterious.

2 egg whites
⅛ teaspoon cream of tartar
⅛ teaspoon baking powder
1 cup firmly packed brown sugar
½ teaspoon vanilla extract
1 cup flaked coconut
2 heaping cups cornflakes
6 ounces milk chocolate chips
1 teaspoon butter

Preheat oven to 325°. In a large bowl beat egg whites and cream of
tartar until stiff peaks form. Beat in baking powder and lightly beat in
brown sugar and vanilla. ("Lightly," like folding, however, still needs the
action of a rotary beater.) Fold the coconut and cornflakes into mixture
with a spatula. Dollop onto greased baking sheet, using about 2 tablespoons per puff. Bake for 15 minutes; should be dry looking. Allow to
cool on the cookie sheet; remove to waxed paper.
Melt chocolate chips and butter together in a small saucepan. Dip
cooled cookies in chocolate to coat top third of cookie. Store uncovered.

CHERRY CHOCOLATE BARS
PARFAIT COOKIES
ANGEL PUFFS

BEST-IN-THE-WORLD OATMEAL RAISIN COOKIES

Yield: 5 dozen
Assemble: 30 minutes
Bake: 7-8 minutes

2 cups raisins
¼ cup water
1 cup butter or margarine, softened
1 cup sugar
1 cup firmly packed brown sugar
2 eggs
1 teaspoon baking powder
1 teaspoon baking soda
2¾ cups flour
2½ cups old-fashioned oats
¼ cup cornstarch
1 tablespoon vanilla extract

Preheat oven to 350°. Bring raisins and water to a boil in a small saucepan. Cover and turn off heat. In a large bowl cream butter and sugars together for 4-5 minutes. Add eggs and beat for 4-5 minutes longer until mixture is light and fluffy. Add dry ingredients and mix well. Drain raisins and add to dough. Stir in vanilla. With a 2-inch ice cream scoop or tablespoon make 2-inch balls and place on a lightly greased cookie sheet. Bake for 7-8 minutes only. (Cookies will be slightly under baked.) Cool.

GLAZED ORANGE COOKIES

Yield: 3-4 dozen
Assemble: 30 minutes
Bake: 12 minutes

1½ cups firmly packed brown sugar
¾ cup vegetable shortening
2 eggs
2½ cups flour
½ teaspoon baking soda
½ teaspoon salt
½ cup sour milk
1 cup chopped pecans or semi-sweet chocolate chips
Grated peel from ½ orange

ORANGE GLAZE:
¼ cup fresh orange juice
1 cup powdered sugar
Grated peel from ½ orange

Preheat oven to 375°. In a large bowl cream sugar and shortening; beat in eggs. Sift flour, soda and salt together. Add to creamed mixture alternately with milk. Stir in nuts or chocolate chips and orange rind. Bake on lightly greased cookie sheet for 12 minutes.

Combine powdered sugar and enough orange juice to make glaze the consistency of very heavy cream; add orange peel. Place a teaspoonful on each cookie as soon as removed from the oven.

WASATCH MOUNTAIN RANGER COOKIES

QUICK
& EASY

Yield: 6 dozen
Assemble: 20 minutes
Bake: 12 minutes

Note: The Wasatch
Mountains rise
majestically from Salt
Lake City and her
sister cities, Ogden to
the north and Provo
to the south. The
mountains form a
geographical
backbone to the
populated adjacent
land, which is often
referred to as the
Wasatch Front.

1 cup sugar
1 cup firmly packed brown sugar
1 cup butter, margarine or vegetable shortening, softened
2 eggs
2 cups flour
1 teaspoon baking soda
Pinch of salt
½ teaspoon baking powder
1 teaspoon vanilla extract
2 cups old-fashioned oats
2 cups rice crispies or cornflakes or ¾ cup all-bran cereal

OPTIONS:
1 cup chopped walnuts or pecans
1 cup unsalted roasted peanuts
6 ounces peanut butter chips
6 ounces butterscotch morsels
6 ounces milk chocolate chips
1 cup flaked coconut
¾ cup golden raisins

Preheat oven to 350°. In a large bowl cream together the sugars, butter and then add eggs. Add the remaining ingredients, fold in choice of cereal carefully. Choose any options or combination of options and add to dough. Spoon by tablespoons onto an ungreased baking sheet and bake for 12 minutes or until very lightly browned.

SOFT GINGER SNAPS

Yield: 5 dozen
Assemble: ½ hour
Chill: 30 minutes
Bake: 6-8 minutes

1½ cups vegetable oil (or ¾ cup butter or margarine, softened)
2 cups sugar
2 eggs
½ cup light molasses
4 cups flour
4 teaspoons baking soda
1 teaspoon salt
1 tablespoon ginger
2 teaspoons cinnamon
Granulated sugar for coating

In large mixing bowl beat oil, sugar, eggs and molasses together well. Sift dry ingredients and stir into butter mixture until blended. Refrigerate dough for 1 hour. Preheat oven to 350°. Form into balls, using 1 heaping teaspoonful of dough. Roll each ball in granulated sugar and bake on ungreased baking sheet for 6 to 8 minutes. Do not overbake. Cookies will be puffy when removed from oven, but will flatten as they cool. Tops will look cracked. Cool on rack.

CHOCOLATY MACAROONS

Yield: 3-5 dozen
Assemble: 1 hour
Bake: 15-18 minutes

2 eggs
1 cup sugar
½ teaspoon vanilla extract
½ cup flour
1½ cups finely chopped macadamia nuts or walnuts
1½ cups flaked coconut
1 cup semi-sweet chocolate chips
2 teaspoons vegetable shortening
¾ cup finely chopped macadamia nuts or walnuts (optional)

Preheat oven to 325°. Grease and flour madeleine pans or tiny cupcake pans. In a medium-size bowl beat the eggs until thick and lemon colored on high speed with an electric mixer for about 3 minutes. Gradually beat in the sugar and vanilla until thick, about 3 minutes. On low speed of mixer, beat in flour until just blended. By hand, stir in nuts and coconut. Spoon about 1 tablespoon mixture into each indentation in pan. Bake for 15-18 minutes or until lightly browned. Cool in pan for 5 minutes; remove to rack to cool. Repeat with the remaining batter. Melt chocolate chips and shortening together in a small saucepan. Drizzle or trim tops of macaroons with chocolate as desired. Sprinkle with additional chopped nuts, if desired. Cool until chocolate hardens.

WALNUT SQUARES

QUICK
& EASY

Yield: 3 dozen squares
Assemble: 30 minutes
Bake: 35 minutes

FIRST LAYER:
1 cup butter, softened
½ cup sugar
2 cups flour
½ cup cornstarch

SECOND LAYER:
4 eggs
1 pound brown sugar
4 tablespoons flour
½ teaspoon baking powder
1 pound walnuts, chopped
1 7-ounce package flaked coconut

FROSTING:
3 ounces cream cheese, softened
1 teaspoon vanilla extract
1 cup powdered sugar

Preheat oven to 300°. Cream together butter and sugar in a large bowl. Add the flour and cornstarch; mix well. Press this mixture into a lightly greased cookie sheet with edges. Bake for 15 minutes. Mix together eggs, brown sugar, flour, baking powder, walnuts and coconut. Spread on top of the first layer. Bake at 300° for 15 minutes, then at 350° for 5 minutes; cool. Mix the frosting ingredients in a small bowl. Frost and cut into squares.

GRANOLA BARS

Yield: 2 dozen
Assemble: 20 minutes
Cool: 40 minutes

2 cups Quaker 100% natural cereal
1 cup old-fashioned oats
1 cup flaked coconut
¾ cup raisins or dried fruit
¾ cup butter
½ cup firmly packed brown sugar
½ cup honey
1 teaspoon vanilla extract
½ teaspoon salt

In a large bowl combine cereal, oats, coconut and raisins; set aside. In a small saucepan combine butter, brown sugar and honey. Cook over medium heat, stirring continuously until mixture reaches about 250° on a candy thermometer or the firm ball stage. Add the vanilla and salt. Pour syrup over the cereal mixture and stir until well blended. Press mixture firmly into a lightly greased 9 x 13-inch pan. Allow to cool and cut into bars.

JUAN VALDEZ MOCHA BARS

Yield: 3 dozen
    squares
Assemble: 30 minutes
Bake: 35 minutes

Note: Great for
tailgate party.

7 1-ounce squares semi-sweet chocolate
½ cup butter
1⅓ cups flour
2 teaspoons instant coffee (decaffeinated, if desired)
½ teaspoon salt
1 teaspoon baking powder
5 eggs
1½ cups sugar
3 teaspoons vanilla extract
1⅓ cups graham cracker crumbs
1 cup pecans

COFFEE GLAZE:
2 tablespoons milk
1 tablespoon butter
3 teaspoons instant coffee
2 cups powdered sugar

In a small saucepan melt chocolate with butter over low heat; cool. Combine flour, instant coffee, salt and baking powder; set aside. In a large bowl beat eggs and sugar at medium speed until light. Beat in chocolate mixture and vanilla. Stir in flour mixture, graham cracker crumbs and nuts. Pour into a greased 9 x 13-inch pan and bake at 350° for 35 minutes.

Heat milk, butter and instant coffee for glaze in a small saucepan. Add powdered sugar and blend until smooth. Glaze bars while warm. Cool and cut into squares.

CHERRY CHOCOLATE BARS (Pictured)

BOTTOM LAYER:
½ cup butter, softened
¼ cup sugar
5 tablespoons cocoa
1 teaspoon almond or vanilla extract
1 egg
2 cups graham cracker crumbs
½ cup chopped pecans

MIDDLE LAYER:
¼ cup butter, softened
2 tablespoons vanilla instant pudding mix
3 tablespoons milk
2 cups sifted powdered sugar
½ cup chopped maraschino cherries, well drained on paper towel

TOP LAYER:
4 squares semi-sweet chocolate
1 tablespoon butter

Place butter in top of double boiler. Add sugar, cocoa, almond extract and egg. Set over boiling water and stir until butter has melted and mixture resembles custard (do not overcook). Combine crumbs and nuts; blend well. Add to custard mixture and mix thoroughly. Pack evenly into a 9-inch square lightly greased pan.

For the middle layer, combine milk and pudding powder in a cup. Cream butter in a medium-size bowl; add pudding mixture. Blend in sugar and maraschino cherries; spread over the base. Refrigerate 15 minutes or longer to harden. Melt chocolate with the butter and drizzle on top with a fork (making lines). Cool and cut into triangles before storing in the refrigerator. This recipe may be doubled and placed in a 9 x 13-inch pan.

CHOCOLATE CARAMEL DELIGHTS

1½ cups flour
1½ cups old-fashioned oats
¼ teaspoon salt
½ teaspoon baking soda
1½ cups firmly packed brown sugar
1⅛ cups melted butter or margarine
14-ounce bag caramels (48)
½ cup whipping cream
1 12-ounce package milk chocolate chips

In a large bowl combine first 6 ingredients to make mix. Melt caramels and whipping cream in a saucepan over low heat. Sprinkle ½ of mix into 9 x 13-inch ungreased pan. Bake at 350° for 10-15 minutes. Sprinkle chocolate chips over baked mixture and top with melted caramel mixture; sprinkle remaining mix on top. Bake at 350° for 15 minutes.

CHOCOLATE LOVERS' FAVORITE MINT BROWNIES

Yield: 2 dozen
Assemble: 30 minutes
Bake: 30-35 minutes

BROWNIES:
2 cups sugar
1 cup butter, softened
4 eggs
4 1-ounce squares unsweetened chocolate,
 melted and slightly cooled
2½ cups sifted flour
¼ teaspoon salt
¼ teaspoon baking powder
2 teaspoons vanilla extract
1 cup broken walnuts or pecans

MINT FROSTING:
4 tablespoons butter, softened
2 tablespoons evaporated milk
2 cups powdered sugar
½ teaspoon peppermint extract
Few drops pink or green food coloring

GLAZE TOPPING:
6 tablespoons butter
2 teaspoons vanilla extract
1 cup semi-sweet chocolate chips

Preheat oven to 325°. In a large bowl cream together sugar and butter until fluffy. Beat in eggs until well blended; then add melted chocolate. Sift flour, measure, sift again with dry ingredients and add to creamed mixture along with vanilla and nuts. Spread in a greased and floured 9 x 13-inch baking pan and bake for 30 to 35 minutes or until no imprint is left when touched with finger. Do not overbake.

Mix all frosting ingredients until creamy and spread on brownies. Refrigerate 1 hour. Combine butter and chocolate chips in top of double boiler; add vanilla and blend thoroughly. Pour gently over pink or green frosting and spread by tipping pan; refrigerate.

BOOZE BROWNIES

Yield: 2 dozen
Assemble: 15 minutes
Bake: 20 minutes
Chill: 2 hours

Note: Rich and unique—copies of A PINCH OF SALT LAKE were purchased before printing on the love of this recipe alone!

1 21½-ounce fudge brownie mix (or use brownie
 base from mint brownies above)
¼ cup bourbon
1 cup butter or margarine
3 tablespoons rum
2 cups powdered sugar
1 6-ounce package semi-sweet chocolate chips
1 tablespoon vegetable shortening

Bake brownies according to package directions (or directions above, if using that base). Drizzle brownies with bourbon as soon as removed from oven; refrigerate.

Cream butter, rum and powdered sugar. Spread on cooled brownies and refrigerate again. When cold melt chocolate chips and shortening together in the top of a double boiler or microwave. Spread quickly on top of brownies; chill.

PUMPKIN PIE SQUARES

Yield: 16 servings
Assemble: 30 minutes
Bake: 1 hour

Note: Try Pumpkin Pie Squares in place of the traditional pumpkin pie for a holiday dessert.

CRUST:
1 18¼-ounce spice cake mix, reserve 1 cup
1 egg
½ cup butter, melted

FILLING:
1 30-ounce can seasoned pumpkin pie mix
2 eggs
1 6-ounce can evaporated milk

TOPPING:
1 cup reserved spice cake mix
3 tablespoons butter, melted
½ cup chopped walnuts or pecans

GARNISH:
Whipped cream or ice cream

Preheat oven to 350°. Reserve 1 cup cake mix. Mix remaining cake mix with egg and melted butter. Pat lightly in a 9 x 13-inch pan. Mix pumpkin, egg and milk. Pour over dough mixture. Add butter to reserved cake mix; add nuts. Crumble on top and bake for 1 hour. Serve hot with whipped cream or à la mode.

CREAMY CHEESECAKE

Yield: 10 servings
Assemble: 25 minutes
Bake: 35 minutes

Note: Many cheesecakes were submitted for testing and this one rated best.... It's a true prize!

1¾ cups finely crushed graham cracker crumbs
¼ cup finely chopped walnuts
½ teaspoon cinnamon
½ cup butter, melted

FILLING:
3 eggs, well-beaten
16 ounces cream cheese, softened
1 cup sugar
¼ teaspoon salt
2 teaspoons vanilla extract
½ teaspoon almond extract
3 cups sour cream

Mix graham cracker crumbs, walnuts, cinnamon and butter. Press mixture along bottom and sides of a 9-inch springform pan; set aside. Preheat oven to 375°.

Combine eggs, cream cheese, sugar, salt, vanilla and almond extracts. Beat until smooth. Blend in sour cream. Pour batter into crumb crust. Bake for 35 mintues, or until filling is set (like a custard). Serve with strawberry or raspberry sauce or a fresh fruit topping.

Yield: 12 servings
Assemble: 2 hours
Chill: 24 hours
Bake: 1 to 1½ hours

CRUST:
½ cup toasted finely chopped almonds
½ cup finely chopped Amarettini cookies
¼ cup butter, melted

FILLING:
1¾ cups heavy cream
16 ounces cream cheese, softened
¾ cup sugar
4 eggs, separated
2 tablespoons flour
½ teaspoon salt
7 tablespoons Amaretto liqueur

GLAZE:
8 ounces semi-sweet chocolate chips
4 tablespoons butter
3 tablespoons raspberry liqueur
1 tablespoon honey
50 whole blanched almonds for garnish

RASPBERRY SAUCE:
20 ounces frozen raspberries
3 tablespoons sugar
2 tablespoons raspberry liqueur
3 tablespoons cornstarch
Fresh raspberries for garnish

Butter a tight-fitting 10-inch springform pan. Invert pan and cover bottom of pan with a large piece of heavy aluminum foil, molding foil to shape of pan. Mix together toasted almonds, Amarettini cookie crumbs and ¼ cup melted butter. Pat onto bottom of pan. Place pan in freezer for 30 minutes.

Scald heavy cream and cool slightly. Beat cream cheese and sugar in a large bowl until smooth. Add egg yolks, flour and salt; beat until smooth. Gradually add the scalded cream and Amaretto. Preheat oven to 300°. Beat egg whites until stiff, but not dry, and fold into cream cheese mixture. Pour filling into chilled crust. Set springform pan in larger baking pan containing ½-inch hot water. Bake for 1 to 1½ hours or until filling is almost set. Remove cheesecake from water bath and cool completely. Refrigerate overnight.

In the top of a double boiler combine chocolate chips, butter and honey. Stir and cook over simmering water until mixture is smooth. Add raspberry liqueur and stir. Remove from water and stir until glaze is thickened (approximately 5 minutes). Remove sides of springform pan from cheesecake. Pour part of the glaze on top of the cake, tilting cheesecake to completely cover with glaze. Use a spatula to cover sides of cheesecake with glaze. Decorate top with whole blanched almonds. Refrigerate cheesecake.

Thaw frozen raspberries completely and drain well; reserve drained liquid. Put raspberries through a fine sieve to collect puree and set aside. Mix sugar and cornstarch with liquid reserved from raspberries and place in a small saucepan. Bring mixture to a boil, stirring constantly. Add

continued

continued

raspberry puree. Stir and remove from heat immediately. Add raspberry liqueur and stir. Cool and refrigerate. To serve, place raspberry sauce on crystal serving plate. Place cheesecake on top and garnish with fresh raspberries.

CHOCOLATE-ON-CHOCOLATE MOUSSE CAKE

Yield: 12-15 servings
Assemble: 1½ hours
Chill: 24 hours

CRUST:
12½ ounces (approximately 1½ packages) Nabisco chocolate wafer crumbs
½ cup butter, melted

FILLING:
16 ounces, high-quality, semi-sweet chocolate, cut into chunks
4 egg whites, room temperature
2 cups heavy cream
6 tablespoons powdered sugar
2 eggs, room temperature
4 egg yolks, room temperature

LEAVES:
8 ounces semi-sweet chocolate pieces or chips, melted
1 tablespoon butter, softened
12-15 small begonia leaves (or other waxy leaves about the size of a 50-cent piece)

GARNISH:
1 cup heavy cream
2 teaspoons powdered sugar

Grind wafer crumbs and melted butter together in the bowl of a food processor or blender. Press into bottom and up sides of a 10-inch springform pan; chill.

Melt 16 ounces of semi-sweet chocolate pieces in a double boiler; cool slightly. In a large bowl beat egg whites until stiff; but not dry. In a medium-size bowl beat heavy cream with powdered sugar until soft peaks form. Place melted chocolate into a large mixing bowl. Add 2 eggs and beat well. Add 4 egg yolks to chocolate mixture one at a time, beating well after each addition. Lighten the chocolate mixture by adding a small amount of beaten egg white and a small amount of the whipped cream. Fold the whipped cream into chocolate mixture. Then fold in the egg whites. Pour filling into chilled crust. Chill uncovered for at least 6 hours or overnight.

Melt semi-sweet chocolate pieces with 1 tablespoon butter in a double boiler. Using a spoon, "paint" the **backs** of the begonia leaves with the chocolate mixture. Place on a plate and chill at least 6 hours.

Beat cream and powdered sugar together until soft peaks form. With a pastry bag, pipe whipped cream around the edges of the chilled pie and make flower-like whipped cream decorations in the center. Peel leaves from the chocolate and arrange around the whipped cream flowers. Loosen crust from pan with a sharp knife and remove pan sides. Arrange any extra leaves around cake on serving tray.

CHOCOLATE YULE LOG

Yield: 16 servings
Assemble: 45 minutes
Bake: 20-25 minutes

CAKE:
6 eggs, room temperature and separated
½ teaspoon cream of tartar
1 cup sugar, divided
1 teaspoon vanilla extract
4 tablespoons cocoa
4 tablespoons flour
¼ teaspoon salt

WHIPPED CREAM FILLING:
1 cup heavy cream
¼ cup powdered sugar
½ teaspoon vanilla extract

CREAMY CHOCOLATE ICING:
¾ cup sugar
¾ cup light cream
1¼ cups shaved chocolate (use 4-ounces German Sweet
  Chocolate and 3 ounces unsweetened chocolate)
Powdered sugar as needed
Maraschino cherries for garnish
Candied red cherries for garnish
Candied green cherries for garnish

CHOCOLATE CUSTARD SAUCE:
2 tablespoons cornstarch
½ cup plus 2 tablespoons sugar
⅛ teaspoon salt
2 cups milk
4 tablespoons butter
2 ounces (2 squares) grated unsweetened chocolate

Beat egg whites in large bowl until frothy. Add cream of tartar and beat until stiff. Gradually add ½ cup sugar, beating constantly, until very stiff peaks form; set aside. Beat egg yolks until thick and lemon-colored. Beat 1 teaspoon vanilla and the remaining ½ cup sugar. Sift together cocoa, flour and salt. Beat into yolk mixture. Preheat oven to 325°. Gradually fold egg yolk mixture into egg white mixture. Spread to ½-inch thickness in shallow 16 x 11-inch jelly roll pan lined with well-greased waxed paper. Bake for approximately 20-25 minutes or until surface springs back when touched. Turn upside-down onto a towel sprinkled with powdered sugar. Immediately remove waxed paper from cake. Roll cake, with towel, lengthwise. (Rolling towel with cake prevents cake from sticking together.) Unroll when cool. Place cake on waxed paper and remove the towel.

For filling, whip heavy cream in a small bowl until stiff. Beat in powdered sugar and vanilla. Spread on cooled cake and reroll carefully; chill.

For icing, in a medium-size saucepan combine sugar and light cream. Cook over low heat just to boiling, stirring often. Pour slowly over shaved

continued

continued

chocolate in a bowl. Beat until chocolate is melted and mixture is smooth. Add powdered sugar as needed for spreading consistency. Spread chocolate icing on rolled cake, pulling spatula down length of roll to simulate log-look. Decorate with maraschino cherries and candied cherries. Make leaves from candied green cherries or use small sprigs of fresh holly or Oregon grape leaves, washed and dried thoroughly. Chill until ready to serve. Accompany with Chocolate Custard Sauce.

For sauce, mix together cornstarch, sugar and salt in medium-size saucepan. Stir in milk and bring mixture to a boil over low heat, stirring constantly, for 1 minute. Add butter and chocolate. Boil, stirring constantly, until thick and smooth (approximately 2 minutes). Cool. Serve spooned over individual slices of yule log.

BOURBON-WRAPPED WHITE FRUITCAKE

Yield: 3 loaves
Assemble: 2 days
Bake: 90 minutes

1 pound red candied cherries, reserve 9
1 pound golden raisins
1½ pounds whole pecans, reserve 30
½ pound green candied pineapple
½ pound citron melon
⅓ cup bourbon
6 egg whites
1 pound butter, room temperature
2 cups sugar
6 egg yolks
4 cups flour
1½ ounces lemon extract (that's right!)

Brown paper bags for pan liners
Cheesecloth
Bourbon for soaking cheesecloth

In a very large bowl marinate all fruit and nuts in bourbon for 24 hours at room temperature, stirring occasionally. Cut brown paper liners for three 5 x 9-inch loaf pans. In a large mixing bowl beat egg whites until stiff but not dry. Cream butter, sugar and egg yolks together in a large bowl. Add flour and lemon extract; mix thoroughly. Fold in stiffly beaten egg whites. Preheat oven to 300°. Lightly dredge the fruit and nuts (except portion reserved for decoration) with a small sprinkling of flour and add to the batter. Spoon mixture into three paper-lined pans. Decorate tops with reserved fruit and nuts.

Place a pan of water on the top rack of the oven. Bake the fruitcakes at 300° for 1 hour and 16 minutes. Reset oven temperature to 350° and bake 7 minutes longer. Turn oven off and continue baking 7 minutes. Remove from oven and allow to cool in pan for 10 minutes. Remove cakes from pans and allow them to cool before removing the paper liners. Wrap cakes in bourbon-soaked cheesecloth (not wet, but slightly damp), then in foil. Refrigerate. Best to make cakes 2 weeks to 1 month ahead of serving or giving. Refresh cheesecloth in bourbon each week and rewrap.

BOSTON CREAM PIE

Yield: 12-16 servings
(2 cakes)
Assemble: 60 minutes
Bake: 25-30 minutes

1¼ cups sifted cake flour
1 teaspoon baking powder
¼ teaspoon salt
1 cup sugar, divided
1 egg yolk
2 eggs
¼ cup orange juice
1 tablespoon grated orange rind
¼ cup water
⅓ cup sifted cake flour
⅛ teaspoon salt
2 eggs, lightly beaten
2 cups scalded milk
1 teaspoon vanilla extract
¾ cup sugar
2 tablespoons butter
Whipped cream
Grated chocolate

Preheat oven to 350°. In a small bowl sift flour once and measure. Add baking powder and salt and sift together 3 times; set aside. In a large bowl mix ½ cup sugar with eggs and yolk and beat until thick and lemon-colored. Gradually add remaining sugar. Add orange juice, rind and water. Add dry ingredients to egg mixture and beat until well combined. Grease and flour two 9-inch round cake pans. Turn cake mixture into pans and bake for 25-30 minutes at 350°. While still warm, very carefully split cakes horizontally and place on rack to cool.

Combine ⅓ cup cake flour, ¾ cup sugar and ⅛ teaspoon salt in the top of a double boiler. Add eggs then a small amount of milk, stirring vigorously. Add remaining milk and place over double boiler; cook 15 minutes or until thickened, stirring constantly. Add butter and allow mixture to cool. Add vanilla (use electric mixer to blend if mixture is too lumpy). Spread filling between 2 cake layers. Top cake with whipped cream and garnish with grated chocolate.

RAISIN CHOCOLATE CHIP BUNDT

QUICK
& EASY

Yield: 12-15 servings
Assemble: 10 minutes
Bake: 55-60 minutes

1 18¼-ounce package German chocolate cake mix
(pudding-in-mix type)
2 teaspoons cinnamon
1 21-ounce can raisin pie filling
3 eggs
1 cup semi-sweet chocolate chips
Powdered sugar to dust

Preheat oven to 350°. In a large bowl combine the cake mix and cinnamon. Beat in raisin pie filling and then add eggs, one at a time, blending thoroughly after each addition. Fold in chocolate chips.

Pour batter into a greased and floured bundt pan. Bake for 55-60 minutes. Cool cake in pan for approximately 10 minutes. Remove cake to cooling rack and dust with powdered sugar.

ELEGANT LAYERED APPLE CAKE

Yield: 10-12 servings
Assemble: 30 minutes
Bake: 30-40 minutes

Note: This triple-layer apple cake makes a very professional looking birthday cake.

3 cups sifted flour
1½ teaspoons baking soda
½ teaspoon salt
3 cups finely grated, pared, tart apples
½ cup chopped walnuts
1 teaspoon grated lemon peel
2 cups sugar
1½ cups vegetable oil
2 eggs

FROSTING:
8 ounces cream cheese, softened
½ cup butter, softened
16 ounces powdered sugar
1 teaspoon vanilla extract
1 cup finely chopped walnuts

Grease well and flour three 9-inch round cake pans. Preheat oven to 350°. Sift flour with baking soda and salt; set aside. In a small bowl combine grated apple, nuts and lemon peel. In a large bowl combine sugar, oil and eggs; beat well with a wooden spoon. Add sifted dry ingredients mixing until smooth. Incorporate apple mixture; stir until well combined. Spread evenly into prepared pans. Bake for 30 to 40 minutes or until surface springs back when pressed lightly. Cool in pans for 10 minutes. Remove from pans and cool thoroughly on wire racks.

Prepare frosting by creaming together all ingredients except nuts. Frost between layers, on sides and top. Press nuts around sides of cake. One may reserve a bit of icing to pipe around the top edge of cake. Refrigerate until serving time.

SOUR CREAM RHUBARB CAKE

Yield: 12-15 servings
Assemble: 20 minutes
Bake: 35-40 minutes

½ cup vegetable shortening
1½ cups brown sugar
1 egg
1 teaspoon baking soda
1 cup sour cream
2 cups flour
1 teaspoon vanilla extract
1½ cups diced rhubarb, uncooked

TOPPING:
½ cup sugar
1 tablespoon butter
1 teaspoon cinnamon
1½ cups chopped pecans or walnuts

Preheat oven to 375°. Grease and flour a 9 x 13-inch pan. In a large bowl cream together the shortening, sugar and egg. Mix baking soda with sour cream and add to the shortening mixture alternately with flour. Stir in vanilla and rhubarb. Pour into pan, sprinkle with combined topping ingredients and bake for 35 to 40 minutes.

ORANGE KISS-ME CAKE

Yield: 12 servings
Assemble: 20 minutes
Bake: 40-50 minutes

1 large orange (squeeze ⅓ cup juice for topping)
1 cup raisins
⅓ cup walnuts
2 cups flour
1 teaspoon baking soda
1 teaspoon salt
1 cup sugar
½ cup shortening
1 cup milk, divided
2 eggs

ORANGE NUT TOPPING:
⅓ cup reserved orange juice
⅓ cup sugar
1 teaspoon cinnamon
¼ cup chopped walnuts

Preheat oven to 350°. Squeeze juice from orange; set aside for topping. In a food processor grind together the remaining orange (pulp and rind), raisins and walnuts. (one may use a blender for this step, using a combination of ¼ of each ingredient at a time). Sift together the flour, soda, salt and sugar. In a large bowl combine the shortening with dry ingredients, alternately, and ¾ cup of the milk. Beat for 2 minutes until batter is well blended. Add 2 eggs and the remaining ¼ cup milk; beat 2 minutes longer. Fold orange/raisin mixture into batter. Pour into a well-greased and lightly floured 9 x 13-inch pan. Bake for 40-50 minutes.

Remove cake from oven and cool slightly. Drizzle reserved orange juice over warm cake. Combine sugar, cinnamon and chopped walnuts. Sprinkle this mixture over warm cake.

GLAZED CARROT CAKE

Yield: 12 servings
Assemble: 30 minutes
Bake: 55 minutes

Note: This recipe originated from California gold rush days when a heavy nutritious cake provided energy and stored well. The glaze makes this an excellent cake for transporting without mess, but a favorite cream cheese frosting over the glaze adds an elegant touch for more festive dining.

2 cups flour
2 teaspoons baking soda
2 teaspoons cinnamon
½ teaspoon salt
3 eggs
¾ cup vegetable oil
¾ cup buttermilk
2 cups sugar
2 teaspoons vanilla extract
1 8-ounce can crushed pineapple, drained
2 cups grated carrots (approximately 5 large carrots)
3½ ounces flaked coconut
1 cup coarsely chopped walnuts or pecans

GLAZE:
½ cup sugar
½ teaspoon baking soda
¼ cup buttermilk
¼ cup butter
1 teaspoon corn syrup
½ teaspoon vanilla extract

continued

continued

Grease and flour a 9 x 13-inch pan. Sift together first 4 ingredients; set aside. Preheat oven to 350°. In a large bowl beat the eggs and add oil, buttermilk, sugar and vanilla; mix well. Add flour mixture, pineapple, carrots, coconut and nuts; mix well. Pour batter into pan. Bake for 55 minutes, or until toothpick inserted in center of cake comes out clean.

Prepare glaze by combining first 5 glaze ingredients in a saucepan. Bring to a boil and cook for 5 minutes. Remove from heat and stir in vanilla. Pour glaze over hot cake.

SURPRISE-FILLED CUPCAKES

QUICK
& EASY

Yield: 2½ dozen
Assemble: 20 minutes
Bake: 20 minutes

Note: What could be better for school lunch boxes?

SURPRISE FILLING:
8 ounces cream cheese, softened
⅓ cup sugar
1 egg
Pinch of salt
6 ounces semi-sweet chocolate chips

CHOCOLATE CUPCAKES:
3 cups flour
2 cups sugar
4 tablespoons cocoa
2 teaspoons baking soda
1 teaspoon salt
2 tablespoons cider vinegar
2 teaspoons vanilla extract
¾ cup vegetable oil
2 cups water

BANANA CUPCAKES:
2¼ cups cake flour
1⅔ cups sugar
⅔ cup vegetable oil
⅔ cup buttermilk
1¼ teaspoons baking powder
1¼ teaspoons baking soda
3 eggs
3 cups mashed ripe bananas (6 medium bananas)
¼ teaspoon freshly ground nutmeg
¾ cup finely chopped pecans or walnuts (optional)

Mix filling ingredients together in a small bowl; set aside. For chocolate cupcakes, combine first 5 ingredients in a large bowl. Gradually add next 4 liquid ingredients and beat for 2 minutes at medium speed.

For banana cupcakes, combine all ingredients in a large bowl. Beat on high speed for 3 minutes.

Use cupcake liners in muffin tins and fill ½ full with batter of choice. Drop ½ tablespoonful of Surprise Filling in cups then cover with more batter (each cup should be ⅔ to ¾ full). Bake at 375° for 20 minutes.

Chocolate batter and banana batter make wonderful cakes baked in 9 x 13-inch greased and floured pans for 45-60 minutes. May also be made in greased and floured bundt pans for 45-60 minutes. Surprise Filling may be dolloped randomly in cake batter, if desired.

PUMPKIN CAKE ROLL

Yield: 16-20 servings
Assemble: 60 minutes
Bake: 15 minutes

CAKE ROLL:
3 eggs
1 cup sugar
⅔ cup pumpkin (not pumpkin pie mix)
1 teaspoon lemon juice
¾ cup flour
1 teaspoon baking powder
2 teaspoons cinnamon
1 teaspoon ginger
½ teaspoon nutmeg
½ teaspoon salt
1 cup chopped pecans

FILLING:
1 cup powdered sugar
8 ounces cream cheese, softened
4 tablespoons butter, softened
½ teaspoon vanilla extract

In a large bowl beat 3 eggs on high speed with an electric mixer for 5 minutes. Gradually beat in sugar. From this point on, fold in all ingredients; DO NOT BEAT. Preheat oven to 375°. Fold in the pumpkin and lemon juice. Fold in flour, baking powder, cinnamon, ginger, nutmeg and salt. Spread this mixture onto a 10 x 15-inch jelly roll sheet that has been heavily greased and floured. Sprinkle with the chopped nuts. Bake for 15 minutes. Immediately turn out onto a dish towel that has been sprinkled with powdered sugar. While still hot, roll the cake in the towel lengthwise to form a roll. Place on wire rack to cool. When cake has cooled, unroll, remove towel and spread on filling.

To prepare filling, combine powdered sugar, cream cheese, butter and vanilla and beat until smooth. Spread filling over cake and reroll. Refrigerate until the filling sets. Sprinkle top of cake roll with powdered sugar. Slice into ½-inch pieces and serve.

PANAMA TORTE

Yield: 8-10 servings
Assemble: 60 minutes
Bake: 45-55 minutes

TORTE:
¾ cup sugar
7 eggs, separated
6 tablespoons grated semi-sweet chocolate
1½ cups grated almonds

CHOCOLATE CREAM:
6 tablespoons unsalted butter
½ cup sugar
½ teaspoon vanilla
3 squares semi-sweet chocolate
2 eggs

⅔ cup sliced toasted almonds for garnish

continued

continued

Preheat oven to 325°. In a medium-size bowl beat egg whites until they form stiff peaks; set aside. Beat sugar and egg yolks together in a large bowl until fluffy. Add grated semi-sweet chocolate. Fold almonds into chocolate mixture, then fold into egg whites. Pour mixture into a greased and floured 9-inch springform pan. Bake for 45-55 minutes, or until torte springs back to touch. Remove sides of pan and allow to cool slightly. Remove bottom of pan and cool completely on rack.

To make chocolate cream, melt chocolate on low heat or in a microwave. Beat butter in a medium-size bowl until creamy. Add vanilla, sugar, eggs and melted semi-sweet chocolate to butter and beat until mixture is smooth, light and fluffy.

Assemble by slicing the torte in half horizontally. Cover the first layer of the torte with ¼ to ⅓ of the chocolate cream mixture. Place remaining torte layer over cream mixture. Cover the top and sides of the torte with the remaining chocolate cream. Garnish with toasted almonds on top and around sides.

GINGERCAKE WITH CINNAMON APPLE RINGS

QUICK
& EASY

Yield: 10-12 servings
Assemble: 20 minutes
Bake: 25 minutes

½ cup sugar
1 cup molasses
½ cup butter, softened
1 teaspoon ginger
½ teaspoon cloves
1 teaspoon cinnamon
1 cup buttermilk
2 teaspoons baking soda
2 cups flour
2 eggs, beaten

CINNAMON APPLE RINGS:
4 Granny Smith apples, peeled, cored whole
** and cut into ¼-inch rings**
2 teaspoons cinnamon
Pinch of freshly grated nutmeg, or to taste
½ cup powdered sugar
3 tablespoons cold unsalted butter, cut into bits

Vanilla ice cream

Preheat oven to 350°. Mix first 6 ingredients in a large bowl. Dissolve baking soda in buttermilk. Gradually add flour and buttermilk to butter mixture. Add beaten eggs to the buttermilk batter, stirring as little as possible. Grease and flour two 8 or 9-inch cake pans. Pour in the batter and bake for 25 minutes. Do not overbake as it is a very light cake. Remove from pans. Cut into wedges and serve with hot cinnamon apples topped with vanilla ice cream.

Arrange apple rings in one layer on a buttered jelly roll pan. Combine the cinnamon, nutmeg and sugar and sift over the apples; dot with butter. Broil apples under a preheated broiler approximately 2 inches from heat source until apples are tender and carmelized. Place apples over individual cake slices. Top with ice cream and drizzle with pan juices.

FUDGE RIBBON CAKE

Yield: 16-18 servings
Assemble: 30 minutes
Bake: 50-60 minutes

2 tablespoons butter, softened
8 ounces cream cheese, softened
2½ cups sugar, divided
1 tablespoon cornstarch
3 eggs
2 tablespoons milk
1½ teaspoons vanilla extract, divided
1 teaspoon salt
1 teaspoon baking powder
½ teaspoon baking soda
½ cup butter, softened
1⅓ cups milk, divided
4 1-ounce envelopes Nestles ChocoBake
2 cups flour

FUDGE FROSTING:
½ cups butter, softened
4 1-ounce envelopes Nestles ChocoBake
2 cups powdered sugar
1 teaspoon vanilla extract

Cream butter and cream cheese in a small bowl. While beating, add ½ cup sugar, cornstarch, 1 egg, 2 tablespoons milk and ½ teaspoon vanilla. Beat on high speed until smooth and creamy; set aside.

Grease and flour a 9 x 13-inch pan. Preheat oven to 350°. In a large bowl combine 2 cups sugar, salt, baking powder and baking soda. Add butter and 1 cup milk. Blend at low speed then beat on higher speed for 1½ minutes. Add ⅓ cup milk, 2 eggs, ChocoBake, 1 teaspoon vanilla and flour. Beat on medium-high speed for 3 minutes. Spread half of the batter into pan, spoon cream cheese mixture over batter and top with remaining batter. Bake for 50 to 60 minutes.

For Fudge Frosting, melt butter in a small saucepan; remove from heat. Add ChocoBake and vanilla. Stir in powdered sugar, blending until smooth and creamy. Frost when cake is cool.

TOFFEE CRUNCH CAKE

QUICK
& EASY

Yield: 12 servings
Assemble: 30 minutes
Bake: 30-35 minutes

Note: This is a heavy cake with the toffee sinking to the bottom. It does not require frosting and travels well.

1 cup firmly packed brown sugar
1 cup sugar
1 teaspoon vanilla extract
½ cup margarine
2 cups flour
½ teaspoon salt
6 1⅛-ounce crushed chocolate-covered toffee bars
  (6 Heath bars work well)
1 egg, beaten
1 cup buttermilk
1 teaspoon baking soda

Preheat oven to 350°. In a large bowl mix together with a fork the first 6 ingredients. Remove 1 cup of this mixture to a small bowl. To the reserved cup, add the coarsely crushed toffee bars; set aside. To the remaining dry ingredients, add the beaten egg, buttermilk and baking soda; mix well.

Pour batter into a 9 x 13-inch greased and floured pan. Sprinkle with remaining dry candy mixture. Bake for 30-35 minutes.

FRESH PLUM CAKE

Yield: 6-8 servings
Assemble: 25 minutes
Bake: 45 minutes

2 cups fresh tart plums, pitted and cut in half
1¼ cups sugar, divided
½ cup butter, softened
½ teaspoon lemon extract or 2 teaspoons fresh lemon juice
2 eggs
1 cup flour
1 teaspoon baking powder
½ teaspoon salt
½ teaspoon cinnamon
2 tablespoons sugar
1 teaspoon cinnamon
Crème fraîche (page 218), sour cream or whipped cream
  for topping

Arrange the halved plums, cut-side up in the bottom of a greased 7 x 11 or 9-inch square pan. Sprinkle with ¼ cup sugar. Preheat oven to 375°.

In a large bowl cream together the butter, lemon extract or juice and remaining 1 cup sugar. Add eggs, one at a time, beating well after each addition. Sift flour into the bowl and add the baking powder, salt and ½ teaspoon cinnamon. Stir until well blended. Spoon batter over the plums. Mix 2 tablespoons sugar with 1 teaspoon cinnamon and sprinkle over the batter. Bake for 35-45 minutes or until cake pulls away from sides of pan. Serve warm or cool, topped with crème fraîche, sour cream or whipped cream.

APRICOT MERINGUE CAKE

Yield: 16 servings
Assemble: 20 minutes
Bake: 60 minutes

1 cup butter, softened
2 cups flour
2 tablespoons sugar
6 eggs, separated
2 cups sugar
4 tablespoons flour
½ teaspoon salt
1 cup light cream
5 cups fresh apricots, pitted and quartered
⅔ cup sugar
2 teaspoons vanilla extract
Flaked coconut (optional)

Preheat oven to 350°. Blend butter, flour and 2 tablespoons sugar in a large bowl. Press mixture evenly in an ungreased 10 x 15-inch pan (or 9 x 13-inch pan). Bake for 10 minutes. In a large bowl blend egg yolks, sugar, flour, salt and light cream. Fold in prepared apricots. Pour mixture over hot crust. Bake for 40 minutes (45 minutes if using a 9 x 13-inch pan).

Beat egg whites in a medium-size bowl until foamy. Gradually beat in sugar until peaks form. Do not underbeat. Stir in vanilla extract. Spread mixture over baked apricot cake. Sprinkle with coconut, if desired. Bake for 10 minutes. Turn off heat and leave cake in oven for an additional 10 minutes. Remove from oven and cool.

HARVEY WALLBANGER CAKE

QUICK & EASY

Yield: 12-15 servings
Assemble: 10 minutes
Bake: 45-50 minutes

Note: A great party cake, transports well, and is fun to decorate with fresh daisies in the center and around the sides.

1 18¼-ounce package yellow cake mix
1 4-ounce instant vanilla pudding mix
½ cup vegetable oil
½ cup sugar
4 eggs
¼ cup vodka
¼ cup Galliano liqueur (exactly 1 mini-bottle)
¾ cup orange juice

GLAZE:
1 cup powdered sugar, sifted
1½ tablespoons vodka
1½ tablespoons Galliano liqueur
1½ tablespoons orange juice

Preheat oven to 350°. In a large bowl mix together cake mix, pudding, oil, sugar, eggs, vodka, Galliano and orange juice. Beat well. Pour batter into a well-greased and floured bundt pan. Bake for 45-50 minutes. Allow cake to remain in pan for approximately 10 minutes before removing.

For glaze, combine powdered sugar, vodka, Galliano, and orange juice. Drizzle glaze over cooled cake.

CITRUS-GLAZED POUND CAKE

Yield: 16 servings
Assemble: 15 mintues
Bake: 1 hour

1 cup butter
2 cups sugar
3 eggs
3 cups flour
2 teaspoons baking powder
½ teaspoon salt
1 12-ounce can evaporated milk
2 teaspoons lemon or almond extract

CITRUS GLAZE:
1½ cups powdered sugar
Juice of 1 lemon
Juice of ½ orange

Cream butter and sugar until fluffy. Beat in eggs one at a time, mixing well. Sift together flour, baking powder and salt. Add dry mixture alternately with milk. Stir in flavoring. Beat until well mixed and light. Pour into greased and lightly floured angel cake, bundt pan or 2 standard-size loaf tins. Preheat oven to 350°.

Bake for 60 minutes or until cake tests done. Cool on rack 30 minutes before removing from pan; remove onto cake plate.

Combine glaze ingredients together and pour over cake while still warm.

CONTRIBUTORS

Sincere thanks to our contributors, individuals who took the time to share their favorite recipes for consideration. All recipes contained in A PINCH OF SALT LAKE came from the kitchens of the following fine cooks:

Jane Abe
Olivia Guerra Agraz
Nina Saffari Akhavan
Coralie Ashton Alder
Kay Rasmussen Alder
Sue Ann Johnson Alder
Julie Cuthbert Allen
Susan Peterson Amoss
Alice Wilkinson Anderson
Jan Tolboe Anderson
Mary Ann Matthews Anderson
Susan Breinholt Anderson
Joey McCollins Archer
Neena Diumenti Ashton
Marilyn Miller Askins
Carolyn Bowers Astin
Robin Temple Bailey
Cindy Elliott Baldwin
Kathryn Ball
Rebecca Nord Bamberger
Diane Thatcher Barlow
Daryl Cameron Barrett
Julie Ashton Barrett
William W. Barrett
DeDe Gorey Barrigar
Mary Moreton Barton
Rosemary Curtis Barton
Lary Ann Forsberg Bateman
Douglas F. Bates
Sandi Alm Becraft
Bobi Birkbeck Bench
Nanette Jackson Benowitz
Karen Luderman Bettilyon
Dennis Bird
Denise Guiney Black
Denise Bondy
Kathleen Miller Bourne
Nancy Ann Cockayne Bowers
Didi Anderson Bowles
Marcia McBride Bown
Clara F. Brennan
Amy Elizabeth Brooke
Penny Simpson Brooke
Janene Cooley Brown
Lynda Hofhein Brown
Marcia Brown
Margaret Roberts Brown
Martha Hancey Brown
Sally Rich Burbridge
Susan Van Voorhis Burdett
Jeanne Bury
Sara Lea Spencer Bury
Camille Tibbetts Bushman
Kim Koller Butler
Marcia Roylance Cameron
Joanne Barber Cassity
Elizabeth Earl Chalmers
Amy Hathaway Christensen
Ann Richard Christensen

Kathlene Hansen Christensen
Estelle Christopulos
DeAnna Thomas Clark
Kathleen Drummond Clark
Mary Brennan Clark
Laura Herring Clinger
Betty Jensen Clyde
Elaine Clinger Clyde
Dena Papanikolas Cocorinis
Cindy Fregulia Collins
Judy Condie
Julie Congdon
Karen Daniels Conley
Elvera Bird Cooley
Alyce Yanik Covey
Joan Nelson Creer
Jan Aland Crockett
Jim L. Crockett
Mona Hirschi Daniels
Peggy Brown Dayton
Genevieve Fontana DePaulis
Deer Valley Resort
Connie Jacobsen Degn
Sidney Bullen Dibble
Karen Hansen Dingman
Helen Roberts Dinwoody
Connie Jo Tomlin Dobson
Andree D. Dreyfous
Mary Driver
Jan Kiehl Duane
Rebecca Dean Duberow
Mitzi Manson Dunford
Catherine Eaker Dunn
June Cloward Dunn
Kathie Erickson Durham
Sandi Dedekind Eberhardt
Karen Becker Edson
Bryan Bird Eldredge
Nanette Kibbe Elliott
Sue Jones Ellis
Susan Johnson Ellison
Drew Ellsworth
Sandra Snow Ellsworth
Connie Lefavor Engh
Diane Crandall Epperson
Adrienne Earl Eskelson
Gwen Knight Eubank
Diane Murdock Evershed
Rolayne Poate Fairclough
Stacy Greenfield Ferguson
Danielle Fielden
Tracie Pastore Fielden
Debbi Fields
Judy Wilcox Fillmore
Susan B. Finegan
Dorothy Denton Folland
Kathy Harr Forgie
Linda MacFarlane Forsey
Melinda Mattsson Fowler

Cathryn Baldwin Francis
Tricia Economou Frech
Cheryl Grubb Frederickson
JoAnn Robinson Freed
Ann Trevithick Fullmer
Barbara Trunnell Gaddis
Irene Covey Gaddis
Carolyn Smith Gardner
Catherine Cannon Gardner
Lynn Daynes Gardner
Katharine Bagley Garff
Mary Ann Goddard Garner
Frances Clark Garrett
Marny Keenan Gaylord
Vicky Turpin Gaylord
Loraine Mitchell Gerovac
Barbara Aspden Gibbons
Jenifer Brennan Gibbons
Virginia Lambourne Gibbons
Bonnie Lindjord Gilley
Barbara Chytraus Gilson
Robin Giovacchini
Rosanne Cline Gordon
Patricia Shurtleff Grant
Katherine Earl Green
Kay Buchanan Greene
Penelope Steele Grikscheit
Mary Lane O'Donnel Grisley
Josie Anderson Groesbeck
Billie Guiney
Karl B. Guiney
Marianne Guiney
Elizabeth Driscoll Guss
Millie Duncan Hagen
Mickey Lieber Hale
Vicki Firmage Halgren
Christina Buxton Halliday
Karren Kelly Hammer
Claudia Russell Hammond
Mary Sweet Hancey
Myra Ullman Hansen
Shanna Bess Hansen
Alice Kirkpatrick Harcrow
Sue Harries
Elizabeth Harte
Margaret Ashley Hatch
MaryLou Murphy Hauck
Suzanne Reed Hawkes
Shonnie Stillman Hays
Jeri Rakow Helgren
Marguerite Marceau Henderson
Noelle Henderson
Susan McRoberts Hermance
Suzanne Swain Hess
Susan Hessler
Judi E. Waters Higginson
DruAnn Stevens Hill
Martha Reilly Hinchman
Carolyn Cushman Hinckley

Ann Butler Hinds
Marilyn Dawson Hinds
Judee John Holder
Patricia Mowatt Holman
Ellen Shott Holmes
Pamela Baldwin Holt
Rosemary Arm Holt
Jolie Coleman Howard
Peggy Howe
Susan Tobinski Howe
Margeo Stiny Howell
Mary Ann Barton Howell
Dorothy Huger
Enid Van Ert Hughes
Elizabeth Miller Huish
Elizabeth Brandis Hunt
Karen Jo Page Hyde
Marian Watkins Ingham
Rhonda Simmons Irvine
Vicky Hawken Jackson
Jeanne Nebeker Jardine
Winnifred Cannon Jardine
Barbara Cecil Johnson
Mary Jane Egan Johnson
Patsy Hicks Johnson
Tanya Hughes Johnson
Pat Patterick Johnston
Susan Cooper Jones
Sonia Jorgensen
Cherie Jeanne Gee Justice
Susan McNair Kartchner
Faye Hooker Keller
Joann Olson Keller
Verda Kessler
Jane Bering Kimball
Patricia Culp Kimball
Julie Killian Kincheloe
Florence King
Elizabeth Stout Kirk
June Patzner Krough
Colleen Manning Kunz
Connie Gill Kwant
Terry Enquist Landa
Marjorie Johnson Lane
Selma Vance-Lauritzen
Barbara Hunt Lehnhof
Toni LaBonte Lehtinen
Catherine Burton Lence
Georgie Eskelson Lewis
Marie Stewart Lewis
Sherlyn Hart Lewis
Judy Bunk Liapis
Mary Malles Lindjord
Deborah Martens Linke
Nettie Simmons Linton
Jackie Diaz Little
Susan Sorensen Litchfield
Susan Null Lockwood
Fran Coltharp Loos

Darlene Lowe
Pamela Loyola
Nancy Sonntag Lyon
Paula Mahan
Florence Ray Malmquist
Colleen Malouf
Judy Jensen Malouf
Jonette Cocorinis Mangum
Betty Lou Cloward Mann
Ann Kolemainen Marlowe
Carol Woods Martin
Molly Mason
Norma Warenski Matheson
Nancy Nortz Mathews
Billie Maxfield
Dorothy Parrish Maxfield
Colleen Hinckley Maxwell
Pinky Brady McBrier
Karen McLeese
Paula Foil McMahan
Grace Dirkle Meldrom
Denise Heinee Metcalf
Kathie Merrill Miller
Diane Colman Mills
Karen Cooley Milne
Karen Burton Miner
Elizabeth Clark Mleynek
Cecilia Mary Coyne Moffat
Susan LeCheminant Montgomery
Donna Lou Morgan
Frances Grundmann Morgan
Vicky Long Mori
Vicki Allen Mortensen
Lynne Morton
Christie Timmons Mullen
Susan Harmston Mullins
Jim Murphy
Berna Roark Murray
Lori Mann Nadeau
Brooke Ence Nelsen
Joan Nielson Nelson
Molly Moore Nelson
Joan Nichol
Suzanne Sutton Nowels
Karen Thatcher Nugent
Gay Lerwill Null
Sandra England Okland
Bonnie Brain Oettli
Marianne Dobson Ogaard
Mary Jane Ogan
Shauna Gardner Olson
Tricia Forsey Olson
Marie Osmond
Barbara Butters Owen
Constance L. Painter
Elizabeth Watson Parker
Diana Rowan Parton
Margie Sesler Patton

Debie Smith Pearl
Catherine Barton Pederson
Maxine Kennedy Pedersen
Vicki Speros Peters
Gayle Cornaby Petersen
Patricia Snyder Petersen
Beverly James Peterson
Karen Fotheringham Peterson
Linda Graham Peterson
Rhea Allen Peterson
Melissa Waters Phillips
Carol Pia
Jacque Jensen Poore
Kathy Larsen Poulson
Merrilee Tanner Preece
Pat Pinder Provost
Sue Purcell
Francine Alvey Quinn
Shari Halgren Quinney
Karen Jorgensen Raemer
John R. Rains
Mary Jane Johnson Rains
Terry Breznick Rampton
Joni Ramsey
T. Upton Ramsey
Lynne Vincent Rasmussen
Marilyn Wilmarth Rasmussen
Annelie Frerking Rathke
Rebecca Painter Ravizza
Sue Johnson Razor
Pat Beck Reddick
Marian Reed
Barbara Hardy Reese
Sunny Henderson Reinhold
Margaret Nelson Reiser
Sherry Douglas Remund
Francis Rich
Nanette Ulricksen Richard
Evelyn Richards
Lesley Painter Rigby
Linda Roberts
Terry Robins
Rosemary Schaefer Roe
Laurel Parker Rohlfing
Marcia Mayhew Rollins
Karen Greene Romney
Linda Rumel Rose
Jacqueline Woolf Rosenblatt
Bette Coleman Ross
Francis Ruf
Lenessa Tingey Rumel
Kathy Lynn Sargent
Margaret Patterson Sargent
Lynda Blackwell Schneiman
Pamela Moeller Schroeder
Dari McQuarrie Scott
Mary Ann Jensen Sheffield
Susan Archibald Sheldon

Alice Neff Shearer
Brenda Moore Shockey
Ann Ferguson Sill
Lynda Mills Simmons
Mary Soter Simos
Joan Ivie Slagle
Denise Rapp Smith
Liz Lloyd Smith
Renee Widner Smith
Sharon Ailes Smith
Marilyn Miller Smolka
Stella Madsen Smoot
Agnes Snow
Beth Snow
Dale Temple Snyder
Cynthia Dix Soderberg
Elizabeth Oblad Sonne
Laurie Ann Sonneborn
Lucy Sorensen
Margaret Sorensen
Stephanie Kunz Spangler
Karen Mann Spencer
Gwen Rowley Springmeyer
Joanne Spruance
Pat Spencer Starkey
Lurlene Romney Steele
Barbara Reeves Stevens
Amy Darger Stewart
Lydia O. Stillman
Kathleen Dunn Stone
Carolee Reinhold Stout
Sherry Christman Stuart
Kay Ritchie Sundberg
JoAnne Call Swindle
Gail Taylor Szykula
Judy Tatton
Rosemary Stuka Tepper
Dian Thomas
Margarethe Schmitt Thomas
Patricia White Thomas
Ruth Orlob Thompson
Joanna Jones Thorne
Jan Hugie Thorpe
Karen Lee Howells Thorsen
Enid Ryberg Thurman
Nancy Calame Tillotson
Connie Langford Timmons
Diane Pew Tolboe
Jeanne Stephens Tolboe
Trisha Lewis Topham
Ellen Dealtrey Toscano
Myrna Helm Towers
Barbara Kowall Treschitia
Belle Hintze Trunnell
Patricia Gareau Tuft
Carol Petersen VanVranken
Wendy Riser Van de Camp
Carlotta Odegard Veasy

Stephanie Pyke Veasy
Paula Miles Wagstaff
Enid Williford Waldron
Jeanne Lambert Walker
Lynn Economou Walker
Merrill Smith Wall
Carol Callister Wallace
Berlene Hunt Ward
Diane Hague Ward
Clare Jackson Watkins
Dave Watkins
Julia Simmons Watkins
Cheryl Wewee
Mary Margaret Webb
Paulette Wallick Welch
Eleanor Ogden Whisenant
Beverly J. White
Sue Ann Whiting
Kristine Eskelson Widner
Lucy Andrus Wilkins
Stephanie Cairo Williams
Sue Williams
Sydney Timmons Williams
Lynn Harner Wilson
Fred Wix
Gretchen Wix
Mary June Vincent Woods
Carol Ritchie Wootten
Minna Frick Work
Diana Nelson Wray
Judy Roberts Wright
Laurel Heath Young
SuSu Granieri Young
Dimmis Weller Zeigler
Barbara Finch Zimonja

TESTERS

The endurance, patience and good humor provided by our testers and their families were valued immeasurably. It took a great bank of time to make certain the recipes in A PINCH OF SALT LAKE are accurate and delicious. Testers, thank you:

Linda Gill Adkins
Coralie Ashton Alder
Kathryn Hunter Alldredge
Julie Cuthbert Allen
Susan Peterson Amoss
Kathryn Bicknell Anderson
Mary Ann Matthews Anderson
Vee Atkinson Anderson
Joey McCollins Archer
Marilyn Miller Askins
Carolyn Bowers Astin
Genevieve Atwood
Robin Temple Bailey
Cindy Elliott Baldwin
Kathryn Ball
DeDe Gorey Barrigar
Rosemary Curtis Barton
Trudy Weixler Beck
Nanette Jackson Benowitz
Karen Luderman Bettilyon
Denise Guiney Black
Harriet Tefft Black
Lisa Ann Blinzer
Nancy Cockayne Bowers
Shauna Bradshaw
Mary Coltharp Brinkerhoff
Janene Cooley Brown
Margaret Roberts Brown
Martha Hancey Brown
Linda Henderson Buchman
Susan Van Voorhis Burdett
Camille Tibbetts Bushman
Kim Koller Butler
Sallie Byer
Genna Vee Brotherson Candland
Carol Rees Carman
Deborah Chelmes
Constance Geiger Chichester
Amy Hathaway Christensen
Ann Richard Christensen
Kathlene Hansen Christensen
Estelle Christopulos
Kathleen Drummond Clark
Marilyn Cowan Clark
Laura Herring Clinger
Elaine Clinger Clyde
Karen Lebsack Coleman
Cindy Fregulia Collins
Toni Davis Cook
Joan Hudson Cottle
Jan Aland Crockett
Leslie Haws Cutler
Frances Johnson Darger
Sheridan Wright Day
Connie Jacobsen Degn
Cindy Edwards Delanni
Sidney Bullen Dibble
Karen Hansen Dingman
Connie Jo Tomlin Dobson

Becky Setta Donald
Shauna Barker Dorius
Andree D. Dreyfous
Mary Driver
Jan Kiehl Duane
Rebecca Dean Duberow
Kathie Erickson Durham
Marcie Nepo Eaton
Karen Becker Edson
Elizabeth Egleston
Bryan Bird Eldredge
Anne Bratt Elliott
Nanette Kibbe Elliott
Diane Crandall Epperson
Adrienne Earl Eskelson
Lori Wirthlin Eskelson
Gwen Knight Eubank
Rolayne Poate Fairclough
Lisa Brodbeck Fall
Judy Wilcox Fillmore
Julie Welch Fillmore
Linda MacFarlane Forsey
Melinda Mattsson Fowler
Cathryn Baldwin Francis
Cathy Bramwell Fraughton
Judy Lenn Evans Fuller
Ann Trevithick Fullmer
Barbara Trunnell Gaddis
Connie Dell Garcia
Carolyn Smith Gardner
Catherine Cannon Gardner
Frances Clark Garrett
Marny Keenan Gaylord
Randall Gaylord
Barbara Bean Gelegotis
Loraine Mitchell Gerovac
Barbara Aspden Gibbons
Jenifer Brennan Gibbons
Bonnie Lindjord Gilley
Kathleen Jarrell Gillman
Barbara Chytraus Gilson
Penelope Steele Grikscheit
Kathleen Callahan Grisley
Josie Anderson Grosbeck
Mickey Lieber Hale
Vicki Firmage Halgren
Deborah Mitchell Hansen
Lisa L. Hansen
Myra Ullman Hansen
Shanna Bess Hansen
Suzanne Raleigh Hansen
Elizabeth Harte
Launa Lee Migliore Harvey
Margaret Ashley Hatch
Shonnie Stillman Hays
Leigh Ann Hayward
Laura Benson Headden
Ann Toombes Healy
Cathy Argus Hemingway

Marguerite Marceau Henderson
Noelle Henderson
Shellie Steenblik Hepworth
Susan McRoberts Hermance
Marcia Anderson Herzog
Susan Hessler
DruAnn Stevens Hill
Carolyn Cushman Hinckley
Pam Baldwin Holt
Donna Payne Hoover
Susan Tobinski Howe
Mary Ann Barton Howell
Betsy Brandis Hunt
Karen Jo Page Hyde
Marian Watkins Ingham
Rhonda Simmons Irvine
Jeanne Nebeker Jardine
Jo May Wight Jessop
Julie Ann Johnson
Patsy Hicks Johnson
Dyan Elizabeth Jones
Kathleen Haight Jones
Mary Dove Jones
Susan McNair Kartchner
Linda Williamson Kempczenski
Patricia Culp Kimball
Elizabeth Stout Kirk
Daneil Maxfield Koncar
Masie Young Lancaster
Terry Enquist Landa
Julia Harmon LaPine
Selma Vance-Lauritzen
Toni LaBonte Lehtinen
Barbara Hunt Lehnhof
Georgie Eskelson Lewis
Sherlyn Hart Lewis
Judy Bunk Liapis
Jackie Diaz Little
Susan Null Lockwood
Fran Coltharp Loos
Nancy Sonntag Lyon
Marjorie Warshaw Mackey
Ann M. Mackin
Jonette Cocorinis Mangum
Phoebe Marashi
Ann Kolemainen Marlowe
Lori Jardine Martin
Molly Lane Mason
Nancy Nortz Mathews
Pinky Brady McBrier
Mary Schubach McCarthey
Julie McKinnon
Sally Ann Morgan Middlekauff
Denise Heinee Metcalf
Kathie Merrill Miller
Karen Cooley Milne
Frances Grundmann Morgan
Vicki Allen Mortensen
Lynne Morton

Christie Timmons Mullen
Susan Harmston Mullins
Patti Davis Murray
Molly Moore Nelson
Suzanne Sutton Nowels
Gay Lerwill Null
Marianne Dobson Ogaard
Sandra England Okland
Lisa Kump Olson
Shauna Gardner Olson
Cyndy Char Ong
Barbara Butters Owen
Margie Sesler Patton
Jeanne Potucek Paulos
Debie Smith Pearl]
Vivian K. Perry
Patricia Snyder Petersen
Linda Graham Peterson
Melissa Waters Phillips
Jacque Jensen Poore
Evelyn Bryant Mooney Quinn
Francine Alvey Quinn
Sharon Sorensen Quinn
Karen Jorgensen Raemer
Mary Jane Johnson Rains
Terry Breznick Rampton
Joni Ramsey
T. Upton Ramsey
Wendy Brower Rath
Sue Johnson Razor
Margaret Nelson Reiser
Sherry Douglas Remund
Nanette Ulricksen Richard
Susan Ridges
Lesley Painter Rigby
Nancy Aland Rigby
Kathy Rampton Rockwood
Rosemary Schaefer Roe
Sheryl Kamstadt Rowlett
Bette Coleman Ross
Lenessa Tingey Rumel
Rosemarie Michael Russell
Margaret Patterson Sargent
Kari Waring Schaerrer

Nata Wade Schneider
Pamela Moeller Schroeder
Carolyn Goodwin Schubach
Nancy Rose Scott
Mary Anne Jensen Scheffield
Brenda Moore Shockey
Denise Rapp Smith
Sharon Ailes Smith
Deborah Shields Smoot
Sheryl Nelson Snarr
Dale Temple Snyder
Cynthia Dix Soderberg
Glenda Solomon
Elizabeth Oblad Sonne
Nancy Greeley Souder
Gwen Rowley Springmeyer
Laurie Wentch Stander
Lurlene Romney Steele
Barbara Reeves Stevens
Kathleen Dunn Stone
Maggie Strasser
Sherry Christman Stuart
Kay Ritchie Sundberg
Julie Sundstrom
Lu Matheson Sweeney
JoAnne Call Swindle
Doree Ann Tateoka
Denise Herrera Taylor
Margarethe Schmitt Thomas
Joanna Jones Thorne
Jan Hugie Thorpe
Karen Howells Thorsen
Barbara Stevens Thurston
Diane Pew Tolboe
Jeanne Stephens
Nancy Owens Tolboe
Trisha Lewis Topham
Ellen Dealtry Toscano
Patricia Gareau Tuft
Wendy Riser Van de Kamp
Carlotta Odegard Veasy
Stephanie Pyke Veasy
Berlene Hunt Ward
Enid Williford Waldron

Jeanne Lambert Walker
Carol Callister Wallace
Shauna Sudbury Warren
Patricia Thompson Washburn
Shauna Hemming Waters
Paulette Wallick Welch
Eleanor Ogden Whisenant
Sue Ann Whiting
Kristine Eskelson Widner
Karen Johnson Wiedenmann
Stephanie Cairo Williams
Karen Blumenthal Williamson
Lynn Harner Wilson
Mary June Vincent Woods
Carol Ritchie Wooton
Jane Hetzel Wright
Judy Roberts Wright
Brenda Yamagata
Laurel Heath Young
SuSu Granieri Young
Dimmie Weller Ziegler
Barbara Finch Zimonja

INDEX

All Quick & Easy recipes are designated with a "Q.E." following the title.